SHAPING SPACE

The Dynamics
of Three-Dimensional Design

SHAPING SPACE

The Dynamics
Of Three-Dimensional Design

Paul Zelanski
University of Connecticut

Mary Pat Fisher

Harcourt Brace Jovanovich College Publishers
Fort Worth   Philadelphia   San Diego
New York   Orlando   Austin   San Antonio
Toronto   Montreal   London   Sydney   Tokyo

Publisher   Susan Katz
Acquisitions Editor   Karen Dubno
Picture Editor   Marion Geisinger
Special Projects Editor   Jeanette Ninas Johnson
Sr. Production Manager   Nancy Myers
Design Supervisor   Gloria Gentile
Interior Design   Caliber Design Planning, Inc.
Composition and Camera Work   York Graphic Services, Inc.
Separations   The Lehigh Press, Inc.
Printing and binding   R. R. Donnelley & Sons, Co.

Cover   *Passage: An Interval of Time*, 1981. 10-¾ × 17″ (27.3 × 43.2 cm), by Peter Aldridge. Steuben Glass.

Photographic and literary credits appear on pp. 287–288.

Library of Congress Cataloging-in-Publication Data
Zelanski, Paul.
  Shaping space.
  Includes bibliographies and index.
  1. Design.   2. Visual perception.   3. Space (Art)
4. Relief (Art)   I. Fisher, Mary Pat, 1943–
II. Title.
NK1510.Z45 1987   745.4   86-12131

ISBN 0-03-001078-0

Printed in the United States of America
  2 039 9 8 7 6 5

Harcourt Brace Jovanovich, Inc.
The Dryden Press
Saunders College Publishing

Preface

Shaping Space: The Dynamics of Three-Dimensional Design is designed to fill a major gap among art textbooks. Unlike most other design books currently available, it serves as an introductory text for three-dimensional design courses. It approaches three-dimensional design with the thoroughness and sensitivity that have until now been granted only to two-dimensional design.

Shaping Space can be used in a variety of three-dimensional courses. It can be used as a core text for the foundation level course in three-dimensional design. As such, it will provide a rich background in three-dimensional aesthetics that broadens students' understanding and creativity beyond the characteristics of the media and methods emphasized in their studio work. It can also be used as a general appreciation text for lecture/survey courses in three-dimensional art, both fine and functional. *Shaping Space* is also an appropriate supplementary text for beginning courses in specific three-dimensional arts, such as ceramics, sculpture, fiber arts, metalsmithing, interior decoration, stage design, applied design, landscape design, or architecture. All of these disciplines are incorporated into the text via discussion and illustration, for they share the same organizing principles and elements of design.

We are excited about three-dimensional design—about the ideas that shape its creation and about how it affects the viewer. We explore these two aspects with care and enthusiasm for both conventional artistic wisdom and new approaches that stretch and transcend the old definitions of what can and should happen in a work of art. Our hope is that students will encounter here ideas that have never occurred to them before and become more aware of the limitless potential of shaping space.

Special Features

Broad Illustration Program. Our book has a number of unique features. One is its graceful intermingling of the fine and applied arts. As we note, the line between the two is no longer clear-cut, and they are based on the same design principles and elements. All three-dimensional art—from cars and soda bottles to marble sculpture, video sculpture, earthworks, and set design—is built from the same elements: form, space, line, texture, light, color, and time. And all three-dimensional art is subject to the same organizing principles and the same practical considerations, such as the effects of gravity and of the setting in which a piece will be seen or used. In exploring these underpinnings of three-dimensional design, we use illustrations that cover the entire range of three-dimensional disciplines.

In addition to blending fine and applied arts, the 292 illustrations are spread among new and established artists and range from prehistory to today's innovators. Wherever possible, we have secured photographs illustrating works in progress or pieces in their human settings, rather than static museum shots, to help give a sense of the dynamics of the creation of and response to three-dimensional art.

Artists' Own Explanations. To enhance understanding of what lies behind creation of three-dimensional works, we have incorporated into the text the actual words of numerous artists, from sculptors and conceptual artists to craftspeople and a stage designer. From young artists who are beginning to be established to long-recognized masters, they explain in their own words what they are trying to do and how they deal with both the practical and the aesthetic considerations that arise in three-dimensional work. Many of these comments are taken from our own interviews with the artists, all of whom have been very gracious and thoughtful in responding to our questions. The quotations from artists on their own work and the artmaking process add an important human dimension to students' perception of successful artists and the students' own potential for achievement.

57 Studio Problems. For those in studio courses, each chapter ends with a set of problems designed to allow direct experimentation with the concepts introduced in the text. The clear relationship of these problems to the text makes the course very teachable and understandable. But solutions are not confined to any specific aesthetic approach or medium. They can be used flexibly according to the background of both teacher and students. An instructor of a basic 3-D course who has a strong ceramics background might emphasize use of clay as a medium with which to study the characteristics of all three-dimensional art. For a ceramics class, all problems could be given in clay. Prearchitecture students might focus on architectural solutions. Here in rural New England, our students often use wood to solve the problems, for wood is readily available and cheap from local sawmills.

More problems are given than can be covered in most one- or two-semester courses; teachers can select those that they feel are most effective in introducing and broadening three-dimensional awareness and technical skills. For courses emphasizing refinement of technical skills, relatively few problems would be assigned, to allow creation of well-finished works. For courses focusing on design potentials, many problems could be assigned, using media such as nonhardening clay, wax, plaster, wood, cardboard, wire, and paper, which are inexpensive and allow quick developmental studies.

Writing Style. The text is easy to read throughout, with brief, clear discussions of the mental processes in making art and the psychology of perceiving art. Many terms relating to how three-dimensional art functions and affects the viewer are introduced, but each is carefully defined not only in the text but also in a glossary provided at the end of the book. We have tried to avoid using jargon that would obscure our points; instead, we use down-to-earth language and references to experiences from everyday life as well as visual illustrations and studio problems to increase awareness of the dynamics of making and responding to three-dimensional art.

Organization of the Book

Fundamentals of Three-Dimensional Art. The book begins with three chapters introducing basic considerations in three-dimensional design. Chapter 1 explores the ways in which we experience three-dimensional art, with discussions of the limitations of photographs in representing three-dimensional experiences, the degrees of three-dimensionality, and techniques commonly used to draw people into approaching and exploring a piece. Chapter 2—"Working in the Round"—discusses a variety of practical considerations encountered in three-dimensional work, such as the pull of gravity, the influence of the setting, and issues of size, materials, costs, planning methods, and balancing of form and function. Chapter 3 applies the classical organizing principles of design—repetition, variety, rhythm, balance, emphasis, economy, and proportion—to the development of unity in a rich assortment of works.

Elements of Three-Dimensional Design. The second part of *Shaping Space* devotes a full chapter to each of seven elements present in most three-dimensional works: form, space, line, texture, light, color, and time. Each element is explored in depth, with careful attention paid not only to standard descriptions of ways the element can be used but also to subtleties such as negative forms, implied lines, activation of the space surrounding a piece, use of shadows, and changes through time. The chapters on space and color are particularly strong in treating these elements seriously as major aspects of three-dimensional design.

Construction Methods. The third section of the book offers a chapter on each of four general construction methods—found objects, addition and manipulation, subtraction, and casting. Each is further broken down into subcategories described enough to pique the student's curiosity into exploring new media and methods but not serving as detailed how-tos. For more specific how-to help, an annotated list of practical reference books is provided at the end of each of these methods chapters.

Studio problems given in these chapters allow students to experiment constructively with media and methods with which they may be unfamiliar. But like the problems elsewhere in the book, they can be solved with simple skills and relatively inexpensive materials. Our assumption is that technical expertise with a particular medium can be developed by choice or by requirements of individual teachers, but that the main emphasis in an introductory course will be placed on mastering the fundamentals of design—what works well—and stretching students' concepts of what is possible.

Adaptations of the Organization. The sequence of the book follows a logical progression from fundamentals, to elements, to experimentation with different construction methods. But the parts and chapters can be assigned in any order, for each is self-contained, with few cross-references. For example, we have introduced the principles of design (Chap. 3) before the elements (Part II), in order to give students a framework for unifying their solutions to studio problems dealing with the individual elements of design. But some instructors might prefer to introduce the elements before the principles.

In a class stressing design concepts, the third section— "Construction Methods"—might be given simply as a reading assignment, with students applying the information as needed in solving problems given in the earlier chapters. In a class that stresses construction methods per se, more emphasis might be placed on exploration of the third section, with the earlier chapters serving as background material to be drawn on in solving problems using found objects, addition and manipulation, subtraction, and casting.

Acknowledgments

We have thoroughly enjoyed writing this book, partly because the subject is fascinating, and partly because so many people have helped so enthusiastically. First credit goes to our editor at Holt, Rinehart and Winston, Karen Dubno, who recognized the need for *Shaping Space* and who has helped in so many ways to bring it into being.

We also feel very grateful to the working artists whom we interviewed: Ralph DiCapua (conceptual art), Robin Fish (industrial design), Donna Forma (classical marble sculpture), Betty Gerich (ceramics), Arthur Hoener (sculpture), James T. Hoffman (computer graphics), Linda Howard (large fabricated sculptures), Robert Mallary (computer graphics, assemblage), John Matt (mixed media fabrication), Norma Minkowitz (fiber arts), Don Murray (stage lighting design), Minnie Negoro (classical ceramics), Jerry Rojo (stage design),

Richard Swibold (architecture and urban space planning), Betsy Utting (fiber arts), Robert Walker (acrylic sculpture), and Elbert Weinberg (casting and wood sculpture). All have been extremely gracious with their time, perceptive in their comments, and enthusiastic about this book.

Special thanks also go to Ralph DiCapua and Sal Scalora for sharing studio problems that they use in their three-dimensional design courses, and to their students, whose work is used to illustrate 30 of the problems. We are highly impressed with both the quality and the originality of these students' work. Jeanne Victor provided excellent photographs of their solutions.

Our reviewers have also been very generous with their time and thoughtful in their suggestions for improving *Shaping Space*. We appreciate their enthusiasm for this book, which they all feel is greatly needed. We particularly want to thank William C. Zwingelberg, Catonsville Community College, MD; Jamie Abbott, Cabrillo College, CA; Foster Marlow, Southwest Texas State University; Horace L. Farlowe, The University of Georgia; Patricia Nelson, Ball State University, IN; Charles W. Smith, University of Washington; Barbara Nelson, Saddleback Community College, CA; Joseph Molinaro, Broward Community College, FL; Mary Frisbee Johnson, Arizona State University; Marilyn Griewank da Silva, Bowling Green State University, OH; Maralyn Dettmann, North Central College, IL; Suzanne Klotz-Reilly, Arizona State University; Ronald D. Ali, Indiana University of Pennsylvania; and Hovak Najarian, College of the Desert, CA.

For special help in preparing the art program we want to thank Michelle Fisher and Elayne O'Donnell for their cheerful and competent assistance. At Holt, Rinehart and Winston we are pleased to work again with a staff dedicated to high quality in art textbooks: Karen Dubno, Marion Geisinger, Gloria Gentile, Jeanette Ninas Johnson, and Nancy Myers.

Finally, we both want to express our love and appreciation to Annette Zelanski, whose moral support and constructive criticism have helped us see our second collaboration to a satisfying and successful completion.

Many thanks to all of you.

Paul Zelanski
Mary Pat Fisher
Storrs, Connecticut

Contents

Contents

PART III

Construction Methods 213

SHAPING SPACE

The Dynamics
of Three-Dimensional Design

PART 1

Fundamentals of Three-Dimensional Art

1

Experiencing
Three-Dimensionality

Three-dimensional art has height and width, as a painting does, plus a third dimension—depth. This stark definition, though true, gives no hint of the excitement of actually experiencing three-dimensional art. To plunge into this experience, try this experiment: Loosely crumple a piece of paper, any piece of paper. Then look at it. Don't just glance at it briefly; really explore it all over with your eyes. Hold it in your hand and slowly turn it, watching how it changes as the parts you can see and the angle from which you are seeing them change.

If you are giving yourself fully to this experience, you will find that your piece of crumpled paper becomes endlessly fascinating. Your eyes and mind will be intrigued by the ever-changing patterns created by the paper forms and the empty spaces they define—the myriad ridges, hollows, and tunnels and their relationships to each other, the gradations of light and shadow, the changing surface textures. If your piece of paper happens to have writing on it, follow what happens to the lines of words as they disappear over the edge of a fold. Spend a long time exploring as many ways of looking at your paper "sculpture" as possible. Let your fingers explore it as well, if they want to.

This seemingly simple exercise will help open you to fully appreciative experiencing of three-dimensional art. At the same time, it will give you some idea of what is lost in looking at pictures of three-dimensional art. No photograph, no matter how well-planned or dramatic, can possibly replicate the highly personal act of experiencing a three-dimensional piece.

In this chapter we will examine some of the ways in which photographs distort the three-dimensional experience, requiring a great leap of imagination on your part to appreciate the works shown in this book. As an introduction to the vast range of possibilities for your own three-dimensional work, we will also look at the many different degrees of three-dimensionality and some of the techniques that can be used to draw viewers into the three-dimensional experience.

Photographs of Three-Dimensional Work

A black-and-white photograph obviously eliminates certain features of a three-dimensional work. The most obvious is color; another is the surface texture, weight, and balance of a piece—its "feel." A photograph in fact eliminates use of all senses other than vision, and then rigidly controls what we can see of a work and how we understand its totality.

Set Point of View

Presenting a single photograph of a three-dimensional piece confines the experience of the work to a single *point of view*—a set distance and angle from which the piece is viewed. Of the almost limitless possibilities, only one viewpoint is chosen to represent the experience of the whole. This approach obviously has its limitations.

The two views of Donna Forma's *Alone with Thoughts* (Figs. 1 and 2) seem so different that they could be photographs of different pieces. But in actuality, if you were to walk around the piece the sculpture would draw your attention at one point to the contrast between the sharp thrust of the shoulder and the full rounding of the buttocks and to the lifting of the figure from the rock, as in the point of view used for the photograph in Figure 1. Then as you continued to walk around the piece, it would pull your eye into the dark hollows beneath the curves of the body and to the embrace between the rock and the human form, as in Figure 2. Making a full circle around the piece would reveal even more views, as would bending down to look upward or standing on something taller to look down on the sculpture. As Forma laments,

1 and 2 Donna Forma. *Alone with Thoughts.* Carrara marble, height 15″ (38 cm).

"You could have twelve photographs of one piece and still feel you didn't fully show the piece. If you can see the whole thing in one view, there's something wrong with the piece." Good three-dimensional work should compel the viewer to walk all the way around it, examining it from many angles.

Flattening Out

Photographs inevitably distort our perceptions of a three-dimensional piece, for they present it on a flat two-dimensional surface. Looking at a two-dimensional photograph and mentally translating it into three-dimensionality is an ability most people in our culture have developed. When Australian aborigines are shown a photograph of an area they know, they cannot make the mental leap from the flat image to three-dimensional reality. But from experience with photographs, you have probably learned to read the clues to depth they provide. These clues include shadows, the overlapping of one area by another, the greater contrast in *values* (or gradations of lights and darks) and in sharpness of edges in areas closer to the viewer than in areas farther away, and linear perspective (the convergence of parallel lines toward a distant vanishing point). By interpreting such clues, we may get some intellectual impression of how deep a piece might be. But the experience

3 FRANK LLOYD WRIGHT, Interior dome, Solomon R. Guggenheim Museum, New York. 1957–59.

4 CHARLES SIMONDS. *Dwelling, East Houston Street, New York.* 1972. Unfired clay bricks, length ½″ (1.3 cm).

remains an intellectual one nevertheless; we cannot fully appreciate the three-dimensional impact of the piece. And in some cases, there are no such clues to depth. In Figure 3, it takes considerable imagination to make the intellectual leap from what appears in the photograph to be an almost flat geometrical design to the actual experience of looking high up into the dome of the Guggenheim Museum.

Though still too expensive a process to replace regular photography of three-dimensional objects, *holography* offers the opportunity to view a three-dimensional object from more than one point of view. The process uses a laser beam that is split into two beams that spread to wrap around a portion of the object they are illuminating. When these beams are converged on a photographic plate, they form an interference pattern that allows the photograph to appear highly three-dimensional. Even though the resulting image—a *hologram*—is presented on a flat surface, movements by the viewer bring new perspectives on the object into view.

Scale

Another distortion introduced by photographs of three-dimensional works is the confusion of *scale*—the relative size of pieces. Many photographs give no clues as to whether the object shown is very small or very large. Charles Simonds' *Dwelling,* shown in Figure 4, looks larger than the similar structures in the pueblo cliff dwellings shown in Figure 5, yet Symonds' work is a miniature of tiny clay bricks placed among the bricks of a building, photographed from close range, whereas the cliff dwellings are vast and photographed from a distance.

If photographers want to give some indication of scale, they will often include in the photograph something of known size—such as a bench or a human being—to serve as a standard of comparison. The photograph of the true cliff dwellings does include the overhanging rock ledge, but this only serves as a clue to scale for those who are familiar with the vast scale of these hollows in the cliffs of the Southwest.

An additional intellectual clue to the scale of a three-dimensional work is the size given in the caption. Reading the captions for Figures 4 and 5 should suggest to you that they are in reality built on extremely different scales. But imagining how different their sizes really are takes a great imaginative leap on your part.

The Photographer's Interpretation

Yet another limitation introduced in photographs is the difference between the photographer's understanding of a piece and the artist's vision of it. Consider the vast difference between the standard museum

5 Cliff Palace, Mesa Verde National Park, Colorado. c. A.D. 1100.
6 (top right) CONSTANTIN BRANCUSI. *Bird in Space.* (1928?) Bronze, unique cast, height 4'6" (1.37 m). Collection Museum of Modern Art. New York. (Given anonymously.)
7 (bottom right) CONSTANTIN BRANCUSI. *Bird in Space.* 1927. Photograph by Constantin Brancusi.

photograph of Brancusi's *Bird in Space* (Fig. 6) and Brancusi's own photograph of the work (Fig. 7). The first gives us some idea of what the piece looks like; the second has a far more dramatic impact. Brancusi's photograph reveals what he was trying to capture: the mystical wildness of flight. At certain times, birds flying overhead express this quality; all you can see is a flash of light. By contrast, the standard photograph, though graceful, has a static quality, as though it were a statement about a still object.

The Photograph as the Work of Art

Despite the limitations of substituting the second-hand experience of looking at a flat photograph for actual involvement with a three-dimensional piece, in some cases looking at a photograph is our only way of experiencing a piece. If the work is not nearby, a photograph will have to do. And in certain pieces of *conceptual art*—that is, works or events existing as ideas in the artist's mind, but not necessarily presented in tangible form—the phenomenon created may be so short-lived or difficult to experience that a photograph must serve as the documentation of the work.

Walter De Maria's conceptual piece *The Lightning Field* can best be appreciated during a lightning storm. Yet few of us would stand in the midst of these 400 lightning rods during a lightning storm to see

8 WALTER DE MARIA. *The Lightning Field.* 1971–1977. Permanent earth sculpture 1 mile × 1 kilometer. 400 stainless steel poles with solid stainless steel pointed tips, arranged in a rectangular grid array spaced 220 feet (67.05 m) apart. Pole tips form an even plane. Average pole height is 20′7″ (6.27 m). New Mexico, Dia Art Foundation.

what happens. We must thank John Cliett, the photographer who took the photograph in Figure 8, for sharing the experience with us.

The artist Ralph DiCapua, noting that most people cannot experience a conceptual piece in person, chooses to make the most of the translation of the three-dimensional experience into a two-dimensional photograph by assuming from the start that the photograph is more than a documentation of the piece—it is the work of art itself. To create *Whole Pieces III* (Fig. 9), he took the poles and mirrors and four rolls of film to the beach and experimented with them for four hours, manipulating not only the objects but also the camera's point of view to produce a tightly controlled statement. As he explains,

> Viewing this piece on the beach was quite different from looking through the lens. In person, you are experiencing the massive scale of the beach. Once you put those mirrors in that space, you've got an infinite sky and infinite space to deal with. Looking at that was really different from closing off and controlling the space with the camera to convey the idea that we humans—represented by the person-sized mirrors and what can be seen in them—reflect a certain part of our environment. The photograph goes beyond being a

Fundamentals of Three-Dimensional Art

mere pictorial documentation to talk about two illusions: the reflection of tangible depth and tangible reality in the mirrors, and the reflection of those images in the image created in the photograph.

For the most part, however, the photographs you see of three-dimensional works were not intended to be the artistic statement in themselves. In most cases, you must pierce through the layers of abstraction and distortion introduced by the photograph and mentally project yourself into the feeling of actually experiencing the piece.

Degrees of Three-Dimensionality

In experiencing three-dimensionality, we are controlled to a certain extent—depending on the success of the piece—by the intentions of the artist. We will be discussing artistic intentions and means of control throughout this book, but here we will be dealing with the initial fact of how three-dimensionally the piece is conceived. Possibilities range from nearly flat works to works designed to surround the viewer.

Experiencing Three-Dimensionality   **11**

10 Detail from gravestone of Polly Coombes, 1795, Bellingham, Massachusetts. Carving attributed to Joseph Barber, Jr. Slate gravestone, size of full stone 29½ × 16¾″ (74.9 × 42.5 cm).

11 ANDREA DEL VERROCCHIO. *Virgin and Child.* 15th century. Polychromed and gilded terracotta. Metropolitan Museum of Art. (Rogers Fund, 1909).

Fundamentals of Three-Dimensional Art

Relief

The term *relief* refers to the raising of three-dimensional forms from a flat background. It appears that this artistic convention began very early, for relief works were carved on cave walls by prehistoric peoples. Perhaps the ancient sculptors noted bulges in the cave wall that already looked something like horses or bisons; a bit of carving brought out the desired form.

The shallowest form of relief is called *low relief,* or *bas-relief.* Although a formal definition of low relief is hard to pin down, the artistic attitude is one of relative flatness. In the gravestone carving in Figure 10, the angel is barely raised from the incised slate. Note that highlights and shadows are created by the ways the raised areas and strongly chiseled grooves reflect or block the light, helping to accentuate the image.

In *high relief,* forms are brought more fully off the flat surface, for a nearly sculptural effect. In Andrea del Verrocchio's *Virgin and Child* (Fig. 11), the figures even protrude in front of the "frame," as though they are starting to come off a flat canvas to appear as truly three-dimensional objects rather than as painted illusions of three-dimensionality. Here the artist has used strong *undercutting*—carving away of material between a projecting area, such as the Child's legs, and the substrate. In areas so worked, the forms are so three-dimensional that lighting inevitably brings out strong highlights and shadows. Look, for instance, at the dramatic difference between the right and left halves of the Virgin's face, and at the play of light and shadow through the deep drapings of her robe.

Reliefs are not limited to figurative works in which the forms and their background are carved or cast from the same material. Witness Robert Mallary's *In Flight* (Fig. 12, p. 14), a relief in which found materials have been affixed to a piece of painted wood. This piece controls the viewer's experience in the same way as the earlier examples: By presenting forms against a flat surface, it defines a limited space for the viewer's attention and a fixed point of view. Reliefs are designed to be looked at more or less straight on, perhaps with the head lifted somewhat, as in the cases of friezes placed above eye level on buildings.

One-Sided Works

The next step in three-dimensionality is work designed to be seen from only one side but not confined to a flat background. Like reliefs, these works are primarily *frontal*—that is, they are organized for viewing from the front. We can move around these pieces to a certain extent, but the artist does not strongly encourage us to do so.

Most jewelry is of this nature: All the visual interest lies on the front side, with the back only minimally elaborated. Instead of moving

around or turning a piece of jewelry to see how its contours change,
viewers would tend to scan it from edge to edge like a two-dimensional
work, following the interplay of patterns on the surface.

Some one-sided pieces are large enough that viewers can walk
along them, examining each section. If you encountered Louise Nevelson's *Sky Cathedral—Moon Garden + One* (Fig. 13), you'd probably
want to examine it in at least two ways: stand back to see the whole
thing from a distance, and walk from one side to the other, looking into
the individual boxes to see what is happening in each one. However,
Nevelson does not encourage you to stand to one side and look across
the whole piece, for the contents of the boxes do not protrude much
beyond the boxes themselves, limiting what you could see from this
angle. Neither does she suggest that you explore the back of the piece,
for it is backed against a wall, with all parts designed to be seen
frontally.

The less flat a piece is, the more the viewer may be tempted to
examine it from positions to either side of a straight frontal approach.
But even when a piece is presented in the *half-round*—180 degrees of
a fully three-dimensional circle—interest in exploring how it looks
from many angles may be intentionally limited by the artist. Edward
Kienholz's *The Wait* (Fig. 14) affects viewers like a stage setting, an
environment that is not to be intruded upon but rather viewed from the
edge of the braided rug. Attention is drawn so strongly to the old
woman seated in the center, waiting for a death that appears to be

13 (left) Louise Nevelson. *Sky Cathedral—Moon Garden + One.* 1957–60. Painted wood. 9′ × 10′8″ × 1′7″ (2.77 m × 3.30 m × 48.26 cm) (private collection).

14 (bottom) Edward Kienholtz. *The Wait.* 1964–65. Tableau: epoxy, glass, wood, and found objects. 6′8″ × 12′4″ × 6′6″ (2.03 × 3.76 × 1.98 m). Collection Whitney Museum of American Art, New York (Gift of the Howard and Jean Lipman Foundation, Inc.).

15 (top) ROBERT ENGMAN. *Untitled.*
1968–69. Bronze,
4′11½ × 4′11½ × 4′11½″
(1.50 × 1.50 × 1.50 m). Hirshhorn
Museum and Sculpture Garden,
Smithsonian Institution.

16 (bottom) WHARTON ESHERICK.
Treelike stairway hewn from solid
logs. 1930. Red oak. Courtesy
Wharton Esherick Museum, Paoli,
Pennsylvania (Ruth Esherick Bascom
Collection).

occurring already, that there is little incentive to examine how the piece looks from any angle other than dead center. Certainly nothing suggests walking around to see what the tableau looks like from the back.

The Full Round

In contrast to reliefs and one-sided works, pieces done "in the round" are designed to be seen from all sides. Instead of being organized like a two-dimensional work, where all spatial relationships are fixed across a flat plane, areas in a fully round work have been organized with consideration of their constantly changing relationship to each other. Indeed, if they are successful, they should make us want to walk all around them, discovering how the forms and relationships change when seen from different angles.

Robert Engman's sculpture (Fig. 15) presents a visual puzzle that lures viewers into walking around and around it, trying to understand how the two circular forms resolve themselves. One fits into the other through ever-changing curves that almost seem to defy our notions of spatial sense. To view the piece only in the static form of a photograph is frustrating, for the piece provokes the urge to explore it in its fullness and perhaps even to bend down to see what's happening below eye level, as though the answer to the puzzle lies down there somewhere. Although Engman's piece is actually round, "in the round" is an expression applied to any fully three-dimensional piece, no matter how large or small or how shaped.

Walk-Through Work

The final degree of viewer involvement with three-dimensionality is the experience of actually being surrounded by a work of art—of walking not only up to and around a piece, but also into it. In so doing, you become the center of the work; rather than your circumnavigating its circumference, it encircles you. This feeling of being surrounded by a 360-degree experience is as impossible to represent in a photograph as the experience of exploring a work from all sides. Again, you must use your imagination to place yourself in the settings pictured.

To experience Wharton Esherick's stairway (Fig. 16), you would probably want to walk up to it and around it to see how the logs create two branching, spiraling pathways and to appreciate the weight, form, and texture of the steps and central support. In addition, you might want to climb the stairs to see where they go and how they get there. At each step toward, around, and up the stairs, your spatial relationship with the stairway and the rest of the interior would change, changing and enriching the experience of being surrounded by this architectural environment.

Fundamentals of Three-Dimensional Art

17 NANCY GRAVES. *Camels VII, VI, VIII* (left to right). 1968–69. Wood, steel, burlap, polyurethane, animal skin, wax, oil paint. 8 × 9 × 4′ (24.4 × 27.4 × 12.2 m), 7½ × 12 × 4′ (22.8 × 36.6 × 12.2 m), 7½ × 10 × 4′ (22.8 × 30.5 × 12.2 m). National Gallery of Canada, Ottawa (Camels VII and VIII gift of Allan Bronfman, Montreal).

Or consider what you would do if you met Nancy Graves' *Camels* (Fig. 17). Unless you have no curiosity whatsoever, you would want to move around these realistic creatures in as many ways as the gallery allowed. You would want to look at them very closely to see how Graves managed to make them look so lifelike in texture and form. You would want to walk all around them and even between them watching their changing relationships to each other—to look between the legs of one to see the head of another, to see the similarities and differences from head to head, leg to leg, neck to neck, hump to hump. If you have retained or remembered a child's ways of appreciating the world, you might even respond to the playfulness of the piece by walking under one of the camel's bellies and gazing upward to see what you can see, discovering in a very personal way how large a camel really is. If the piece called forth these kinds of reactions from you, you would be participating in it fully, rather than simply standing aside as a passive observer.

For a walk-through experience, a piece must obviously be large in scale, large enough for people to fit inside. And depending on the artist's intent, it may control the ways in which people can walk

Experiencing Three-Dimensionality

18 ROBERT MORRIS. *Labyrinth. 1974.* Plywood, masonite, oil paint. Height 8′ (2.44 m), diameter 18″ (9.14 m), 1′6″ wide passageway (45.72 cm). Collection Dr. Giuseppe Panza.

through it. Architecture often has defined passageways—such as halls and doors and stairs—that limit the ways we can move through its interior spaces. We may or may not find the means of control pleasant. For many people, walking through Robert Morris' *Labyrinth* (Fig. 18) would be a disturbing or even frightening experience. Caught in the endless curves of this maze, one would have no sense of getting anywhere. The 8-foot-high (2.44 m) walls would both frustrate attempts to find the way into the center—or out—and also press in uncomfortably closely along the sides. Whatever emotions are invoked in those who choose to try to find their way through the maze create the drama of the piece.

Involving the Viewer

If it is effective, art in the round invites some kind of participation by the viewer. Depending on its size and nature, a piece may encourage us to pick it up and turn it over in our hands, feel its weight, stroke it, use it, sit on it, walk around it to see what it becomes on the other side, explore its passageways.

In its very three-dimensionality, art in the round has a direct impact on us. Whereas a two-dimensional piece, such as a painting, is

Fundamentals of Three-Dimensional Art

like a window that we must take the time to look through, a three-dimensional piece occupies space and time in our immediate environment, like a wall that we must either walk around or else bump into.

Yet even three-dimensional art can be ignored by the viewer. To a certain extent, people can walk past three-dimensional pieces without really seeing them, for the viewers' thoughts are elsewhere. One of the tasks facing you as an artist is, therefore, to draw attention to your creations, to invite people to notice and respond to them.

Techniques for provoking a direct response from viewers will be explored throughout this book. In this section we examine some general categories of involvement-encouraging factors: tactile/visual appeal, engaging curiosity, realism, abstraction and stylization, scale, content, personal interaction, the unexpected, and verbal statements about the work.

Tactile/Visual Appeal

Involvement in three-dimensional art begins with the artist who creates it. As children, many of us begin exploring three-dimensional art by shaping claylike materials into forms that please our hands and perhaps our eyes. Witness the comments of eight-year-old Ruth Zelanski: "I like to work with clay because it feels mushy—and then when it's glazed and fired it feels nice and glossy." As she talks about her work, her fingers explore it constantly, following its contours, fitting themselves into its concavities, caressing its smoothnesses, noting the grooves made by fingernail marks. Her description of how she works is studded with highly physical verbs: "pound," "roll," "poke," "pinch," "rub," "mush." Although she explains that when faced with a block of clay she draws a form out of it by "sort of seeing it inside my head," she notes that the forms that evolve are "what my body wants to do."

The joy in touching expressed in children's clay modeling may often be part of what draws viewers into involvement with a piece. If you encountered Marvin Lipofsky's blown glass piece *California Storm Series* (Fig. 19), you would probably want to explore it with your hands as well as your eyes, caressing its smoothnesses, questioning its barely glimpsed interiors, following its sinuous organic curves. To trace its unnamable forms with hand and eye would be a highly pleasant and, therefore, inviting experience.

Art does not always appear to us as beautiful or provoke pleasant sensations, however. Artists may use subject matter, colors, and surface treatments that may trigger unpleasant emotional responses. Lois Knobler's heads of fallen angels (one of which is shown in Fig. 20) are fashioned of materials that are otherwise innocently soft and familiar—stuffed stockings, gloves, t-shirts, string. But the artist has presented these materials in such a way that viewers may be afraid to touch or even to look for long, for they may bring to light a highly discomforting

19 Marvin Lipofsky. *California Storm Series*. 1982. Blown glass. 11½ × 13″ (29.21 cm × 33.02 cm). Made at the California College of Arts and Crafts with the help of Carol Schreitmueller (private collection).

20 Lois Jean Knobler.
Dubiel. 1983. Mixed media.
14 × 9 × 10″
(35.56 × 22.86 × 25.4 cm),
base 5½″ (12.7 cm).

awareness of the dark side of ourselves. Art historian Joyce Brodsky responds to the heads thus:

> Never touch them for they are dangerous. Enough to see them—and some cannot be seen. The highest rank can be seen for only an instant. These heads are on the edge of deep and dark mysteries of psyche and flesh, of nerve pain beneath and sensuous—that unshared ache . . . . I cannot stand it for too long.

Yet even in turning away from such pieces, we are responding to them. They have touched us personally, and we must react.

Engaging Curiosity

Many works involve us by piquing our curiosity, by making us stop in our tracks to wonder "What is that?" or "How did the artist do that?" or "What keeps that thing from falling?" or "What happens on the other side?" A common device to lure people to explore a piece in the full round is the use of forms that disappear around the edge of what can be seen from a single point of view. We human beings are simply too curious to glance at a figure like Aristide Maillol's *The River* (Fig. 21)

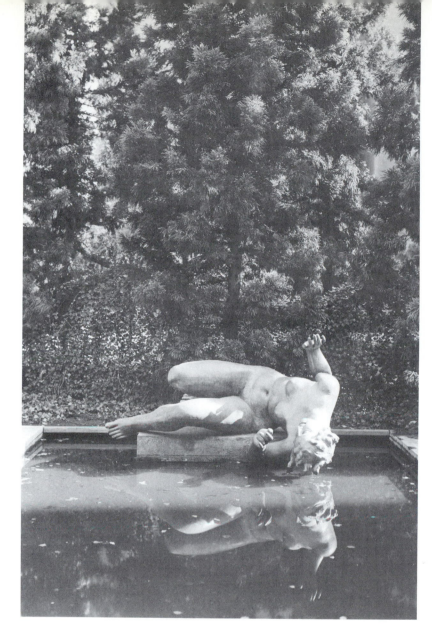

21 ARISTIDE MAILLOL. *The River.*
Begun 1938–39, completed 1943.
Lead, 4′5¾″ × 7′6″ (1.35 m × 2.29 m).
Collection Museum of Modern Art,
New York (Mrs. Simon Guggenheim
Fund).

from a fixed position and let it go at that. From the angle from which
this photograph was taken, our native curiosity would make us want to
find out where the "missing" foot is and what it is doing.

Our knowledge of the human body creates a vague dissatisfac-
tion that is not quieted until we've "found" all the expected parts. If we
see one hand or foot, we look for a second one; we want to follow the
arm line out from the shoulder to complete the suggestion that an
elbow lies just out of view. Sculptors frequently twist torsos into

Experiencing Three-Dimensionality   **21**

extreme positions, not only for the sake of the visual excitement thus created, but also to hide parts of the anatomy from view, piquing viewers' curiosity. An effective piece of three-dimensional art may change continually as we move around it, beckoning the curious onward.

Pieces may also engage our curiosity by presenting us with visual puzzles we don't immediately understand. In *The River,* the woman clearly seems to be off balance, moving so playfully that she is likely to fall off her perch. What keeps her from falling? From the angle that the photograph is taken, there is no way of telling. Many people would therefore be drawn into walking around the sculpture to try to see how and where the woman is anchored.

Realism

Certain works engage our attention by accurately replicating forms with which we are familiar. This approach is called *realism*—visual accuracy in artistic representation of objects from our three-dimensional world. Such works are recognizable, bringing a satisfying sort of involvement if the piece reminds us of something we know.

There are many degrees of realism. Artists may not try to copy all details of an object precisely, concentrating rather on certain features that convey the intended content of the piece. John Rogers' *Wounded to the Rear, "One More Shot"* (Fig. 22) emphasizes the wounds—arm in sling, leg being bandaged—of the Union soldiers but not the sweat, dirt, blood, and terror actually experienced in war. The artist's intent seems to be to evoke pride in heroism, rather than horror.

In extremely realistic work, the artist may be attempting to describe the visual characteristics of an object precisely, without any editing or sentimentalizing. In such cases, viewers' interest in recognizing the real may take the form of amazement that such artful duplication is possible. Marilyn Levine's *Spot's Suitcase* (Fig. 23) so perfectly replicates a worn leather suitcase—down to the limpness of the strap, the patina of the old hardware, the slightly scuffed texture of the

22 John Rogers. *Wounded to the Rear, "One More Shot."* American Civil War period. Bronze, height 23½″ (60 cm). Metropolitan Museum of Art, New York (Rogers Fund 1917).

23 Marilyn Levine. *Spot's Suitcase.* 1981. Ceramics, 7½ × 28 × 15″ (17.78 cm × 71.12 cm × 38.1 cm) (private collection).

Fundamentals of Three-Dimensional Art

leather surface, and the lighter area where half of one clasp used to be—that it is very difficult to grasp the fact that the piece is actually ceramic. If you saw it in a gallery, you would want to touch it to verify its nature. We are intrigued by that which successfully fools us.

Abstraction and Stylization

A third way of involving viewers is to eliminate all but a few characteristics of a figure, forcing people to use their imagination to link this highly simplified form with the more detailed object they know. This technique is called *abstraction*—reduction of details in order to focus on a thing's essence. In the ancient *Venus of Willendorf* (Fig. 24), the female form is reduced to its procreative features—the great breasts and rounded belly of pregnancy, the essence of fertility. Everything extraneous—arms, feet, even the face—is deleted to center focus on the fecundity of woman.

In addition to eliminating nonessential features, artists may *stylize* a form, subordinating accurate representation to a desired way of design. In Figure 25, the horse has been transformed into a few arched cylinders, yet it is still recognizable as a horse. In general, the more an artist abstracts or stylizes a representational figure, the more viewers must bring to the work, drawing on memories, imagination, and intellect to make sense of what they see.

Scale

Viewers may be drawn into responding to a work because of its *scale*—its size in relationship to its surroundings. The very small draws us in, for we must get close in order to see it. The people shown in Figure 26 have stopped on the street, lured by the tiny scale of the miniature cliff dwellings Charles Simonds has constructed among the bricks (detail shown in Fig. 4). Like most of us, these passersby are fascinated by miniaturization, especially when craftsmanship produces a precise replica of something that is much larger in real life.

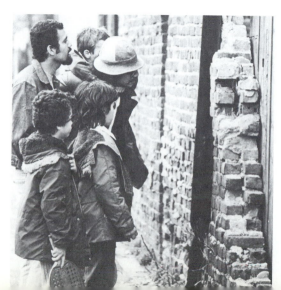

26 CHARLES SIMONDS. Passersby with *Dwelling, East Houston Street, New York.* 1972. Unfired clay bricks, ½″ (1.3 cm) long.

24 (top) *Venus of Willendorf.* c. 30,000–25,000 B.C. Stone (cast of original), height 4⅜″ (10.16 cm). Naturhistorisches Museum, Vienna.
25 (bottom) Haniwa figure—*Horse,* Japanese, III–VI Centuries. Terra cotta, 23½ × 26″ (58.42 × 66.04 cm). Cleveland Museum of Art (Norweb Collection).

23

The very large provokes an emotional response as well. Claes Oldenburg elicits strong reactions from viewers by vastly enlarging objects as mundane as a clothespin (Fig. 27). A vast cathedral, such as Chartres (Fig. 28), dwarfs viewers, filling them with awe at the soaring vastness and grandeur of the universe. And some works are so huge that viewers cannot comprehend the whole from their limited point of view. The mysterious Nazca lines in Peru cannot be comprehended from the ground at all; only an aerial photo reveals the ancient patterns created by removing rocks to expose the lighter soil. In Figure 29, a Nazca line forms a gigantic monkey whose left hand alone is 40 feet (12.2 m) across.

Scale can thus be manipulated to involve viewers by making them feel *they* are changing in size. When presented with a Lilliputian village, we become towering Gullivers; when presented with works that have the appearance of being created by giants, we become like Lilliputians.

Content

We are also drawn into experiencing what a work is "about." In contrast to its form, the *content* of a piece is its subject matter (e.g., "a woman") plus all its emotional, intellectual, symbolic, spiritual, and/or narrative implications, if any (e.g., "the love and creative energy of

27 (left) Claes Oldenburg. *Clothespin.* 1976. Cor-Ten steel, height 45′ (13.72 m). Centre Square, Philadelphia. Commissioned by the developer, Jack Wolgin, in compliance with the Philadelphia Redevelopment Authority's One-Percent Fine Arts Program.
28 (bottom) *Chartres Cathedral.* c. 1194–1221. View through nave, looking toward the apse. Chartres, France.

29 Monkey figure, Peru, c. 100 B.C.–A.D. 700.

the Divine Mother of the world"). Unless the artist provides explicit statements about the intended content of a piece, its nature can only be described subjectively. Two people may interpret the content of a given work quite differently.

Consider responses to spiritual connotations, for instance. Certain works suggest themes that are universally understood. Chartres Cathedral (Fig. 28) was designed to uplift the consciousness of worshipers, helping them to transcend their narrow personal viewpoint to experience a more cosmic awareness. The spaciousness and height of the interior and the upward thrust of its columns and arches will tend to convey the same connotations to people of all cultures.

Although the grand scale of Chartres would have an impact on anyone's consciousness, many religious pieces have spiritual connotations only for those who are personally imbued with a particular spiritual tradition. For those familiar with the mystical Christian tradition, *The Ecstasy of St. Theresa* (Fig. 30, p. 26) narrates a known story and evokes personal memories of the feeling of spiritual ecstasy. The statue of *Coatlicue* (Fig. 31, p. 26), goddess of earth and death, must have inspired awe or even terror in her Aztec worshippers.

It is possible to become involved with such pieces on levels other than what was originally intended, however. There is the intellectual challenge of interpreting ideograms and symbolic messages on pieces such as *Coatlicue* (Fig. 31). We can also admire the artfulness with which religious works were created, such as Bernini's skillfulness in sculpting the hardness of marble to look like the softness of fabric in *The Ecstasy of St. Theresa* (Fig. 30). But if we not only appreciate the artfulness of a work but also respond to it as an evocation of a tradition that has deep personal meaning for us, the content we perceive in the work includes emotional and spiritual implications.

Experiencing Three-Dimensionality

30 (top left) GIANLORENZO BERNINI. *The Ecstasy of St. Theresa.* c. 1645. Marble, life size. Cornaro Chapel, Rome.

31 (top right) *Coatlique,* goddess of earth and death. Aztec, 15th century, Andesite, height approx. 8½″ (20.32 cm). Museo Nacional de Antropologia, Mexico City.

The spiritual content of a work is not limited to specifically religious connotations. Pieces growing out of the artist's personal exploration of life may speak volumes to the viewer who is similarly searching.

Personal Interaction

There are numerous ways of drawing people into a living encounter with a work of art. Some art is designed to be worn, such as Louise Nevelson's necklace (Fig. 32). Wearing a work of art takes what is usually a private experience between the viewer and the piece into the public domain. Now one responds not only to his or her feelings about the piece but also to other people's reactions. Others may come unu-

Fundamentals of Three-Dimensional Art

sually close to examine the worn art; the wearer may not even be able to see it.

Architecture involves "viewers" by forcing them to walk through fixed passageways and experience environments of varying degrees of openness and confinedness. Stairways in architect Louis Kahn's *Salk Institute for Biological Studies* (Fig. 33) lead people through boxlike enclosures opening into catwalks and halls surrounded by deep plunging spaces rather than walls. Some may experience these spaces as liberating; others may find them dizzying. Yet it is impossible not to respond.

Large *installation pieces*—designed environments installed in museums, sometimes temporarily—may have a similar way of involving viewers. Michael Asher's installation piece (Fig. 34, p. 28) offers little visual interest, instead inviting viewers into an experience: what it feels like to walk into a narrowing, angled passageway and emerge into unknown territory beyond. Such intrigue has often been used as a come-on in roadside folk art, luring customers into shops by disguising the stores as oversized lobster traps, tipis, chickens, wheels of cheese, hot dogs, derby hats, or even open-jawed fish.

Performance pieces involve viewers in a live experience conducted or set up by the artist. Street theater is performed for anyone who passes by on the street—at clear risk of being ignored. Larger-scale performance pieces may be staged for captive audiences. Laurie Anderson draws on elements of popular culture for this purpose, using vehicles already proved to have mass appeal. Her epic performance series *United States* combines punk rock music, video effects, voice-altering electronic devices, scenes from video games, and surprising theatrical gestures. One of the backdrops to her *United States Part II* (Fig. 35) was a giant map of the time zones of the United States with all

32 Louise Nevelson. *Neck Piece.*

33 Louis I. Kahn. *Salk Institute for Biological Studies*, La Jolla, California. 1968.

27

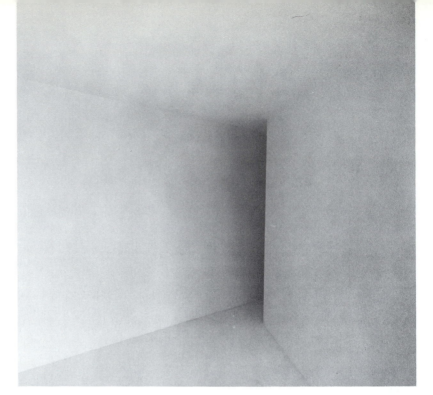

34 (right) Michael Asher. March 1970. Installation at Montgomery Gallery, Pomona College, Claremont, California.
35 (bottom) Laurie Anderson. *"Let x = x,"* part of *United States Part II.* October 1980, Orpheum Theatre, New York.

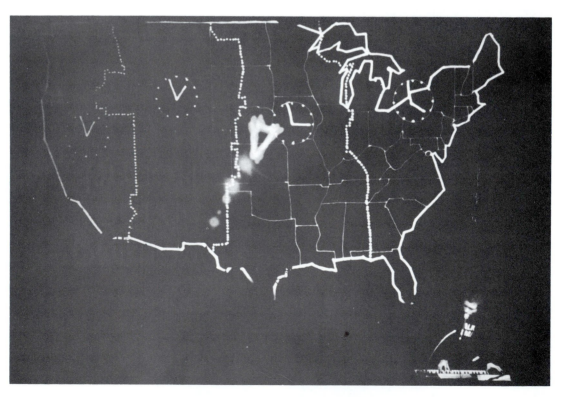

Fundamentals of Three-Dimensional Art

the clocks out of synch. Viewers may be both entertained by her often humorous use of popular media and chilled by the underlying warnings about the dangers of our culture.

Similarly, *video art* uses the apex of popular culture—the familiar but ever-compelling presence of television—to draw people into an artistic event. In his videotape *Global Groove,* video artist Nam June Paik juxtaposes multicultural images such as Allen Ginsberg chanting "Om," Japanese Pepsi commercials, performances by Korean, Japanese, and American popular dancers, electronic distortions of Richard Nixon's face, and John Cage telling a joke with clips of Charlotte Moorman playing a *video sculpture*—a "TV Cello" made of three TV monitors (Fig. 36). In Paik's hands, rapidly evolving video technologies are used vigorously and at times ironically to create three-dimensional sculptures that are in turn shown on televisions, both capitalizing on and subverting the mesmerizing, frantic effects of the medium.

The Unexpected

Some artists provoke involvement from viewers by surprising them. Something may suddenly be perceived in an unexpected place, like

36 Charlotte Moorman playing a *TV Cello* by Nam June Paik in *Global Groove* by NAM JUNE PAIK and JOHN GODFREY. 1973. 30-minute color/sound videotape. Produced by the Television Laboratory at WNET/Thirteen.

37 DANIEL SINCLAIR. *Aegyptus.* 1978. Marble, height 36″ (91.44 cm).

the Nazca lines in the Peruvian desert (Fig. 29). Coming upon such an anomaly provokes people to wonder, "Why?"

Some art startles us with seemingly incongruous elements that defy our stereotyped notions of how things "should be." Sculptors often raise a smooth-chiseled figure from a bed of rough-cut marble; it is surprising to see this convention reversed in Daniel Sinclair's *Aegyptus* (Fig. 37). Similarly, faced with Meret Oppenheim's fur cup (Fig. 38), viewers find themselves incapable of fitting together their mental associations with "fur" and with "cup." Such works become visual puzzles, luring viewers into the mental exercise of trying to figure out what is going on.

Verbal Statements

Though not strictly part of a work of art itself, written statements about a piece or about a particular artist's work may also help draw people into the experience the artist intended. Sometimes these statements are written by art critics or museum curators; sometimes they are written by the artists themselves. Those working in *applied design* disciplines—the creation of functional projects, such as interior design, landscape design, and industrial or product design—are often required to give verbal explanations of their ideas to prospective clients.

Many artists find it very difficult to articulate what they are trying to do, for they have chosen a nonverbal medium to express their nonverbal ideas. Often the impulses that lead them to work in a certain way are as mysterious to them as to others. But Linda Howard, whose

38 MERET OPPENHEIM. *Object* (Fur-covered cup, saucer, and spoon). 1936. Cup, 4⅜″ (10.16 cm) diameter; saucer, 9⅜″ (22.86) diameter; spoon, 8″ (20.32 cm) long; overall height 2⅞″ (7.6 cm). Collection Museum of Modern Art, New York. (Purchase).

Fundamentals of Three-Dimensional Art

monumental works will be shown later in this book, observes that making the effort to define what one is doing may be as beneficial to the artist as to the viewing public. Howard explains,

> I work intuitively, preconsciously, nonverbally. Creating the work brings it to a more conscious level, because then there is a visual, tangible form. Then the next step of responsibility—which most artists don't take, but which is very important for me and actually for all artists—is to try to figure out from this statement, that is the piece, a verbal statement: 'What is it that I'm trying to do?' It's really important for me to sit down and try to figure out my words for what it is I think I'm doing. I may not be right, but at least it brings that much more clarity to my work. You have to figure out what it is that you're doing—no one is going to tell you. You can't just say the work should speak for itself. You should either have the answers or try to seriously search for the answers. Putting your ideas into this even more conscious verbal form then frees your creativity as you return to the preverbal process of creation again.

STUDIO PROBLEMS

1.1   From Three-Dimensionality to Two-Dimensionality

Using the medium of photography—perhaps with a Polaroid-type camera for instant prints—transpose a three-dimensional experience of an actual object or sculpture into a two-dimensional visual experience. How can you photograph the piece to best indicate its three-dimensionality? Its size? What features of the original object are enhanced or lost in the photograph? In a class situation, each student could take one photograph of the same object on campus and then the class could compare the results.

39   From Two-Dimensionality to Three-Dimensionality. Construction with plastic egg, branches, and thread; charcoal drawing. Student work.

1.2   From Two-Dimensionality to Three-Dimensionality

First draw a simple nonobjective design on an 8 1/2 x 11" piece of paper. Then translate the drawing into a three-dimensional piece of sculpture of any material(s) you choose, such as wood, cardboard, fabric, or wire. How can this be done? What aesthetic differences can be seen in the two versions of the design? What factors do you have to deal with in the three-dimensional piece that were not at issue in the two-dimensional drawing? In the example shown (Fig. 39), the student had to reckon with the force of gravity by finding some way of suspending an oval form amid a grid of horizontals and verticals. The solution used—only one among many possibilities—was to create a triangular form by tying thin branches together with thread, including a platform for the egg to rest on, and to use a lightweight plastic egg to avoid putting too much stress on the branch structure.

1.3 Modular Low Relief

Use two pieces of foam core (plastic-coated foam sold in quarter-inch sheets at art supply stores) to create a low-relief work. One is to be the backing; cut the other into a series of identical or similar flat shapes and attach them to the backing to build up a low-relief design. These *modules* (the series of similar pieces) can be joined to each other and to the backing in any way you choose—glue, cut grooves, pins, even some form of tying. What visual effects develop as the flat shapes begin to move outward into three-dimensional space? The solution shown in Figure 40 creates visual excitement with the dark shadow line produced by placing two strips of foam core so close together that they block out almost all light.

1.4 The Wrapped Object

Choose an everyday functional object and wrap it with some other material, such as string or lace, so that no portion of the object remains uncovered. Then do the same thing with an object from nature, perhaps wrapping it with a different material. How can you solve this problem in a way that will draw viewers into looking at the solution? Could the object and the wrapping be antitheses of each other, such as a hammer wrapped with lace? Is there a sense of mystery about what the wrapping conceals? What about evoking a sense of humor or intellectual curiosity? Can the underlying shape be easily recognized within a wrapping that creates a visual pun? You might work with contrasts, such as hard and soft, or with a close relationship between the object and the wrapping.

40 (top) Modular Low-Relief.
Foamcore. Student work.
41 (bottom) Walk-Through Work.
Wood and shavings. Student work.

1.5 Walk-Through Work

Given or choosing a specific location, create an installation piece that controls how people move through the space. You can use any material(s) you choose, such as cardboard or fabric or sand. Part of the problem is figuring out how to set up the piece and how to take it down. Your control of people's movement through the space can be physical or psychological. This problem could be done by individuals or by groups of three to five students working together.

The student who created the solution shown in Figure 41 effectively controlled the movements of other students through a heavily traveled turn in a corridor by laying out lumber, shavings, and puzzlelike pieces of cut wood in such a way that people respected the design enough not to disrupt it. The pieces are not fastened to each other or to the floor in any way; a slight kick would have thrown the whole thing askew. But the installation was up for a week and was not disturbed the whole time. Most people went out of their way to walk across the ends rather than the middle, which crossed the normal path of traffic. Those who did walk across the middle did so very carefully.

2

Working in the Round

All art begins as an idea in the mind of the artist. To bring this idea into reality, to create the form imagined, requires dealing successfully with a number of technical details. Each idea demands certain specific practical considerations and specific skills. Yet it is possible to look at general considerations that arise in every attempt to create art in the round. The care and ingenuity with which artists approach these technical details will make the difference between pieces that fall apart or simply don't do what the artist intended and those that give high-quality expression to the artist's vision.

Gravity

We are so accustomed to accommodating the force of gravity in our everyday existence that we usually give it little thought. Yet this downward pull must be dealt with very consciously and carefully by the

42 Antonio Pollaiuolo. *Hercules Crushing Antaeus.* c. 1475. Bronze, height with base 18″ (45.72 cm). Museo Nazionale, Florence.

three-dimensional artist. Over a period of time, the sheer heaviness of things begins to tell. Even seemingly lightweight objects are surprisingly gravity-bound. Have you ever tacked a poster to a wall, nice and flat, only to discover later that it has bowed out as it slid downward, enlarging and perhaps eventually tearing the upper tack-holes? Or try holding your arm out parallel to the floor; as time passes, its heaviness becomes increasingly apparent and difficult to resist. The pull of gravity may present the artist with difficult challenges, but in some cases the successful defying of gravity's tendency to pull things down may be a major ingredient of the excitement of a work.

Some artists learn to accommodate the force of gravity by trial and error; others conceive ideas that require extensive intellectual knowledge of physics. At the simplest level, any three-dimensional artist learns that whatever projects from the vertical axis is subject to downward pressure and must be firmly anchored to prevent its breaking off and counterbalanced to prevent its pulling the whole piece over. Antonio Pollaiuolo's *Hercules Crushing Antaeus* (Fig. 42) is only

18 inches high, including its base, and yet the weight of Antaeus' outstretched leg would be enough to topple Hercules off the pedestal. In addition to building up a strong vertical mass from other parts of the two figures to help anchor the leg on the left and thrusting Hercules' back far to the right as a counterbalance, the artist's ultimate solution to offset the pull of Antaeus' raised leg was to add a secondary form behind Hercules. The sculpture would probably be more exciting and aesthetically pleasing without the prop, for then Hercules would seem to be the strong force holding Antaeus in the air, but given the state of the art of bronze casting at the time, Hercules himself had to be propped up.

At a more complex level, certain works require great engineering skill if they are to counter the force of gravity successfully. To hang a 200,000 square foot (61,000 sq m) orange nylon curtain across Rifle Gap in Colorado (Fig. 43), Christo had to hire consulting engineers and contractors to help devise ways to support the weight of the curtain from above. The initial solution involved cables running from 7-ton

43 CHRISTO. *Valley Curtain.* 1971–72. Span 1250′ (381 m). Height 185–365′ (56.39 m–111.25 m). 200,000 square feet (18,587 square meters) of nylon polyamide, 110,000 pounds of steel cables. Grand Hogback, Rifle, Colorado. Project Director: Jan van der Marck.

Working in the Round

44 Olivier Mourgue. *Double Chair.*

concrete anchors on either side of the gap, but geologists' tests showed that these would have been pulled right out of the mountain. Instead, construction crews had to construct 200-ton concrete top-anchors to offset the anticipated pressures of gravity and wind on the curtain.

Adding the weight of a person to a piece adds additional considerations. Even if the *Double Chair* shown in Figure 44 holds its curves through time without sagging or its balance without falling over, what happens when one person or even two sit on it? Will it support their weight without caving in? Will it tip over if they both lean forward? What will happen if they lean back? The designer had to take these possibilities into account, or the chair would have unnerved—as well as unseated—potential buyers.

45 Claes Oldenburg. *Soft Toilet.* 1966. Vinyl filled with kapok painted with liquitex, and wood. 4'4″ × 2'8″ × 2'6″ (1.33 m × 81.28 cm × 76.2 cm). Collection Whitney Museum of American Art, New York (50th anniversary gift of Mr. and Mrs. Victor W. Ganz).

Gravity is not necessarily a disagreeable force to work with, however. For the artist who understands it, calling viewers' attention to this everyday phenomenon can be central to the idea of a piece. Claes Oldenburg presents a humorous glimpse of what would happen to a familiar object—the toilet—if it were too soft to resist the pull of gravity (Fig. 45). And in Kenneth Snelson's *Free Ride Home* (Fig. 46), the metal tubes seem to defy gravity like an acrobat flipping high through the air. Even though the cables holding them aloft are somewhat visible, the mastery with which they have been rigged from only three points touching the earth creates the drama of the sculpture.

46 KENNETH SNELSON. *Free Ride Home.* 1974. Aluminum and stainless steel, $30 \times 60 \times 60'$ ($9.14 \times 18.29 \times 18.29$ m). Collection Storm King Art Center, Mountainville, New York. (Purchase).

The Setting

In many cases, a second major consideration is where a piece will be presented. In recent years, there has been a noticeable shift from regarding art as a private or museum experience to presenting large pieces in public settings. Town planners, architects, politicians, and corporations are recognizing that art presented in public spaces may enhance the appeal of those spaces. Despite negative public responses to some pieces, state and municipal governments and private businesses are increasingly setting aside a percentage of the cost of new buildings to be used for the purchase of works of art. The setting of such pieces—foyers of large buildings, public plazas, and the like—dictates a very different approach than the assumption that a piece will be displayed on a mantel or desktop, or behind glass in a museum.

Awareness of whether a work is to be shown inside or outside

47 Great Mosque, Djenné, Mali. 1908. Mud.

makes a big difference in the design process. In general, considerations of safety and vandal-proofing dictate simpler designs for outdoor sculptures, for people are more likely to try to climb on them. Indoor works can be more delicate. For large outdoor works, engineering consultants may be needed to help calculate specifications for factors such as wind loads, snow loads, seismic stability, and the necessary size and depth of footings.

Anything to be used outdoors will also be exposed to weathering processes. If the material used will age, the change should be one that the artist considers desirable. For example, some artists value the shiny brown or green patina that develops on bronze as the surface corrodes. The *Great Mosque* at Djenne, Mali (Fig. 47) could only have been built in a desert climate, for it is constructed of mud. In the absence of significant rains, it has stood for over 75 years, with its surface restored after the yearly rainy season.

If a piece is to be used in a specific place, the lighting of the area should also be determined and perhaps controlled by the artist. Daniel French, sculptor of the *Abraham Lincoln* for the Lincoln Memorial, complained that the lighting in the building did not bring out the strength and drama of the face as he had conceived it. To prove his point, he made two photographs of a full-size model of the head, one with natural light cast upward, as through the east door entrance of the building (Fig. 48), and the other with artificial lighting shining down on the sculpture from a 45-degree angle (Fig. 49). The characteristics thus revealed were so strikingly different that French's requests for artificial lighting were finally granted.

Pieces designed for a particular setting must of course take its

Fundamentals of Three-Dimensional Art

size and characteristics into account as well. Parameters for commissioned works are usually defined by the client. A typical project description—this one appearing in a competition for artworks for a renovated vocational-technical school—was prepared by the Percent for Art in State Buildings, Connecticut Commission on the Arts:

> The commissioning of a three-dimensional work suspended from the lobby ceiling or the commissioning of flat glass for the clerestory windows extending across the front of the lobby. The piece should be conceived to provide color and warmth for a space where predominant materials are brick and wood. It should also serve as an identifying factor for this school.

The challenge to the commissioned artist is to exercise creativity in conceiving pieces that work well not only in themselves but also in relationship to the scale and nature of their surroundings.

To relate a work to its environment does not necessarily mean copying the style of the surroundings, as we saw in Claes Oldenburg's erection of a giant clothespin in historic Philadelphia (Fig. 27). Artists have highly individual ways of relating their work to its environment— yet none ignore it. One version of a successful relationship between art and its surroundings is Henry Moore's placement of his large sculptures in the pastures around his home in England. Moore finds architecture too distracting a background for his work, preferring the sky as a backdrop. He explains,

> There is no background to sculpture better than the sky, because you are contrasting solid form with its opposite space. The sculpture then has no competition, no distraction from other solid objects. If I wanted the most foolproof background for a sculpture, I would always choose the sky.

In Moore's *Sheep Piece* (Fig. 50, p. 40), the coexistence of art and nature is enhanced by the presence of the sheep who share a pasture with the piece. The distinctively rounded, huddled bulks of the live sheep visually reinforce the essence of Moore's sculptural forms.

Size

Size is of importance not only in scaling a work to its surroundings but also in the practical details of creating, transporting, and displaying the work. Look back at Kenneth Snelson's *Free Ride Home* (Fig. 46). Its scale is aesthetically successful in its open outdoor setting, leaping into the sky above the low walls. But imagine the process of assembling the piece. Obviously, it could not be built in a studio or workshop and then transported intact, for it is far too large to fit through a door or onto a truck. Since he chose to work on this large scale, the artist had to make the parts separately and figure out how to assemble

48 (top) DANIEL CHESTER FRENCH, head of *Abraham Lincoln*. 1921. Plaster model of the white marble original, head over 3′ (91.44 cm) high, total figure 19′ (5.79 m) high. Lincoln Memorial, Washington, D.C., architect Henry Bacon. Photographed under replication of original lighting conditions.
49 (bottom) DANIEL CHESTER FRENCH, head of *Abraham Lincoln*. Photographed under desired artificial lighting.

50 Henry Moore. *Sheep Piece.* 1971–72. Hoglands, Hertfordshire, England. Courtesy Henry Moore Foundation.

51 William Stumpf, for Herman Miller. 1976. *Ergon Operational Chair.* Courtesy Herman Miller, Inc.

them on-site. If artists envision circumstances in which they will not be on-site to supervise the assembly and setup of their works, they must also prepare detailed instructions for others to follow.

The size chosen will also determine whether a piece can be constructed by the artist working alone or whether help will be needed. Even relatively small pieces of very dense materials such as marble or glass may be too heavy for one person to maneuver; works made of lighter materials such as aluminum can become much larger before assistance is needed. Some three-dimensional pieces, such as marble sculptures, need not be carried around while they are being worked, and the artist can mount them on a revolving stand for easy access to all sides. But the problem remains: How then to transport such works of art out of the studio to be displayed?

For functional designs, the size of the piece relative to the size of the intended user is a major practical consideration. For instance, if the handle of a mug is too small, large-handed users drinking hot liquids may burn their knuckles. Older people find low sports cars or high vans difficult to climb into and out of. And the relatively new science of *ergonomics*—the study of how people relate physically to their environment—has led to design of office furniture that minimizes fatigue and improves work efficiency by properly fitting and supporting the human body. The *Ergon Chair* (Fig. 51) designed by William

Fundamentals of Three-Dimensional Art

Stumpf for Herman Miller has a shortened seat to prevent restriction of the blood vessels in the thighs, an anatomically contoured back and seat to support the user's upper and lower back, open sides that encourage people to move somewhat instead of getting cramped and numb from sitting still, and armrests that double as backrests when the person is sitting sidewise in the chair. The model shown is designed specifically for people who work long hours seated at computer terminals or other office machines, offering the support of a high seat back with adjustable height, and height and angle adjustments for the chair as a whole to help fit it to the individual user. Despite the many functional aspects of the chair, it also works well aesthetically, with a soft curvature of the back, seat, and armrests that complements the upward curve of the armrests from the base.

Materials

In choosing and working with materials, artists range between two extremes: crafting the material to look like something else, or presenting the material in such a way that its own nature is emphasized. Either way, the unique qualities of each material must be taken into account.

In Chapter 1, we noted that the viewer-involving device in Marilyn Levine's *Spot's Suitcase* (Fig. 23) is the use of clay to look exactly like worn leather. At this extreme, the denial of the characteristics of the medium is sometimes called *trompe l'oeil,* or "fool the eye." Similarly, some artists have developed great skillfulness in sculpting the hardness of marble to look like the softnesses of skin, hair, and draped clothing, as in Bernini's *Ecstasy of St. Theresa* (Fig. 30).

At the other extreme, artists may choose to work a material as little as possible, presenting it in a form closely resembling its natural state. Elyn Zimmerman's *Marabar* (Fig. 52) presents the natural tex-

52 ELYN ZIMMERMAN. *Marabar.* 1984. Plaza and Garden Sculpture, National Geographic Society, Washington, D.C. Shown: 5 natural cleft and polished carnelian granite boulders ranging in height from 3′ to 10′ (91.44 cm to 3.05 m), surrounding a pool constructed of polished carnelian granite.

tures and forms of carnelian granite boulders as an interesting contrast to the straight lines of the National Geographic Society building, and as a reference to the interests of the society. Zimmerman further accentuates the weather-worn and grainy outer surface of the boulders by splitting them and polishing their cleft faces to an utterly smooth and reflective sheen that is the exact opposite of their exteriors.

Another approach to a material is to work it in such a way as to bring out its inner beauty. In its uncut state, marble has a rather rough, dull surface. But carving and smoothing it reveals a softly glowing, fine-grained luster. As in Jean Arp's marble piece *Aquatic* (Fig. 53), artists sometimes choose to simplify the contours of a piece so that this natural inner beauty of their material is not obscured by details.

Each material has its own unique qualities that artists must understand and respect, whether they choose to emphasize or deny these qualities. Claes Oldenburg's statement about materials illustrates a healthy respect for their cussedness:

> I like to work in material that is organic-seeming and full of surprises, inventive all by itself. For example, wire, which has a decided life of its own, paper, which one must obey and will not be ruled too much, or cardboard, which is downright hostile, or wood with its sullen stubbornness. I am a little afraid of metal or glass because they have the capacity like a lion to gash and kill, and if I gave them the freedom I give my other materials they probably would.

Use of different materials in combination requires particular skills and knowledge of their unique properties. John Matt's *Wind Chant* (Fig. 54)

53 JEAN ARP. *Aquatic.* 1953. Marble, 13 × 25½ × 9″ (33.02 × 63.5 × 22.86 cm). Collection Walker Art Center, Minneapolis (gift of the T. B. Walker Foundation).

combines the reflective surfaces of polished aluminum with the warm feel and colors of woods—Philippine mahogany, walnut, and rosewood. Matt notes that wood can always be expected to move—to shrink, expand, and perhaps crack—no matter how thick, old, or dense it is. Metals have very different properties that allow them to bend and to span distances without being very thick. In this piece, all wood parts are allowed to move independently of each other and of the metal. It is also possible to join wood to metal without the wood's cracking, but careful craftsmanship is essential.

The wealth of new materials available to the artist today and the flexibility of today's aesthetics allow artists to use anything they choose—from plastics to camel fur—so long as it works, carrying out the role for which it was chosen. Robert Walker encourages exploration of the potentials of new high-tech materials such as the absolutely clear acrylics he uses in his color sculptures, to be pictured in Chapter 9 ("Color"). He notes that many sculptors today have become "techno-freaks," in that they are thoroughly absorbed in the unique qualities of their chosen medium. Admitting, "I can't deny that I'm in love with this material," he points out that his work with dyed and cast acrylics requires not only appreciation for the material but also highly specialized training. He feels that it is important for artists to develop their mastery of whatever medium they choose, "so they can produce what their minds conceive of."

Respect for the material cannot be overemphasized, for carelessness in this area can undermine even the most elegant of designs. Witness the initial fate of Christo's *Valley Curtain.* After months of elab-

54 John Matt. *Wind Chant.* 1979. Aluminum and hardwood, 6'2½" (1.88 mm) tall, 6'9" (2.06 m) long, 2'7" (78.74 cm) wide (collection the artist).

43

orate preparations and hundreds of thousands of dollars of expenses, the huge curtain unfurled itself prematurely during its test run, snagging and tearing on the rocks. Why? Workmen tying the knots that were to hold the curtain bundled around the cable until everything was ready ran out of the tape they were supposed to be using. Rather than climbing down to get a new roll of tape, they simply used old tape they found stuck to the curtain. Under stress, first the tape gave way, and then the knots, and then the curtain itself. No detail—including the suitability of each material for its intended purpose—is too small to be overlooked.

Planning Three-Dimensional Work

Sometimes artists work directly with their chosen material, manipulating it until it approximates their vision. But when a piece will be large, use costly materials, or require time-consuming techniques of construction, the artist will usually begin by experimenting with its form, using some medium that is cheaper and more easily manipulated.

Often drawings are used in the planning stage. If so, the artist must learn to translate a three-dimensional idea into two-dimensional sketches and, in turn, envision them three-dimensionally. Usually many sketches are required, studying the form from many different points of view. Before beginning construction of *Wind Chant* (Fig. 54), John Matt filled pages of his sketchbook with drawings such as those shown in Figure 55, "thinking nonverbally" about forms, their relationships to each other, and ways of putting them together.

In fields such as architecture and landscape or interior design, plans may include *layouts* viewed from overhead, requiring an additional leap of the imagination to envision the three-dimensional reality of the projected work. Pieces that must be *fabricated*—constructed using industrial techniques—by someone other than the artist may require mechanical drawings to scale for precise duplication. Views from the top, end, side, and sometimes cross-section specify exact sizes and fittings for the craftsperson to use. Often cross-sections are included with dotted lines to indicate the inner construction of joints that will not be apparent on the surface, as in Figure 56. It is an excerpt from the mechanical drawings for Linda Howard's *Rectangles,* a 25-foot-long (7.62 m) hanging redwood sculpture put together with nuts, bolts, washers, and steel rods.

For *site-specific* works—those to be installed in a particular location—drawings of the piece in place as the viewer will see it are usually necessary. They are helpful in judging how well the piece fits into its surroundings, not only in form but also in scale. In Claes Oldenburg's drawing for a *Proposed Colossal Monument to Replace the*

55 (top) JOHN MATT. Excerpt from preliminary sketches for *Wind Chant.* Black fine-point ball-point pen on white drawing paper.
56 (bottom) LINDA HOWARD. Section of blueprint detail drawings for *Rectangles.* 1982. Finished piece redwood, 25 × 14 × 7′ (7.62 × 4.27 × 2.13 m). Collection Pacific Lumber Company, San Francisco, California.

Working in the Round

57 CLAES OLDENBURG. Drawing for *Proposed Colossal Monument to Replace the Washington Obelisk, Washington, D.C.: Scissors in Motion.* 1967. Crayon and watercolor, 30 × 19¾″ (76.2 cm × 50.2 cm). Collection Philip Johnson, New Canaan, Connecticut.

58 SKIDMORE, OWINGS & MERRILL. Computer Study of a Roof Covering Considered for the Haj Terminal, King Abdul Aziz International Airport, Jeddah, Saudi Arabia.

Washington Obelisk (Fig. 57), we really get the sense of what it would be to see these scissor blades thrusting far above the trees into the sky. Such drawings, when done by famous artists such as Oldenburg and Christo, become collector's items in themselves and are often sold to help finance the massive projects they propose.

Computer technology now offers the potential for planning by program—for creating computer programs that will generate two-dimensional drawings of projected three-dimensional projects in perfect perspective. Computer-aided designs such as Skidmore, Owings and Merrill's computer study of a roof covering considered for the International Airport in Jeddah, Saudi Arabia (Fig. 58), can be rotated, shrunk, or enlarged for viewing from any angle or distance. In effect, the varying graphics displays that can be called up allow the artist to walk around a work before it is even constructed. The programs also allow the designs to be changed in specific dimensions, as variations on a basic theme. The rapidity of changes once the initial program is created makes it possible for artists with a knowledge of computer programming to experiment with a great variety of solutions to any visual problem they can conceive, changing specifications until they find the design that works best.

Planning can also be carried out in a variety of three-dimensional modes, allowing direct apprehension of the intended forms. Sculptors often mold a small *maquette* of soft clay as they do their initial nonverbal thinking about a piece. The work itself may be a further evolution of the idea rather than a literal translation of the maquette into a larger scale and more durable material. Sometimes, however, construction of the final work may be done by assistants copying the model. In this case, the model may be small-scale, with enlargements carried out by exacting caliper measurements, or it may be full-scale. Frederick

Fundamentals of Three-Dimensional Art

59 Frederick Hart working on a detail of a plasticine model for *Ex nihilo,* tympanum to be carved over entrance to the National Cathedral, Washington, D.C.

Hart's 2-ton full-scale plasticene model for *Ex nihilo* (Fig. 59) will be carved in stone above the entrance to the Washington Cathedral by master stonecarvers. The model itself was preceded by a traditional planning process: Hart first sketched the design and made a small plasticene model of it. The model was then cast in plaster and enlarged by an "enlarger" to a rough full-scale plasticene copy. After Hart finished the detail work on the model, as shown, it was cast in plaster by sections. The stonecarvers work from this cast, taking its measurements to carve the final piece.

Maquettes may be made of anything the artist finds suitable. John Matt's maquette shown in Figure 60 is made of paper and thread, hanging from a 2-foot-high (.61 m) stand. Matt explains that if he were seeking a commission for the piece, his next step would be to construct a larger model—perhaps 10 feet (3.05 m) high—of aluminum and stainless steel for a more realistic preview of what the actual piece would look like. In his vision, the piece would be 50 to 100 feet (15.25 to 30.5 m) high, perhaps soaring and floating through the foyer of a large building. Even in the 2-foot-high (.61 m) maquette Matt includes the small paper figure of a human dwarfed by the sculpture, to create a sense of the vast scale he envisions.

Some artists prefer to do their experimenting directly, learning from a piece itself what is possible as it evolves. Arthur Hoener, whose sculpture shown in Figure 61 was one of a series based on repetition of same-size wooden modules, explains this way of working:

> So many decisions are made as I go along that each piece becomes a sketch for the next piece. I'm already turning the next piece over in my mind as I see what develops on an individual piece. I find that trying to do any drawings ends up restricting what form I can make. So rather than restrict the form to drawings, I allow my mind and the work in progress to develop new ideas.

Hoener's way of working does not imply a lack of planning, however. In his mind, he determined the general plan: "This time I'll use alternating pieces of dark and light wood that are an inch and a quarter thick, and this time I'll use a 45-degree angle and then cut them and sand them for a tight sensuous surface that exposes the interior form." With this coherent pattern in mind, Hoener could then work freely with the individual modules, "weaving" them together in the ways that seemed to work best as the sculpture took shape.

Form vs. Function

Traditionally, a distinction has been made between the fine arts and the applied arts. *Fine art,* such as sculpture, is meant only to be looked at; the *applied* or *functional arts,* such as architecture, interior design, landscape design, and product design, are meant to be used. Although these definitions seem distinct in theory, in actuality the line between the two is imprecise.

Crafts—functional pieces made by hand—help to blur the dis-

60 (top left) JOHN MATT. Maquette for a proposed sculpture. Paper and thread, height 2' (60.96 cm).
61 (bottom left) ARTHUR HOENER. *Standing Figure No. 2.* 1969. Honduras mahogany and poplar, 7'5" × 2'6" × 1'9" (2.26 m × 76.2 cm × 53.34 cm) (collection of the artist).

Fundamentals of Three-Dimensional Art

tinction between form and function, for while they serve some useful purpose they are typically also designed with an appreciation of aesthetic considerations. That is, they are created with attention to the *elements of design*—form, space, line, texture, light, and color—and the *principles of design*—repetition, variety, rhythm, balance, emphasis, economy, and proportion—that are explored in the next chapters of this book. For example, Oskar Sørensen's *Silver Liqueur Decanter*, shown in Figure 62, has been handcrafted with loving awareness of the effects of form, line, surface texture, and light.

Techniques developed for use in creating functional works are sometimes adopted in construction of nonfunctional works designed solely as artistic experiences. Diane Sheehan carried her skill as a weaver into the area of art for art's sake, creating in *Like the Wind* (Fig. 63) a piece of fiber art. It becomes a sculpture in the round, enticing the viewer to investigate its forms, textures, and inner spaces from all sides. One is drawn in partly by curiosity about how this familiar non-rigid craft medium has been coaxed to hold an upright form.

Similarly, to create monumental aesthetic experiences such as the *Valley Curtain* (Fig. 43), Christo draws on methods and materials not traditionally linked with art—from excavation, drilling, concrete pouring, curtain fabrication, and cable-hanging to the great complexities of "nonart" activities such as obtaining permits from landowners, highway departments, environmental protection agencies, and local officials, and raising the funds necessary to support his visions.

62 (top left)   Oskar Sørensen for Tostrup. *Silver Liqueur Decanter,* bird-shaped. 1937. H. 27 cm (10.6″). Marks: "830 S. J. Tostrup, Oslo." Collection Oslo Museum of Applied Art. Acquired through the Grosch Fund 1938.

63 (top right)   DIANE SHEEHAN. *Like the Wind.* 1983. Linen and cotton, 11 × 11 × 11″ (27.94 × 27.94 × 27.94 cm) (collection of the artist).

Working in the Round   **49**

64 Krone Company, West Germany. Krone-a-Phone Compact 1000. Thermoplastic, 8″ long, 2½″ wide, 2¾″ high (20.32 × 6.35 × 7.1 cm).

Another variation on the form/function relationship appears in *industrial design*—styling of the functional, often mass-produced, products that fill our environment, from appliances to office interiors, with consideration of their aesthetic appeal. The telephone, once a contraption obviously concocted of wires and bells, has become an object of art, with designs ranging from French Baroque to the elegant lines of the *Krone-a-phone* (Fig. 64), designed by a West German design firm. Even home computers are developed and judged partly on the basis of exterior design characteristics. Manufacturers consider design an important marketing tool, a way of increasing sales. Industrial designers have been commissioned to enhance the visual appeal of everything from automobiles and refrigerators to soda bottles.

In some cases, and in some historical periods, form has been the primary consideration in creating functional pieces. The saltcellar that

65 Benvenuto Cellini. *Saltcellar of Francis I.* 1539–43. Gold, 10¼ × 13″ (26 × 33 cm). Kunsthistorisches Museum, Vienna.

66 ALMA SLEDHOFF-BUSCHER. *Bauhaus/ Blocks,* designed 1923. 21 wood pieces, $10 \times 2\frac{1}{2} \times 1\frac{3}{4}''$ (25.4 cm × 6.35 cm × 4.57 cm).

Benvenuto Cellini created for Francis I (Fig. 65) elaborates form far beyond what is strictly necessary in a vessel for salt. By contrast, rather than elaborating form for its own sake, some artists have felt that in a functional piece, form should evolve alongside functional considerations. At the *Bauhaus,* a famous German design school that opened in 1919 with the statement "There is no essential difference between the artist and the craftsman," form and function were seen not as isolated considerations but as a single unity, an organic whole. In this approach to integrity in design, industrial designers may enhance the way a product functions. The streamlined locomotive that Raymond Loewy designed for the Pennsylvania Railroad reduced wind drag by a third. And the *Bauhaus/Blocks* designed by Alma Sledhoff-Buscher (Fig. 66) are at the same time classically appealing in form, texture, and color, and also well suited to the function of entertaining and educating children. Scaled for manipulation by small hands, they fit seamlessly into the rectangular package and can be combined to create a great variety of representational and nonrepresentational forms.

On a grander scale, the marriage of computer-aided mathematics, modern technology, and artistic sensitivity allows creation of technically and artistically elegant structures such as the *Brotonne Bridge* (Fig. 67, p. 52). Designed by Jean Muller, the cable-stayed plan is free from the clutter of overhead trusses. Instead, the precise calculation of stresses allows the bridge to be hung from only two central towers, a design that is at once structurally sound, inexpensive, and lyrically graceful.

Certain pieces we now appreciate as fine art were initially created not as art but as useful objects. The Shaker furnishings (Fig. 68, p. 52) many now admire for their beauty of form were created under strictly functional considerations. Lines were sparse and storage recessed to avoid cluttering or pampering the senses so that all thoughts could be directed toward God. Pegs on the walls allowed chairs to be hung out of the way when the floor was being cleaned. Paint was usually not applied to the native wood for to do so was

67 (top) JEAN MULLER. Brotonne Bridge over the Seine near Rouen, France, completed 1977. Campernon Bernhard Engineering Firm, Paris.
68 (right) Shaker dwelling room. Early 19th century community, Enfield, New Hampshire. Courtesy Henry Francis du Pont Winterthur Museum, Winterthur, Delaware.

Fundamentals of Three-Dimensional Art

thought unnecessary. From our vantage point in time, we judge these Shaker rooms as aesthetically pleasing, but at the time, the preferences of the larger society were for the ornate.

Despite all these exceptions and variations, the fact remains that an artist designing a functional piece does so with a slightly different attitude than one designing a piece that is not meant to be used. A functional piece must work. If it doesn't, it is not successful on a practical basis, no matter how successful it is aesthetically. In some cases, aesthetics must be sacrificed somewhat in the interests of functionality. A case in point: The *Max II Cups and Saucers* (Fig. 69) were designed by Vignelli Associates to be both highly functional—the pieces stack neatly in a small space, can be used indoors or out, and are mass-producible of high-quality plastic—and aesthetically elegant. However, one of the strong points of the cup design, from an aesthetic point of view, proved to be nonfunctional and had to be abandoned. This was the open-channeled handle, presenting a negative (or unfilled) space that flowed intriguingly up the handle and disappeared down into the interior of the cup. Unfortunately, when users unpredictably filled the cup to the brim, as American coffee-drinkers were wont to do, the hot liquid would use this convenient channel to flow out onto their hand. Consequently, the design had to be changed to place a dam at the top of the handle, arresting the flow not only of coffee but also of the eye. The version shown in Figure 69 is the original one, still the designer's favorite.

69 Massimo and Lella Vignelli, Vignelli Associates, for Heller Design. *Max II Cups and Saucers.* 1970. Melamine. Cup: height 2¹¹⁄₁₆″ (68 mm), diameter 3³⁄₁₆″ (80 mm), width at handle 4½″ (110 mm). Saucer: diameter 5¾″ (145 mm). Permanent Collection of Design, Museum of Modern Art, New York.

Cost and Audience

Finally, many artists are forced to be aware of who might buy their pieces and how much they can afford to pay. There are some who create works of art chiefly to satisfy their own curiosity or inner compulsion; they may or may not connect with buyers who like their work. Others must pay some or a great deal of attention to the marketplace or to specific clients or employers.

The costs of producing a piece depend on three factors: the time, materials, and tools involved. If a potter designs a cup with a handle that takes an hour to pull, the piece cannot be sold for $5. A fine piece of marble is a beautiful medium to work with, but it is not inexpensive. An industrial designer might have wonderful ideas for products that must be set aside because the company has already invested heavily in some different technology and cannot afford to retool for the processes required. As a student, you will be working chiefly with inexpensive materials and readily available tools; if you become successful as an artist, the prices you can get for your work may allow you to move into more expensive materials and processes.

Who is the audience? Must a piece be mass-producible for

70 Gianlorenzo Bernini, *Triton Fountain,* Piazza Barberini, Rome. 1642–1643. Travertine.

instant appeal to a mass market? Or, at the other extreme, is the audience a profitable corporation willing to spend a large sum to bring art to its employees and customers? What are the artistic tastes of this audience? Aesthetic preferences change, sometimes rapidly. Today there is an appreciation of simple, clean lines, perhaps as an antidote to the busy clutter of our lives. There is also an attraction to honesty in design. For example, public fountains were once expected to be graceful, highly ornamental works like the *Triton Fountain* in Rome (Fig. 70). The water coming out of a figure was secondary to the figure itself. By contrast, in Isamu Noguchi's *Dodge Memorial Fountain* (Fig. 71)

71 Isamu Noguchi. *Horace E. Dodge and Son Memorial Fountain.* Civic Center Plaza, Detroit. 24' (7.32 m) high, stainless steel loop, granite well, 35 sprays and light sources.

the water and the fountain cannot be separated. The water pipe is one with the water; together they create a dramatic statement that reflects the technologically advanced character of the Civic Center, itself designed to present Detroit as a forward-looking city. The new aesthetic that allows appreciation of Noguchi's fountain accepts a thing for what it is: a fountain MOVES WATER, and in this case, it even responds to changes in the weather by moderating the flow.

Or take another example: the *Notch Showroom* (Fig. 72) for Best Products, a discount appliance chain. To overcome the monotonous boxiness of the standard warehouse, the architects came up with a

72 SITE PROJECTS, INC. for Best Products Co., Inc. *Notch Showroom,* Arden Fair Shopping Center, Sacramento, California. 1977. 65,279 internal square feet (6067 square meters), two floors. Consulting architects: Simpson/Stratta Associates, San Francisco, California.

witty and functional solution: a 14-foot high corner of the store slides out 40 feet on tracks as an entrance that can be opened and closed daily. Open, it creates an interesting jagged edge. It is highly successful in drawing attention. People bring their out-of-town friends to the store to show off its zany approach, whether they like it or not. And the daily opening and closing of the 45-ton notch always draws a crowd of onlookers. In the past, would people have accepted a building that appeared to be coming apart? Today, the freshness of this approach is appreciated in contrast to the tedium of look-alike shopping centers.

Despite changes in tastes and values, certain pieces transcend the mood of their times to invoke a more timeless appeal. They become classics because their excellence in design—both aesthetic and functional—is unquestionable. The *Bauhaus blocks,* for instance (Fig. 66) were designed in 1923 but are still being sold today, for they work on every level. In this chapter, we have examined some of the practical considerations that determine whether a piece works well; in the next chapter we will look at the general aesthetic considerations that determine the success of a work of art.

Fundamentals of Three-Dimensional Art

STUDIO PROBLEMS

2.1 Good and Bad Design

Bring in a functional piece that you consider well-designed and a functional piece that in your opinion is poorly designed. If you can't bring in the pieces themselves, photographs will do. Consider both aesthetic appeal and functionality, or lack thereof, and describe for the class the characteristics that enhance or detract from the aesthetics and functionality of the pieces you have selected.

2.2 Working with the Setting

Using whatever materials and as many forms as you choose, create a site-specific piece that controls all space within an existing indoor or outdoor environment. That is, all the space within certain obvious boundaries should appear to "belong to" the work. The piece shown in Figure 73 controlled a pitlike area surrounded by low walls by creating an atmosphere within it of a sacred Indian circle, bringing the feeling of the outside inside. The atmosphere worked so well that most people stayed out of the pit, choosing to look at the piece over the walls instead. To help with clean-up, opened plastic bags were placed beneath the dirt; the branches were just laid across each other and held in place by their own weight.

This problem can be solved in any size, from a large-scale designed environment to a small-scale model within a scaled-down indication of an

73 Working with the Setting. Dirt, branches, stones. Student work.

environment, and by individuals or small groups. An alternative would be for several students to use pieces created as solutions to an earlier problem and explore ways to combine and present them so they work well together and in relationship to a specific setting.

2.3 Defying Gravity

Using any materials you choose, create a piece that appears to defy gravity and by so doing, draws the force of gravity to the viewer's attention. For instance, the piece might fly or appear to be about to fall. If it flies, it should not look so much like a standard kite that the viewer takes its ability to fly for granted. If it is earthbound and seemingly about to fall, whatever keeps it from falling should not be apparent to the viewer to preserve the illusion of defying gravity. The graceful wood piece shown in Figure 74 stands without any hidden means of support. Although the upper part encompasses a large volume of space, it is actually very lightweight. The plywood arc into which the legs of the piece are sunk is just barely wide and heavy enough to counterbalance the curve of the upper part. If the base were larger and heavier, the fragile and living sense of balance would be lost.

74 Defying Gravity. Steam-bent pine. Student work.

2.4 Working on a Large Scale

The point of this problem is to create the largest three-dimensional piece you can using no more than $5 for materials. At the instructor's discretion, a time factor might even be specified; that is, the piece might have to be sturdy enough to stand up on its own for a certain number of hours—perhaps 6 to 8 hours. The student who turns in the largest work that holds up for the duration "wins"—perhaps a prize might be offered. This problem may get you thinking about the economics of materials and size as well as the artistic challenge of creating a large piece.

Fundamentals of Three-Dimensional Art

3

Organizing
Principles
of Design

The characteristics that make a piece work well are difficult to define. Each piece is different and created with different intent. The *intent* of a work is the central idea or problem with which the artist is working. This idea forms the intangible focus of the work, that which underlies its form. One artist's intent may be to create an extremely lifelike representation of some object; another may be trying to reveal the beauty of a material or of pure form. The intent might be to evoke a particular emotional atmosphere or intellectual realization. Or it might be the solving of a visual problem the artist has created, such as the studio problems suggested at the ends of chapters in this book. It is what the piece is "about." Without some initial sense of intention, the artist has nothing around which to unify a piece.

Working from a central intention, artists have traditionally striven for *unity*—the coordination of all parts of a work to expression of their intent. To unify a work is to make its many parts appear as one coherent whole. Despite vast differences in intent and style, artworks whose aesthetic value holds up over the centuries tend to have certain unifying characteristics in common. These have traditionally been labeled the *principles of design.* These aesthetic considerations—repetition, variety, rhythm, balance, emphasis, economy, and proportion—are general ways of organizing a work. They satisfy the mind's desire to create order out of chaos. Although **unity** is sometimes treated as a separate principle of design, the term is used here to connote the combined result of all organizing principles of design.

The principles to be discussed in this chapter are not absolute rules. A successful piece need not conform to all of them, and many artists use them more intuitively than intellectually. The principles can also be interpreted in many different ways. Art is a living field; it changes with its times. And three-dimensional design today does not represent a single, unified approach to art. Rather, contemporary three-dimensional expression ranges from the strictly representational to totally nonrepresentational, from efforts to create beauty to attempts at social commentary, from sculpture to functional pieces. Although the same principles are relevant to all these works and to all historical periods, to define and use the principles in a narrow sense is to ignore their limitless potential.

Before we examine the principles one at a time, note that they are artists' ways of unifying their manipulation of the *elements of design*—form, space, line, texture, light, color, and time. These elements will be explored in detail in subsequent chapters.

Repetition

Repetition is the use of similar design features again and again. This device gives the mind of the viewer an obvious way to understand what the eye is perceiving: "They're all alike," or "Oh, look, this one is like that one, and here's another one." Looking down the stairwell at the Guggenheim Museum (Fig. 75), one is immediately struck by the repetition of similar lines, creating what appears to be a series of nested triangles. We don't perceive one line in isolation; instead, we "read" from one to the next to the next, grouping them logically into a pattern.

Repetition tends to tie things together whether they are touching or not. Although the mind likes to categorize—and perhaps even count—similar objects, if the task is too obvious it may search for some more subtle line of reasoning. Encountering Ursula von Rydingsvard's *Untitled* (Fig. 76), we quickly perceive that the work consists of twelve small, similar, mountainlike wooden forms. Its unity is so apparent that the mind may quickly create a new mental puzzle: Why? Why did she do this? What does it mean? In the absence of a title,

75 (left)   FRANK LLOYD WRIGHT. Stairwell, Solomon R. Guggenheim Museum, New York.
76 (bottom)   URSULA VON RYDINGSVARD. *Untitled.* 1978. Laminated cedar, 2½ × 15 × 16′ (76.2 cm × 4.57 m × 4.88 m). Photographed at Manhattan Psychiatric Center, Ward's Island, New York (collection the artist).

77 MOSHE SAFDIE. *Habitat,* Montreal. Built for the 1967 Expo. 354 modular construction units comprising 158 houses. Each modular box is 17′6″ × 38′6″ × 10′ (5.33 × 11.12 × 3.05 m), pre-cast in concrete with metal reinforcements.

we are stuck with a conundrum that may successfully engage our attention for a while.

Repetition is often handled more subtly, satisfying our desire for order without calling attention to itself. Moshe Safdie's *Habitat* (Fig. 77) is built from a series of identical 70-ton rectangular modules. But since they can be put together in different ways—with different ends facing the viewer, and with varying degrees of overhang—the fact of their repetition may be intellectually discovered but does not announce itself at first glance.

As is true of other organizing principles of design, repetition is a framework within which the artist may feel a paradoxical sense of freedom. As Arthur Hoener, whose work was shown in Figure 61, explains,

> I've found that I have the greatest freedom if I use certain restric-
> tions—if, for instance, I make up my mind to use repetition of light
> and dark modules of the same size to develop a form. Most such
> decisions are based on one's knowledge of the principles of design:
> I know that if I use repetition, for example, the piece will hold
> together. Then I have tremendous freedom in developing the form—
> in pushing it as far as I can.

Fundamentals of Three-Dimensional Art

Variety

While our minds can apprehend repetition with some facility, they can also create order from the chaos of incoming sensations when they can discern some unifying theme among disparate inputs. The organizational principle of variety does not refer to total chaos, for few people can tolerate total meaninglessness—unless perhaps randomness is itself the organizing theme of a work. Rather, *variety* is a form of order in which the organizing principle must be discovered by the viewer. In works organized on the principle of variety, parts that are seemingly different from each other nonetheless have something in common.

Variety is often expressed as variations on a theme. In Sol LeWitt's *All Variations of Incomplete Open Cubes* (Fig. 78), we are shown a multitude of wooden units with a consistent similarity: All are variations on a cube form. While a full cube would have twelve edges, LeWitt has left out varying pieces and varying numbers of pieces. Analysis of the variations shows that from the eleven-legged unit to the three-legged unit, all can be interpreted as "cube." The three-edged piece is the absolute minimum that can be used to convey the cube

78 Sol LeWitt. *All Variations of Incomplete Open Cubes.* 1975. 122 wood sculptures painted white, each 26 × 14″ (66.04 × 35.56 cm). Also 131 framed photographs and drawings of the units in the series, each 26 × 14″ (66.04 cm × 35.56 cm). Base: 1 × 10 × 18′ (30.48 cm × 3.05 m × 5.49 m). Courtesy Saatchi Collection, London.

idea, but given three pieces of wood connected at right angles to indicate a figure of equal height, width, and depth, we can perceive an implied cube. Variations with more sides reinforce this interpretation. The variations on the incomplete cube theme are continued in the wall-hung photographs and drawings of the individual units on the table. Another approach to appreciating the similarities would be to search for pieces that are identical but turned a different side up.

In contrast to the obvious cube-ness of LeWitt's variations, the unifying theme in some works is almost beyond the viewer's grasp. Confronted with William Wiley's *Sea Man Awl Works* (Fig. 79), we may have an intuitive sense that these crazily juxtaposed objects fit together somehow, but our mind cannot easily get hold of the unifying principle of the piece. We are drawn into trying to figure out the visual puzzle— "What on earth is going on here?" The mind hunts for clues: "It feels like a waterfront; maybe that's a fishing pole—or is it a mast of some sort? And what's all that string? Is it fishing line all fouled up or is it rigging? What's that paintbrush doing in there? And there's a palette— the guy must be an artist, too." Presented with such a great variety of parts, we look from one to the next, trying to figure out what each thing is and how it relates to other parts of the whole. The sense of the whole itself is elusive, hovering right on the edge of our consciousness but

Fundamentals of Three-Dimensional Art

80 Cynthia Boyer. Hand-felted jacket with knit sleeves. 1984.

just beyond our reach. Our inability to quite grasp what is going on does not mean that the piece has failed, however; in presenting just enough information to suggest some hidden unity, the piece forces us to try to pull the parts together into a coherent whole.

Variations may also be seen as variations in the elements of design. Artists may present us with *contrasts*—juxtaposition of dissimilar areas. These contrasts engage our participation in comparing, for instance, light and dark areas, wide lines and thin lines, heavy forms and lightweight forms, filled spaces and unfilled spaces. In the *Hand-felted jacket* shown in Figure 80, Cynthia Boyer invites us to explore the sensual contrasts among a variety of textures. Although the contrasting features presented—very loose-knit vs. very tight-felted areas—may seem to be polar opposites of each other, they can be perceived as an organic whole, for the poles are related as ends of the same continuum. Boyer's piece is unified by its persistent reference to texture; a piece that contrasts very light areas with very dark areas is unified by its persistent reference to value. Filled and unfilled areas complete each other like yin and yang.

Variety may be handled boldly, as in the juxtaposition of dramatically contrasting areas. Or it may be handled gently, with a dark area gradually blending into a light area, wide gradually dwindling to

Organizing Principles of Design　　**65**

narrow. This gradual introduction of variety is known as *transition*. Transitions obviously help to tie a work together, for they gently lead the mind from one quality to another, revealing the logic of their relationship.

Rhythm

Repetition and variety in art tend to create a certain visual *rhythm*—a more or less regular pattern created by the elements of design as they seem to move and change through time and space. It is actually the eye that moves across the changing surfaces of the piece. Movements in and out, up and down, flowing and pausing, and sudden changes in size, value, or complexity create visual effects that can be compared to music. As the eye explores a three-dimensional piece, the viewer may get a sense of accented and unaccented beats or of crescendos and decrescendos. Rhythm exists as a substratum that usually does not call attention to itself, but nonetheless helps to unify the viewer's perception of a piece.

Beats may be quite distinct. The forms of the Easter Island statues (Fig. 81) can be seen as accented beats, separated by the unfilled spaces between them. The statues suggest a series of dramatic single pulses, like heavy individual beats played on a deep-throated drum or gong. In Frederic Remington's narrative sculpture *Comin' Through the Rye* (Fig. 82), individual visual beats are less distinct, but a rapid staccato rhythm is set up nevertheless as the outlines of the forms abruptly shift direction up and down, in and out through space. The many hooves striking the ground in succession, punctuated by the upraised arms, make this a very "noisy" piece of sculpture.

In some pieces, there may be a sense of movement that has no

81 Six of the seven statues of Ahu-Akivi, Easter Island. 17th century or earlier. Height 30′ (9.14 m).

82 FREDERIC REMINGTON. *Comin' Through the Rye (Off the Range).* c. 1902. Bronze, 27⅜″ (70.6 cm) high. Metropolitan Museum of Art, New York (Bequest of Jacob Ruppert, 1939).

beginning and no end. The curving lines of Max Bill's *Monoangulated Surface in Space* (Fig. 83) set up a continuing song, endlessly flowing back into itself. As it rises, the "sound" swells in a gentle crescendo; as the two sides meet and flow downward again, the rhythm resolves temporarily into a decrescendo and then rises again with barely a

83 MAX BILL. *Monoangulated Surface in Space.* 1959. Gilded brass, 15 × 18 × 26″ (38.1 × 45.72 × 66.04 cm). Detroit Institute of Arts (Gift of W. Hawkins Terry).

67

pause. The piece almost becomes a visual mantra, like a continually chanted "Om."

Some works echo—or contrast with—the rhythm of their surroundings. Pieces that suggest a single beat are sometimes very effective in contrast with the cacophony of an urban environment. Michael Singer's *First Gate Ritual Series* (Fig. 84) fits in with the soft rhythm set up by its natural environment—the whispering ripples and highlights of slow-moving water. The work gently adds its own lightly sustained, overlapping notes to the passing flow of shimmering reflections.

Balance

The sense that a three-dimensional work is visually balanced is another way in which a work may satisfy the mind's search for order. If pieces were not in fact balanced or anchored, they would fall over. But beyond the physical fact of their remaining as placed, works convey a sense of *visual balance.* Each area suggests a certain *visual weight,* a certain degree of lightness or heaviness. Factors such as value, texture, form, size, and color affect our perception of visual weight. For example, light colors appear lighter in weight than dark colors; transparent areas seem to weigh less than opaque areas. Yellow areas seem to expand in size whereas blue areas tend to contract. To balance a work is to distribute the visual weight of its parts in such a way that the viewer is satisfied that the piece is not about to pull itself over.

One form of visual balance is *symmetrical balance*—the formal

84 Michael Singer. *First Gate Ritual Series.* 1976. Oak and rock. Installed at the Nassau County Museum of Fine Art, Roslyn, New York.

85 Pirro Ligorio. *The Fountain of the Organ,* Villa d'Este, Tivoli. c. 1550.

placement of identical parts of each side of an imaginary *vertical axis,* a central line that could be drawn vertically through the piece. In *The Fountain of the Organ* (Fig. 85) the organ pipelike jets of water are exactly the same on both sides, like mirror images of each other. Such a configuration tends to create a secure, safe feeling, a sense of solidity that transcends the fluidity of the medium.

    Asymmetrical balance is a trickier balancing act. Here, areas on either side of a central vertical axis are not identical but appear to have the same visual weight nonetheless. To balance forms asymmetrically, a *thrust* away from the vertical axis in one area may be balanced by a *counterthrust* in the opposite direction on the other side of the vertical axis. In Jacques Lipchitz' *Prometheus Strangling the Vulture* (Fig. 86),

86 Jacques Lipchitz. *Prometheus Strangling the Vulture.* 1944–1953. Bronze, 8′4″ × 8′4″ × 4′9″ (2.29 × 2.29 × 1.45 m). Walker Art Center, Minneapolis (Gift of the T. B. Walker Foundation).

87 (top left)   Richard Sapper. Tizio
Table Lamp. 1972. Black metal, 44″
(1.12 m) maximum height, 4½″
(11.43 cm) diameter at base. Manufacturer: Artemide, Italy. Collection
the Museum of Modern Art, New
York (Gift of the manufacturer).
88 (top right)   Vico Magistretti.
Atollo Table Lamp, 1977. Aluminum
with nextel finish, 27⅝ × 19¾″
(69.60 × 50.29 cm). Manufacturer:
O-Luce Italia. Collection the Museum of Modern Art, New York (Gift
of the manufacturer).

the projection of the vulture and Prometheus' head to the right are
offset by the thrust of the form billowing out to the left, making it
appear logical that Prometheus could indeed be balancing his considerable weight atop the small ball at the base. Here, the central axis is
suggested by presentation of an actual *balancing point*—a fulcrum at
the base upon which the entire upper portion of the composition
seems to be balanced.

   In asymmetrically balanced pieces, the balancing point may not
fall in the exact center of the work. In the *Tizio Lamp* shown in Figure
87, there appear to be two balancing points—the lower one to the left
of center and the upper one to the far right. By contrast, the symmetrically balanced *Atollo Lamp* shown in Figure 88 has a single balancing
point in dead center.

   Designs must be balanced vertically as well as horizontally; that
is, if an imaginary line is drawn horizontally through the center of a
piece, representing its *horizontal axis,* the area above the line must be
balanced by the area below the line. In judging this *vertical balance,*
we may feel that absolute symmetry—the same weight above as

below—is actually unbalanced. Based on our experiences in the three-dimensional world, we expect that greater weight is needed on the bottom to support the area rising above the horizontal axis. In John Storrs' skyscraperlike *Forms in Space* (Fig. 89), we sense that the great height of the figure relative to its width is possible only because of the "support" of the shorter outer columns for the tallest central columns.

The complexities of visual balancing are compounded by the fact that the components of the balance change as one walks around a three-dimensional piece. Although our view of Lipchitz' *Prometheus* (Fig. 86) is frozen by the photograph, the projection of forms on either side of the balancing point is quite different from other points of view, but equally well balanced. Because balance is often too complex to be determined intellectually, artists are more likely to work with it intuitively, manipulating the elements of design until areas feel balanced in relationship to each other.

Can a piece of three-dimensional work be visually unbalanced? It depends on the intent of the artist. In some cases, a suggestion of imbalance is central to the excitement of a piece. In *Prometheus* the lack of a broad base for Prometheus' great bulk makes his struggle with the vulture all the more exciting, for he seems to have precise balance as well as considerable strength. In Arthur Hoener's *Standing Figure No. 2* (Fig. 61), the fact that the sculpture seems slightly off balance adds to its sinuous quality, as though it were in motion.

Emphasis and Economy

Many works are successful because they adhere to the principle of *emphasis*—stressing of a particular area or characteristic rather than presentation of a maze of details of equal importance. One method of achieving emphasis is to make one area or quality *dominant,* or most important visually, with other areas contributing but subordinate. That area to which the eye is drawn most compellingly may be the largest, brightest, darkest, or most complex part of the whole, or it may be given special attention because it stands out for some other reason. In Naum Gabo's *Linear Construction* (Fig. 90, p. 72), we could see the oval void in the center as the *focal point*—the place where our gaze tends to center. Though consisting of unfilled space, it stands out because it runs through the physical center of the work and because its simplicity contrasts with the fine lines of the filled areas that surround it.

Although focal points are commonly used as unifying characteristics in two-dimensional art, three-dimensional works may not have a single focal point, since there may be no one point that can be seen from all sides. Gabo's piece is transparent, thus allowing the central

89 JOHN STORRS. *Forms in Space.* Metals in combination. Without base, height 20¼″ (51.30 cm), greatest width 4″ (10.16 cm). With base, height 25″ (63.5 cm), base height 4¾″ (11.68 cm), width 5½″ (13.71 cm), depth 3⅛″ (8.12 cm). Metropolitan Museum of Art (Bequest Fund, 1967).

90 NAUM GABO. *Linear Construction, Variation.* 1942–43. Plastic with nylon thread, height 24⅛″ (61.46 cm), length 24⅛″ (61.46 cm), narrowest width 2¼″ (5.58 cm), widest width 9⅞″ (25.14 cm). Phillips Collection, Washington, D. C.

void to be seen from all angles. But in works that must be walked around, the eye may be led from one area to another, so the notion of focal *point* is not easily applied. One-sided works may be organized around a single dominant area, however. And in works that physically surround the viewer, such as gardens, a contrasting element such as a fountain or piece of sculpture may be used to draw people into or through the work. In Lawrence Halprin's *Auditorium Forecourt Fountain* in Portland, Oregon (Fig. 91), a series of waterfalls is used as a dominant feature, an unusual focus within the urban environment.

Another form of emphasis is the directing of all elements of design toward the intended goal. In Antoni Gaudí's *Church of the Sagrada Familia* (Fig. 92), the aesthetic intent is to uplift the awareness of the viewer. To this end, the major forms rise in slender spires, making the cathedral's height much greater than its width. The visual accent is on the vertical, creating a pronounced upward thrust. The gingerbread cutouts make the materials appear much lighter than they actually are, creating an airy effect, as though the building were actually stretching upward in a spiritual reaching that defies the pull of the earth's gravity.

Yet another way of creating emphasis is to limit the viewer's focus to only a few elements of design. This device is called *visual economy*—stripping away all nonessentials to reveal the essence of a visual idea. In pieces such as the pot shown in Figure 93, the late British potter Hans Coper limited his use of colors and textures to leave the viewer room to experience the bare essence of abstract form. This austere aesthetic eliminates clutter, allowing the mind to focus on the beauty of the seemingly simple.

Fundamentals of Three-Dimensional Art

91 (top) Lawrence Halprin & Associates, *Auditorium Forecourt Fountain,* Portland Open Space Sequence, Portland, Oregon. 1968.
92 (left) Antoni Gaudi. *Church of the Sagrada Familia.* 1903–26. Barcelona, Spain. Photo from collection Museum of Modern Art, New York.
93 (bottom) Hans Coper (1920–1981). Ceramic pot. Height 8″ (20.32 cm).

To use the principle of visual economy is not simple, however. To reduce an aesthetic statement or a form to its simplest components requires an elegant mental feat. It also asks much of the viewer. For *minimal art*—art based on the idea that less is more—to work, precisely enough information must be given, in the right scale and proportion, and the viewer has to be willing to fill out the picture from his or her own experiences in the three-dimensional world. In Ellsworth Kelly's *Blue-White Angle* (Fig. 94), the bare bones of a rectangle—two planes at right angles to each other indicating height, width, and depth—can create the wholeness of RECTANGLE in the mind of the viewer willing to make the imaginative leap with the artist. It is much more difficult to emphasize by understating than to emphasize by overstating, for in understatement the artist is open to ridicule since directing of the viewer's understanding is reduced to an absolute minimum. Many may not understand, or care to try.

Proportion

A final, subtle organizing principle of design is *proportion*—the size relationships among parts of a work. When proportions are correct, when they "feel right," the work as a whole will tend to fall into place with a satisfying sense of order in the mind of the viewer.

The issue of proportion can be approached mathematically. The ancient Greeks felt that the most aesthetically perfect size relationship between two unequal parts of a whole was 1 to 1.618. In a rectangle whose short side was one foot (.3 m) long, for instance, the length of the long side would be 1.618 feet (.49 m). Enshrined as the *golden section*, these proportions were thought to be the epitome of beauty and were used in the designing of buildings such as the Parthenon. The same size ratio can be found in many natural growth patterns, such as the size relationship of successive florets in the center of a daisy, or stages of growth in a nautilus shell.

Parts of the human body also exist in specific size relationships to each other. The representational artist must bring the ratios between parts of the body into conscious awareness to satisfy viewers' sense of proper proportion. Students usually learn, for example, that the body as a whole is seven and a half heads high. Finger joints, hands, and arms exist in predictable mathematical relationships to each other.

Even when an artist is working with the human figure on a more abstract level, use of the familiar proportions will help viewers make sense of the piece. In creating *Dancing Torso* (Fig. 95), Betty Gerich worked more intuitively than intellectually to create a semblance of female proportions. Yet even in this stylized reference to the female figure, with the difference in width of waist and hips exaggerated to emphasize the feminine quality, we are impressed with the correct

94 (top) ELLSWORTH KELLY. *Blue-White Angle*. 1966. Painted aluminum, 6 × 3 × 6′ (1.83 m × 91.44 cm × 1.83 m) Private collection.
95 (bottom) BETTY GERICH. *Dancing Torso*. Unglazed porcelain, 23½ × 10 × 8″ (59.69 cm × 25.4 cm × 20.32 cm).

"feel" of the parts of this body turning in space. The vertical distances from "shoulder" to waist to knees, and the height of the piece in relationship to its width remind us of the familiar—and carry us beyond, to appreciate its form.

Aside from known associations with the proportions of the human body or other familiar figures from our three-dimensional world, we have a subtle intuitive sense of what looks correct. This sense of perfect correctness was captured by the Zen monks who designed the *Ryoan-Ji Garden* in Kyoto (Fig. 96). The outer dimensions of the garden, the height and distance between rocks, the distances between the rocks and the viewer, the mountainlike height of the rocks from this distance, the width of the furrows in the raked sand, and the proportion of the sand raked in concentric circles around the islands of stone—all aspects of the composition exist in such perfect relationship to one another that the viewer feels a great sense of peace, of everything being as it must be. One feels that if a single proportion were changed, the unity of the piece would be destroyed.

Although the principles of design have been examined separately, they work together to create an impression of unity. Satisfying proportions are not the only unifying feature of the Ryoan-Ji Garden.

96 Rock Garden of Ryoanji Temple, Kyoto, Japan.

Organizing Principles of Design

Reconsider the other principles discussed in this chapter—repetition, variety, rhythm, balance, emphasis, and economy. How is each reflected in the organization of this classic work, making it a coherent, aesthetically pleasing whole rather than a series of unrelated rocks stuck in some sand?

STUDIO PROBLEMS

Problems for this chapter are based on varying arrangements of identical or similar forms, from cubes or slabs of wood or clay to scissors, cups, or paper bags. To aid exploration of the effects of each principle of design, the same forms could be used to solve each problem and simply disassembled and rearranged, if bonding techniques used allow their reuse; if not, one could start with many identical forms and use some of them for each problem. The decision whether to require that all problems be done with the same forms rests with the instructor. If you are required to use the same forms, you might want to review all problems assigned for this chapter before deciding what forms to use.

3.1 Repetition

97 Repetition. Wooden coffee stirrers, wood. Student work.

Assemble four or more identical or similar forms, either found objects or forms made from some easily worked material such as wood or clay. Use them together to create a piece that is more than the sum of its parts. The viewer should be aware that the same unit is being repeated, but the real excitement should be the overall form. The coffee stirrers painted black and glued together in Figure 97 seem to be moving as a unit in stop-action sequence toward the area left open on the right end of the base.

Fundamentals of Three-Dimensional Art

98 Variety. Wood construction. Student work.

3.2 Variety

Again using four or more identical or similar forms, assemble them in such a way that they give an impression of variety. For instance, they might be piled together in varying amounts or placed in varying directions. The pieces used in Figure 98 were cut by hand to be almost identical, but each varies slightly and is placed at a slightly different angle, creating visually interesting variations in edges coming out and planes shifting through space but yet maintaining a clear overall cohesiveness. Variety also adds interest to the edges of the individual pieces: The lower edges are sanded round, while the other edges are squared off.

3.3 Visual Rhythm

Using four or more identical or similar forms, set up a visual rhythm that gives the viewer a distinctive way to "read" the work. A certain rhythm may well appear in the solutions to the first two problems, but here the emphasis is placed on a rhythmic effect. Note that apparent movement that varies through space and time—in and out, up and down, flowing and pausing—can be used to create the impression of rhythm.

Organizing Principles of Design

99 Emphasis. Split and stacked firewood, tree trunk. Student work.

3.4 Visual Balance

Using four or more identical or similar forms, assemble them in two ways: (1) a symmetrically balanced structure; (2) an asymmetrically balanced structure.

3.5 Emphasis

Using four or more identical or similar forms, assemble them in a way that emphasizes some aspect of their nature or some area of the sculpture. The object is to give the viewer a visual tool for organizing the whole. If necessary, the forms can be altered to emphasize some characteristic, or an auxiliary part—such as a base—may be added. The modules used in Figure 99 are pieces of split cordwood, stacked around an uncut chunk of a tree trunk, with the pile rising higher toward the back in this picture and chips surrounding the outside of the pile. Emphasis is thus given to the nature of tree as a source of firewood. "Treeness" is suggested by the organic growth upward, the uncut core of "heartwood," and the "bark" which rings it; the sawed-off stump with a crack already starting across it and the many split logs and chips surrounding it give a sense of the process of breaking down the tree's massive structure into many small parts.

Fundamentals of Three-Dimensional Art

PART 2

Elements of Three-Dimensional Design

4

Form

Form is perhaps the most obvious element of three-dimensional design, for *form* defines what three-dimensional art is: It is that which occupies three-dimensional space. Yet defining form itself is not so simple. A limited definition of form is the actual physical contour of a work, the volume or mass that it carves out of space. In Tony Smith's *Die* (Fig. 100), the form is clearly a 6-foot (1.83 m) cube. But in certain works the question of what constitutes the form of the piece is less obvious.

100 TONY SMITH. *Die*. 1962. Steel, 6'(1.83 m) cube. Courtesy Fishbach Gallery, New York.

101 SYLVIA STONE. *Another Place.* 1972. Plexiglas, 6'8" × 17' × 28'2" (203 × 518 × 859 cm). Collection Al Held.

In Sylvia Stone's *Another Place* (Fig. 101), the form of the piece could be said to be a sprawling assembly of flat Plexiglas panels. By such a definition, its form is almost nonexistent, since the thin Plexiglas occupies very little space and is also transparent. Stone's work almost transcends form in the literal sense. But to limit understanding of form to its physical existence is to overlook the fullness of the experience of such a piece. To broaden our understanding, we could say that the form of the work includes the interior spaces it encloses and the varying but barely visible Plexiglas configurations that can be grasped at the very edge of perception as the viewer shifts position.

The elements of design can be understood as dynamic aspects of three-dimensionality that the artist manipulates in order to create desired effects. The words we use for these elements—form, space, line, texture, light, color, and time—are simple and familiar terms in everyday language. Yet their use to describe what happens in a work of art vastly expands the potential of their meaning to encompass a world of

Elements of Three-Dimensional Design

nonverbal experience that can only be poorly hinted at through the use of words.

In these chapters on the elements of design, we hope to indicate something of the great range of effects that can be created through use of each element. Although artists work with many elements of design at once, directing them toward a unified goal, we must study them by isolating each element and exploring what it can do. For form, we consider interior as well as exterior forms, secondary as well as primary contours, negative as well as positive forms, static forms and dynamic forms, and representational, stylized, abstract, and nonobjective forms.

Exterior vs. Interior Forms

We normally think of form as referring to the outside of a piece—its *exterior form*—but works may also reveal an *interior form.* Comparing the relationships between the two may be a major part of the aesthetic experience.

At the most literal level, the inner form is simply the reverse of the outer form of a hollow piece. A bowl has both a convex exterior form and a concave interior form. In some vessels, such as Eilene Sky's whimsical bowl shown in Figure 102, the interior form is elaborated as much as or more than the exterior form.

Sometimes artists create the illusion of revealing a hidden inner

102 Eilene Sky for Neiman-Marcus. *Bowl.* 1975. Low-fire white earthenware, hand-painted with underglazes and underglaze pencil. 13 × 18 × 6″ (33 × 46 × 15 cm).

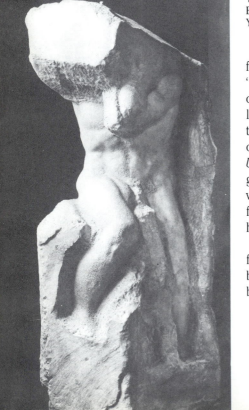

104 (bottom) Michelangelo. *Bound Slave* (Unfinished). Marble Galleria dell' Accademia, Florence.

103 Arnaldo Pomodoro. *Sfera con perforazione* ("Sphere with perforations"). 1966. Bronze, one-half cast, diameter 23½" (60 cm). Courtesy Marlborough Gallery, New York.

form. In *Sphere with Perforations* (Fig. 103), Arnaldo Pomodoro has "opened" a gleaming bronze sphere to show its secret core, mysterious interior forms of which the exterior form gives no hint. On another level, sculptors often feel that in removing excess stone from a block they are revealing a form that was hidden inside all along. This process of bringing the interior form to light is illustrated in Michelangelo's *Unfinished Bound Slave* (Fig. 104). It is not known whether Michelangelo intended to finish bringing the inner form out of the marble or whether the piece is intended as a completed statement of the outer forces almost totally constraining the inner life and freedom of a human being.

Another expression of the contrast between interior and exterior forms appears in pieces in which one form is physically separate from but contained within another. When all or part of the interior form can be seen through the exterior form, the relationship between the two and the discovery of the inner form can be quite exciting. A classic example is the traditional Japanese "package" for bringing five eggs home from market (Fig. 105). Through the horizontals and verticals of the exterior reed form, we can see the elegance of what many designers consider the perfect natural form: the egg.

In architecture, glass walls may allow us to see the interior forms, such as stairwells and furniture, encased within the exterior framework of the building. Similar effects are sometimes created in sculptures with exterior forms that either contain visual openings or are transparent. In Mario Merz's *Double Igloo* (Fig. 106) the glass panes clamped to the exterior framework allow us to see the yurtlike igloo within. We are invited not only to explore the juxtaposition of seemingly modern and primitive ways of constructing the same form, but also to wonder what is hidden inside the inner igloo, pierced by or sending forth the electric energy represented by the glowing blue neon rods.

In contrast to works in which we are invited to compare inner and outer forms, some pieces present an outer form which is hollow, implying an inner form that cannot be seen. There may be a sense of a force bulging outward, forcing the walls of the piece into outer shapes by pressure from within. Or in the case of jewelry, masks, or medieval body armor, a piece may be made to fit over the form of a body. When shown without a body inside, the outer form is both interesting in itself and reminiscent of the inner form it once enclosed. The suits of armor made for Henry VIII from 1511 to 1545 (Fig. 107, p. 88) reveal his physical evolution from the slenderness of youth to middle-aged paunch.

106 Mario Merz. *Double Igloo*. 1979. Glass panes, metal pipe, clamps, clay, neon. Height 9' (2.75 m), diameter 18' (5.49 m). Installation at Sperone Westwater Fischer, New York. Staatsgalerie, Stuttgart.

105 (top) *Tamago no tsuto* (the egg package). Rice straw, 16" (40 cm). Collection Hideyuki Oka.

107 Tournament armors for Henry VIII. c. 1511, 1515, 1540, 1545. Silver and steel. Tower of London.

Primary and Secondary Contours

In any form with surface elaboration, a distinction can be made between the *primary contour* of the piece—the shape of its outermost extremity—and its *secondary contours*—the forms developed on its surface. In the white jade miniature "mountain" from 18-century China (Fig. 108), the primary contour of the piece is its outer boulderlike form. The secondary contours are the complex forms carved across and even deep into the face of the stone.

In many cases there is no clear distinction between primary and secondary contours but rather an ever-changing interplay between them. In the famous Greek statue *Laocoön* (Fig. 109), the primary contour is the complex outline of the piece; the secondary contours are the details of the snake and the bodies of Laocoön and his sons. But what is not apparent from a photograph is that the primary contour of the sculpture will change as the viewer moves around it, seeing different areas created by the "secondary contours" as outermost.

The words "primary" and "secondary" do not have any hierarchical significance, either. Neither is automatically more important. In *Laocoön* the real excitement lies in the relationships between secondary forms—parts of the snake to parts of the humans, arm to arm, leg to leg.

Elements of Three-Dimensional Design

108 *Mountain Scene.* Chien-Lung Dynasty (1735–1796). White Nephrite jade boulder, 10″ (254 cm) high × 14″ (36 cm) wide, excluding stand.

109 HAGESANDROS, ATHANODOROS, POLYDOROS. *Laocoön.* 2nd or 1st century B.C. Marble, 6′ (1.84 m) high. Vatican Museums, Museo Pio Clementino.

Positive and Negative Forms

Another set of polarities that arises in three-dimensional work with form is the distinction between *positive forms*—solid areas that occupy space—and *negative (or implied) forms* or *voids*—the shapes of spaces that are enclosed or delineated by positive forms. The difference between the two is apparent in Barbara Hepworth's *Wave* (Fig. 110). Here the positive form is the wave; the negative form is the oval space contained within it. The viewer is invited to experience both. Although the negative form cannot be seen, its shape is almost totally defined by the encompassing wave, and the two complete each other as a single unit. For Hepworth, this sense of unity between mass and void grew out of her personal experience of the wholeness of life. She writes,

> All my early memories are of forms and shapes and textures. Moving through and over the West Riding landscape with my father in his car, the hills were sculptures; the roads defined the form. Above all, there was the sensation of moving physically over the contours of fulnesses and concavities, through hollows and over peaks—feeling, touching, seeing, through mind and hand and eye. This sensation has never left me. I, the sculptor, *am* the landscape. I am the form and I am the hollow, the thrust and the contour.

Although negative forms actually consist of empty space, they can be as active and important in a piece as the positive forms. In Le Corbusier's *Notre Dame du Haut* (Fig. 111), the negative window forms

110 Barbara Hepworth. *Wave.* 1943–44. Plane wood with color and strings, interior pale blue. Length 18½" (47 cm). Collection Mr. and Mrs. Ashley Havinden.

Elements of Three-Dimensional Design

in the thick walls are highly active, for they are both channels for light and intriguingly varied volumes in themselves. A void in a piece of sculpture allows the exposure of inner surfaces, creates spatial relationships among forms that would not otherwise occur, and invokes playful or curious attempts by viewers to look through the piece. In Erwin Hauer's *Inversion of Volumes* (Fig. 112), the opening of a void in the lower area creates lovely interplays of rounded positive and negative forms. Note that the artist has created a visual game in which the viewer may discover that the upper portion is a re-creation of what has been carved away below—the positive of the negative, if you will.

111 (top) Le Corbusier. *Notre Dame du Haut* (interior south wall). 1950–55. Ronchamp, France.
112 (bottom) Erwin Hauer. *Inversion of Volumes*. 1965. Bronze, 24 × 8 × 8″ (61 × 20 × 20 cm). Kunsthaus, Basel, Switzerland, Collection Margarite Hagenbach-Arp.

Static Forms and Dynamic Forms

Certain works have a stability of form that can be called *static*, in the sense of appearing stationary, nonmoving. One of the most static forms is the pyramid (Fig. 113, p. 92). The base is so much broader than the top that no inner force could conceivably cause the form to move or fall over. But although these silent, permanent forms are

113 (right) The Great Pyramids at Giza, Egypt. After 2700 B.C.

114 (bottom right) CARL ANDRE. *Way North/South.* 1975. Three Western red cedar uncarved blocks, 3 × 3 × 4′ (91 × 91 × 122 cm).

115 (bottom left) *Gudea Woshiping.* Telloh, c. 2100 B.C. Dolerite, height approximately 42″ (107 cm). Louvre, Paris.

grounded in eternity, standing at their base and gazing up to their summit and the vastness of the sky beyond also inspires awareness of another aspect of reality: infinity.

Like pyramids, architecture with straight walls and ground-hugging proportions gives a sense of visual stability. So does Carl Andre's *Way North/South* (Fig. 114). Here, though, the artist offers a

Elements of Three-Dimensional Design

paradoxical visual suggestion that these heavy, inert blocks of wood are like a child's building blocks. They are not moving, but once we notice that they are the same size, we may begin subconsciously to rearrange them in our mind's eye. We may also become involved in tracing the textures of the rough-cut cedar. What is static in appearance is not necessarily lacking in interest or active participation by the viewer.

Although many static forms are straight-sided geometric solids, some have curving edges and may even represent living beings. The energy of life is obvious in *Gudea Worshiping* (Fig. 115), and yet the figure does not appear to be in motion. Rather than presenting a stop-action image of a moving person, the sculptor of this ancient piece presents us with a still image of a still figure. Feet, hands, and shoulders are at the same position on both sides. Nothing suggests physical movement.

By contrast, *dynamic* forms are those characterized by motion, change, or energy that will lead to motion and change. Victor Horta's *Door handle* (Fig. 116) is a highly *dynamic* form, for it appears to be in a state of constant motion. Although it is made of metal, it has the flowing quality of a plant form, as do many similar Art Nouveau pieces from the same period.

Even buildings can be shaped into dynamic forms, as in architect John Lautner's *Marbrisa* (Fig. 117) overlooking Acapulco Bay. The

116 (top) VICTOR HORTA. *Door handle in the Hotel Solvay,* Brussels, Belgium. 1895–1900. Museum of Modern Art, New York.
117 (bottom) JOHN LAUTNER. *Marbrisa,* Acapulco, Mexico. Interior view.

118 Michelangelo. *David*. 1501–04. Marble, height approximately 18′ (5.49 m). Galleria dell' Accademia, Florence.

walls and massive concrete roof of this house curve with such apparent ease that the structure seems to have the energy and ability to continue the flowing visual motion set up.

Or compare Michelangelo's *David* (Fig. 118) with *Gudea Worshiping* (Fig. 115). While the latter seems to be fixed in an attitude of worshipful concentration, David watching Goliath's approach bespeaks a reserve of energy like a coiled snake ready to strike. Although he is moving only slowly, if at all, nothing in his body is at a passive place of rest. The two sides of his body are asymmetrical to each other, suggesting a readiness to spring into action, foreshadowed by the swelling tension in the sinews of his anchored foot, clenching lower hand, and neck. The dynamism of this form is understated, but a perceptive observer can read tremendous power waiting within it.

Representational, Abstract, and Nonobjective Forms

A final range of effects that can be created using form involves degrees of likeness to known objects. Distinctions among these kinds of forms are not easily made, but the terms and ideas are useful, for they indicate different attitudes toward form on the part of the artist.

Representational or *figurative* forms are those that refer directly to an object from the three-dimensional world of our experience. The highest degree of representationality is sometimes called *superrealism*. An example of this attitude toward form would be Carlin Jeffery's nude (Fig. 119), a body casting that faithfully reproduces the contours of a specific human body in all its naked imperfection. The artist is uncompromising in details, including even the wart on the model's foot.

119 Carlin Jeffery. Installation view. 1972.

Though we may not be aware of it, we are more accustomed to forms that are slightly *idealized.* That is, contours and proportions are directed toward an idea of what the object would look like in its imagined or inner perfection, rather than its less than perfect superficial appearance. In sculpture, the ideal may exist in the mind of the artist, who may extract qualities from a variety of human models to serve his or her vision rather than trying to represent a single model realistically. Michelangelo's *David* (Fig. 118), for instance, is clearly a representation of a young man. The master has not chosen to reproduce every detail of a living human body, however. David—known Biblically as the chosen of God—is presented as an idealized conception of the perfect body, strong, lithe, and without blemish. He is seen as a giant among men, and the statue itself is a colossal 18 feet (5.49 m) high. The sculpture is still regarded as a classic representation of male beauty almost five hundred years after it was created.

In some cases, the ideal in the artist's mind is an emotion rather than a specific form. Here realism in outer form is subordinated to representation of what that emotion would look like if projected to its fullest through a being the viewer can identify with.

Another variation from reality occurs in representational works that are highly *stylized.* In these pieces, the form has been simplified and altered to conform to a particular historical style or to stress a particular design characteristic. If you look back at *Gudea Worshiping* (Fig. 115), you can see that even though this figure is recognizable as a man, his contours have been reduced to the simplified outline of a standing, draped figure, and his robe falls straight to his feet with only a few stylized folds. In a more realistic piece, the draping would be more complex, following the more complex forms of the human body. In addition to simplifying contours to create a strong design, the ancient Mesopotamian sculptor used the stylistic conventions of the times: a direct frontal pose, large eyes, and thick eyebrows. Despite all these stylizations, this very old piece conveys the impression of a unique and genuine personality as well as elegance in design.

The next remove from superficial reality is *abstract* works—those in which the artist has reduced a real form to its bare essence. Constantin Brancusi's *White Seal ("Miracle")* (Fig. 120) has no eyes, mouth, or flippers, but Brancusi's genius in abstracting the essential qualities of "sealness" leaves no doubt as to what the creature is. These qualities seem to include its streamlined contours and a form that while ideal for underwater travel appears slightly bulky on land. For all the awkwardness of its locomotion on land, the seal still has surprising facility at balancing its bulky body on small surfaces, so the balancing of this marvelous seal form on a small stone seems both wonderful and believable. As we noted in Chapter 2, the more the artist leaves out, the more the viewer must bring to the work in order to understand and appreciate it.

120 CONSTANTIN BRANCUSI. *White Seal ("Miracle").* (1936?) Marble height 43″ (109 cm). Base of two stone sections, height 21⅝″ (56 cm). Solomon R. Guggenheim Museum.

121 ANTOINE PEVSNER. *Developable Column.* 1942. Brass and oxidized bronze, height 20¾″ (53 cm), base diameter 19⅜″ (49 cm). Collection, Museum of Modern Art, New York. Purchase.

Works that do not refer at all to any object from our three-dimensional world are called *nonobjective* or *nonrepresentational.* This approach to three-dimensional art can be traced back to the Constructivist Movement that developed in Russia between 1914 and 1922. As explained in the Realistic Manifesto of Naum Gabo and his brother Anton Pevsner, this new approach to art set aside the old attempts to imitate nature through descriptions of human figures and other tangible objects. Rather, the Constructivists sought to explore the characteristics of materials themselves and of the intangible realities of space and time. This "nonobjective world" beyond sensory experience is suggested by pieces such as Pevsner's *Developable Column* (Fig. 121). Its nonobjective form seems to be in perpetual motion through time and space. Without suggesting any known object, it draws us into a sense of movement through space and evokes interest in the texture and colors and lines of the bonded brass and bronze rods.

Nonobjective forms are sometimes unfamiliar shapes growing out of the artist's inner imaginings; sometimes they are elaborations of geometric shapes, suggesting the orderly mathematical structures that form the building blocks of life. While viewers will judge representational works partly on the basis of how well they re-create the sense of a known object, nonobjective forms may invite viewers to move beyond mental associations and experience the impact of form, line, texture, value, color, space, or time directly.

STUDIO PROBLEMS

4.1 From Flat Material to Volume

Experiment with paper folding to develop an understanding of *planar construction*—creation of flat-sided forms. First use an 8½ × 11 sheet of paper, creasing or scoring it along one or more lines and then folding it along the creased lines to raise the flat surface into a series of planes angling away from or back toward each other in three-dimensional space. Do as many as you like, choosing the one that is most effective as a low relief or free-standing sculpture. A minimum of tape can be used to fasten edges together if necessary. Then do the same thing with the additional option of cutting the original sheet to see what forms can evolve. The forms need not be symmetrical, and the fold lines can be either straight or curving.

4.2 Curvilinear Form

Using any media, accent the strong horizontality or verticality of a piece by using curvilinear form. In Figure 122 the downward curve in the slab of

Elements of Three-Dimensional Design

122 Curvilinear Form. Wood. Student work.

lumber seen against the straight horizontal surface of the next slab in the "bench" accentuates its straightness by contrast and its length by leading the eye rather slowly along the length of the piece rather than allowing its form to be grasped at once.

4.3 Exterior and Interior Forms

Using any method and material you choose, create a piece that reveals both external and internal forms and uses their interplay as the major focus of the work. The solution in Figure 123 contrasts the organic qualities of a tree trunk with the perfect geometries of pillars carved from it, as if revealing the pillars as interior forms hidden within the exterior form of the trunk.

123 Exterior and Interior Forms. Tree trunk. Student work.

124 Metamorphosis. Plasticene on wire. Student work.

4.4 Metamorphosis

Using plasticene clay, transform one representational form into another in five stages. First create the two representational forms in a realistic manner; then create an abstraction of each in which its form approaches the other. Finally, construct the middle stage using the two abstracted forms as reference, so that it becomes an abstraction of abstractions. To make the transition from man to vacuum cleaner shown in Figure 124, the form had to be gradually turned upside down, a humorous shift that is handled plausibly as the form itself changes.

4.5 Fill-a-Bag

Fill a bag of any sort with some loose material—such as sand, sugar, water, or stones—in such a way that the bag controls the form of the loose material. In the example shown (Figure 125), a transparent plastic bag has been filled near the bursting point with semitransparent blue marbles, twisted, and tied with gold cord. Solutions need not be tightly bound—floppiness is a possibility, provided that it is under control.

125 Fill-a-Bag. Plastic bag, marbles, cord. Student work.

98

5

Space

Space is a very real and important element of three-dimensional design, but it is difficult to conceptualize. *Space* is the three-dimensional field with which the artist works. It may include unfilled as well as filled areas, or what are referred to respectively as *negative* and *positive* areas. The positive area is the part of the work that physically occupies space; the negative area is all unfilled space that is activated by the piece. Although a good artist works with both kinds of space at once, viewers' experiences of negative space are so subtle and subjective that it is hard to define and measure. The use of two-dimensional photographs further limits understanding of spatial concepts, for these subtle experiences change as the viewer moves.

Within these limitations, this chapter will explore some of the ways in which artists work with space. These include delineated shapes in space, activated surrounding space, confined space, spatial relationships, scale, and illusionary space.

Delineated Shapes in Space

In addition to physically occupying space, forms may carve shapes out of the unfilled spaces within and around them. In David Smith's *Cubi XII* (Fig. 126), the angle from which the photograph was taken reveals triangular shapes framed within the sculpture. We can also discern a series of partial shapes formed where the surrounding space meets the sharp edges of the piece. For instance, at the edges of the two small balanced cubes in the upper right, unfilled space seems to thrust inward to 90 degree points as a sort of counterforce to the triangular spaces pointing outward from within. Below the broader but thinner block jutting out farthest to the right is a notched shape in space. If you follow the edges around the piece, you will be struck by the dynamic shapes meeting these edges in space. In a sense, these strong shapes created in unfilled space help to maintain the tense visual balance of the blocks, giving cohesiveness to the precariously balanced structure.

Delineated spaces, those shapes carved out of space by positive forms, may serve a variety of aesthetic functions in a work. In Naum Gabo's *Linear Construction* (Fig. 90), the elegant delineated space in

126 (top) David Smith. *Cubi XII.* 1963. Stainless steel, 9′ 1⅝″ × 4′ 1¼″ × 2′ 8¼″ (278.5 × 125.1 × 81.9 cm). Hirshhorn Museum and Sculpture Garden, Smithsonian Institution.
127 (right) William King. *Victory.* 1977. Sheet aluminum, height 9′ (2.75 m).

Elements of Three-Dimensional Design

the center is the focal point of the work. He explains that in such sculpture,

> space is not a part of the universal space surrounding the object; it is a material by itself, a structural part of the object—so much so that it has the faculty of conveying a volume as does any other rigid material.

Often delineated spaces are visually interesting or appealing in themselves, whether the viewer is conscious of "seeing" them or not. To make these unfilled shapes more visible, three-dimensional works are often photographed against a plain background, as in *Cubi XII*. In the photograph of the work shown in Figure 126, the delineated spaces show up as dramatic white areas whose presence is heightened by contrast with the dark edges of the forms. If William King's *Victory* (Fig. 127) were photographed totally against a plain background such as the sky, it would be easier to perceive the interesting space delineated between the two figures. It might also be easier to perceive the shape of this shape if we were looking at the piece itself, no matter what the setting, for our eyes automatically focus on that which interests us and let areas closer or farther away fall out of focus. Those whose awareness is not awakened may see "nothing" in any case.

Activated Surrounding Space

Somewhat different from the carving of identifiable shapes out of space is the tendency of some works to activate an area larger than their own physical confines. This happens when the visual statement made by the piece draws the viewer's attention to a broader area or charges the surrounding atmosphere with a subtly active energy. The *spatial presence* of a work is something that can only be sensed; it usually cannot be seen unless it is limited to the contours of the piece. Judgments as to how large the presence of a work is are quite subjective; they depend not only on the work but also on the awareness and personality of the viewer.

One way of activating surrounding space is to draw the viewer's attention to *eye lines* through space. In Picasso's *Head of a Woman* (Fig. 128), enough information is given for us to perceive the likeness of a woman looking downward. If we follow the direction of her gaze, her visual path through the space in front of her face becomes for us an activated area that extends beyond the edges of the head itself. Picasso also suggests form in the space surrounding the woman's head without physically filling it. What he presents is a series of deep indentations; what we may perceive is a convex-surfaced form, fleshed out in our imagination. In this case the *Gestalt,* or whole, of what we perceive is more than the sum of the work's parts.

128 Pablo Picasso. *Head of a Woman.* 1909 (cast 1960). Bronze, 16 × 9⅜ × 10⅜″ (40.9 × 24 × 26.2 cm). Hirshhorn Museum and Sculpture Garden, Smithsonian Institution.

129 GEORGE RICKEY. *N Lines Vertical.*
1967. Stainless steel, 98 × 9¼ × 5¼"
(248.9 × 22.8 × 12.7 cm)
San Diego Museum of Art.

In *Wind Chant* (Fig. 54), John Matt activates surrounding space by filling it with "music." The open lines of the sculpture invite space to flow through the harplike section, in lyrical curves suggested by the curving line in the piece. The presence of *Wind Chant* may therefore be perceived as a mystical presence—a suggestion of unseen winds playing subtle music beyond human perception. Matt describes this aspect of the piece he has created:

> The music that I feel when I see that piece is like sound in three dimensions. The sound covers a large or small space, depending on where the piece is shown. The image itself is like a scale, a note; it almost reminds me of a harp, a stringed instrument with a sounding board. There is an aura encompassing it, an airyness about it, a very lyrical nature—it suggests the vocabulary we usually associate with music.

George Rickey's *N Lines Vertical* (Fig. 129) activates a large area in yet other ways. One is its use of pointing lines, for their sharp outward thrust directs the viewer's vision infinitely outward; the lines given in the sculpture seem to be only the beginning of implied lines that continue far out into space.

A second reason for the great presence of Rickey's sculpture is the sharp points of the piece. They would tend to hold viewers at some distance in healthy respect for the possibility of being pricked. A third presence-enlarging factor cannot be appreciated in a still photograph: It is the movement of the piece with the wind. The rotation of the sharp-pointed lines through space would activate an even larger space that seems to belong to the sculpture. Psychologists have found that people tend to do the same thing: They subconsciously establish a certain distance around their bodies as their "personal space." If you have ever intruded on the personal space of a person who is feeling angry or sharp-edged, you will know what the word *activated space* can mean.

The spatial presence of a work is not necessarily a hostile environment, of course. But to the sensitive, it may engender a certain respect. *Stonehenge* (Fig. 130) has such colossal spatial presence that even from a distance people are touched and awed by it. Its great size and mysterious appearance against the vastness of bare plain and sky give it a presence that radiates far outward.

By contrast, some large works are designed to welcome people, to draw them in rather than creating an outward-expanding spatial presence. *Participatory sculpture* is meant to be touched, climbed on, or swung from by viewers. Public sculpture may weigh tons, but if its contours are low and rounded people may treat it like familiar furniture, leaning against it and perching all over it. Some people are drawn to sit on public sculpture even if they have to go to some trouble to do so. The pair eating lunch on Clement Meadmore's *Upstart* (Fig. 131)

Elements of Three-Dimensional Design

130 (top)   Stonehenge. c. 2000–1500 B.C. Height of stones 13′6″ (4.11 m) Salisbury Plain, England.
131 (left)   CLEMENT MEADMORE. *Upstart*. 1967. Welded Cor-Ten steel, height 20′6″ (6.25 m). Fabricated at Lippincott, Inc., New Haven, CT. Collection Mrs. Harry Lynde Bradley, Milwaukee, Wisconsin.

Space   103

had to hoist themselves far above normal sitting height to attain their perch, apparently unintimidated by the looming bulk of this large piece.

Confined Space

Some three-dimensional pieces are developed within clearly defined boundaries. Within these boundaries, the artist controls not only filled areas but also the remaining unfilled areas.

In an installation piece, the artist attempts to incorporate an entire room of a gallery or museum into the aesthetic experience. The characteristics of the existing space must be dealt with in order to create a controlled environment with no elements that distract people from the intended experience. For instance, heating pipes and floor joists overhead may be busy visual distractions from the lines of a work, or they may be used creatively as places from which to hang things. Low ceilings may not allow enough visual room for the upward thrust of some pieces. High ceilings may create a space bigger than the work can control; a false ceiling or other visual barrier may be needed to stop the eye and shrink the space. Noise from adjacent areas may intrude on the mood the artist intends; some artists use sounds as part of an installation to cover background noise and/or to create the desired atmosphere.

132 JOSEPH CORNELL. *Suite de la Longitude*. 1955–57. Box construction of painted wood, papers, glass, marbles, cork, metal rings, ink wash and pencil, 13¼ × 19¾ × 4⅜″ (34 × 50 × 11 cm). Hirshhorn Museum and Sculpture Garden, Smithsonian Institution.

Elements of Three-Dimensional Design

In a relief work, the panel from which figures are raised delimits the spatial world of the images. In Joseph Cornell's boxes, such as *Suite de la Longitude* (Fig. 132), the space with which the artist is working is confined within the dimensions of the glass-fronted box. The shadows on the back wall reveal how shallow this space is. Note that in this piece, Cornell makes reference to further confinements within the box: marbles confined within glasses, like planets confined within their orbits, and orbitlike rings whose freedom of movement is limited by the rod from which they hang. Here the confinement of aesthetic space is a paradox, for we associate the images of globe and planetlike spheres with the vastness of "outer space," but yet everything is small-scale and contained. Cornell draws us in very close by piquing our curiosity with what looks like old scientific writing; one discovers it to be French, so English-speaking viewers with some knowledge of French may be held close to the work even longer as they try to understand the writing.

Instead of standing on the outside looking in, as in Cornell's work, viewers may find themselves within the confined space of a work. Sometimes the artist's intent seems to be to emphasize the feeling of confinement, either physically or psychologically. Tony Smith's *Smoke* (Fig. 133) so monopolizes the space within the Corcoran Gallery of Art that it practically forces viewers to walk beneath its own bulk. Not only does it crowd onlookers; it also seems to be overpower-

133 TONY SMITH. *Smoke*. 1967. Plywood (to be made in steel), 24 × 34 × 48′ (7.32 × 10.37 × 14.64 m). Photographed at the Corcoran Gallery of Art, Washington, D.C.

105

ing the delicacy of the gallery itself, pushing outward at its Grecian columns and upward into the space of the second floor balcony.

How will those who walk through such a work respond? Our experience of being confined within a controlled space is highly subjective. If we find ourselves sharing a space with an object we don't like, the space will feel too small, crowded, since we cannot put enough distance between ourselves and the object. Confinement within certain spaces may seem like welcome refuge, however. A place that we love to come home to surrounds us with an intimate environment of our own choosing. Urban plazas are often designed to lure people into the shops opening onto them by suggesting a sense of enclosure, a friendly oasis set off from the disorder of city streets. Toronto's Nathan Phillips Square (Fig. 134) is "protected" by the twin towers of its City Hall, rising like cupped hands, and by the viewing platform surrounding the plaza on three sides, providing a band of shelter for those just stepping off the street or exiting from mass transit. The life-filled plaza is so popular that it is booked every day of the year for events ranging from drum majorette demonstrations to rock concerts. The atrium within the *Ford Foundation Building* (Fig. 135) is a restful change from the busy street scene outside. The contrast in environments when one steps down into this parklike space is quite dramatic and is highly unlikely to be perceived as unpleasantly confining.

134 Nathan Phillips Square.
Toronto, Canada.

106

135 KEVIN ROCHE, JOHN DINKELOO & ASSOCIATES. Interior, *Ford Foundation Building*, New York. 1967.

   While our focus is directed inward in some spatially confined works, such as Cornell's box (Fig. 132), some confined works invite us to compare the confined space with what surrounds it, finding either contrasts (as in the Ford Foundation atrium) or similarities, as in Eero Saarinen's *TWA Flight Center* (Fig. 136, p. 108). Designed to suggest the excitement of air travel, the building surrounds participants with soaring interior spaces shaped by concrete structures whose winglike appearance is even more evident in the outer form of the building (Fig. 137, p. 108). The interior "confined" space refers us not only to the outside of the Flight Center but also to the airplanes on the runways beyond, in an extended comparison of inner and outer space.

136 (top) EERO SAARINEN. Interior, *TWA Flight Center*, Kennedy International Airport, New York. 1962.
137 (right) EERO SAARINEN. Exterior, *TWA Flight Center*, Kennedy International Airport, New York. 1962.

Spatial Relationships

Another aspect of space with which the artist works is the spatial relationships between forms, between forms and the setting, and between the forms and the viewer.

Landscape designers and architects may work together to bring outdoor structures, walkways, and plantings into harmonious relationship with buildings and users of buildings, and both landscape design and architecture into spatial harmony with the greater environment. Space planning is often influenced by economic and political constraints, however. The increase in real estate costs in cities has led to construction of taller and taller buildings on small plots of land, sometimes at considerable sacrifice to the quality of life perceived by the person on the street. Zoning requirements about setbacks have sought to ensure "sunrights," but overall planning of spatial relationships among buildings is often lacking. Architectural critic Paul Goldberger describes the kind of thinking necessary to create pleasing spatial relationships within urban settings:

> A city, physically, represents a kind of social contract. There must be a common agreement as to the way in which buildings work together, the kinds of uses to which they will be put and the physical form that they will take. . . . Light, a sense of space, quiet, visual variety, modest scale—we may not be able to quantify the effects of these things, but we can know that we can have no civilized city without them. They are disappearing fast. . . .

On a smaller scale, effective installation of three-dimensional works of art requires consideration of their spatial relationships to each other and to their setting. Their placement nearer or farther, to one side or the other, higher or lower, has a direct impact on how well pieces work. Museum curators find it more difficult to set up a show of three-dimensional works than of two-dimensional works such as paintings, for if one three-dimensional piece is moved, it affects not only the things on either side but everything within the space. Since three-dimensional works interact with each other and with what is around them, many artists prefer to take on the time-consuming job of arranging their pieces themselves.

When Erwin Hauer displayed his condor sculptures at the Choate School (Fig. 138), he was careful to keep them all in the highest space available rather than under the mezzanine shown in the foreground, for these high-flying creatures of open spaces would have seemed crowded beneath the low ceiling. The condors are placed in varying relationships to each other and to the ground, each assuming a different pose, creating an impression of the movement of take-offs and landings as one looks from one bird to the next. The space-embracing wings and pointing wingtips of the condors activate the areas around

138 Erwin Hauer. *Project California Condor*. 1978–1983. Plastic laminate, 9 to 10′ (2.75 to 3.05 m) wing-tip to wing-tip. Collection the artist.

them, almost as though one could feel the air pressure created by motions of the heavy wings.

As the viewer moves through the space activated by the condors, the visual relationships of form to form and filled to unfilled spaces will change constantly. So will the viewer's spatial relationship to the forms. Seeing a sculpture of a condor at a distance is quite different from a close encounter with one of these imposing birds, much less being surrounded by six of them. Life-size, the sculptures have wing-spans of up to 10 feet (3.05 m). Some of Hauer's condors (though not those in this exhibit) are set on platforms that revolve very slowly, constantly changing the spatial relationships among the condors and between the viewer and the long wings.

The viewer's spatial relationship to objects within the three-dimensional field may be carefully controlled by the artist. In Hauer's placement of the condors, the inward-turned focus of the condors themselves and their placement to either side of a central corridor tend to compel the viewer to use this corridor as a path through the work.

Elements of Three-Dimensional Design

Architecture and interior design control passageways and viewing points by corridors, furniture placement, and openings in walls. Japanese gardens such as the one shown in Figure 139 lure people to walk along winding paths, pausing at specified intervals to look at tableaux created from natural and manufactured forms. They do so by skillfully planned placement of stepping stones, visual barriers and openings, and use of visual accents. When such designs are successful, we are not aware of being manipulated. Other gardens, such as the formal garden at Blenheim Palace (Fig. 140), allow continual appreciation of the entire panorama. Although the pathways control the way we can walk through the garden, the absence of visual obstructions allows us to continually gauge where we are in space in relationship to the whole garden, as well as to the vista beyond.

139 (left)   Japanese garden. From *House and Garden Guide*, copyright © 1968 by Condé Nast Publications, Inc.
140 (above)   Blenheim Park, Oxford, England. 18th century. Garden renovated in 1920s with landscapist Achille Duchene.

Scale

The effective use of space also involves consideration of *scale*—the size of an object in relationship to other objects and to its surroundings. We human beings tend to judge sizes relative to our own size and to the sizes we have learned to associate with the objects in our three-dimensional world. Some works may challenge our notion of our own size and importance in the three-dimensional field, however.

   Some representational works are presented in life-size scale. Hauer's condors (Fig. 138) awe us with their realistically great size, perhaps making us feel somewhat smaller than usual because we are not accustomed to such large birds. When works offer realistic representation of humans in life-size scale (as in Carlin Jeffery's nude in Chap. 4, Fig. 119), even without the distance of a wax-museum or display case barrier we may feel strangely excluded from their spatial field since being lifeless, they ignore us.

A work may be presented in miniature scale, either relative to human scale or to the scale of the actual object being represented. Miniatures often make us feel like giants, since they are so much smaller than what we expect that we mushroom in relative size. In Robert Graham's *Girl with Towel* (Fig. 141), the woman has been shrunk to only a few inches but yet appears so realistic that we assume monstrous proportions peering in at her. Other miniatures assign us a tiny size. David Kraisler's 18-inch-high (45.7 cm) *Stonehenge Series, The Theatre-2* (Fig. 142) has a massive, boulderlike quality that appears quite monumental in a photograph. And the artist has added a miniature human figure to show the relationship of the sculpture's size to the size of Stonehenge. We are asked to judge the apparent size of the work by reducing our notion of our own size.

The largest end of the scale spectrum is *monumental works.* They may be nonobjective works that are so large in relation to human scale that they dwarf us, such as Stonehenge (Fig. 130), or larger-than-life representations of familiar objects. In the past, monumental sculptures conveyed the idea of the heroic grandeur of the human spirit. In Michelangelo's *David* (Fig. 118), a man preparing to slay a giant was himself represented as an 18-foot-tall giant. More recently, artists like Claes Oldenburg have elevated mundane objects from our everyday life to monumental scale, such as the 45-foot-tall (13.72 m) *Clothespin* in Philadelphia's historic Centre Square shown in Figure 27, reflecting the antiheroic materialism of our culture. Scale can thus be used to make political statements about the degree of importance and power we grant to the object represented, as well as to fascinate us with that which is much smaller, much larger, or exactly the same size as ourselves. For this reason, some people are disturbed by the political implications they read into Robert Graham's reduction of a woman into a tiny specimen within a see-through box (Fig. 141).

Spatial Illusions

We are so accustomed to dealing with space in our three-dimensional world that we have learned to make certain assumptions about the spatial implications of what we see. For instance, if several identical objects are presented at varying distances from us, we see them as being different sizes but automatically override that visual impression with the mental assumption that they are probably all the same size. Artists can use these assumptions to advantage in situations that call for fooling the viewer about the size or relative distance or objects.

Elements of Three-Dimensional Design

141 (top) ROBERT GRAHAM. *Girl with Towel*. 1968. Wax, balsa wood, paper, and plexiglas, 11 × 20 × 20″ (28 × 6 × 6 cm). Hirshhorn Museum and Sculpture Garden, Smithsonian Institution.

142 (left) DAVID KRAISLER. *Stonehenge Series. The Theatre-2*. Bronze, 12 × 14 x 18″ (30 × 36 × 46 cm).

143 JERRY ROJO. Set design for *Going Away* by Tom Dulac, for UConn Nutmeg Theatre, University of Connecticut, Storrs, Connecticut. 1973. Watercolor, 18 × 12″ (46 × 30 cm).

In Japanese gardens such as the one shown in Figure 139, certain artistic conventions allow creation of the illusion of nature's peaceful spaciousness within what is actually a small space. This spatial illusion is necessitated by the fact that Japan has long had a dense population occupying a limited amount of land, most of which is mountainous and unsuitable for building. Within the walls of the small garden, one can experience a world of a different scale, in which rocks become mountains and areas of sand or water become the ocean. This reduction of scale is not just symbolic. Many illusionary devices are used to make the space appear larger than it is. For example, trees with relatively few leaves, such as white birches, are planted close to a house; viewing the garden through their open branches helps to push it back in space. Use of trees, screens, or boulders to obscure parts of the garden from immediate view also creates an illusion of depth, and the use of stepping stones of varied sizes winding around these barriers to discover new vistas makes paths appear longer and wider.

Elements of Three-Dimensional Design

The art of stage design makes considerable use of spatial illusion, for the designer must often use the small actual space of the stage to create the impression of a much larger area. Many plays have been written for *box sets*—for the appearance of action taking place within rooms. The immediate spatial illusion is that you are peeping into a removed fourth wall, seeing people within a room. Set designer Jerry Rojo's design for Tom Dulac's play *Going Away* (Fig. 143) illustrates other devices used for spatial effects. One is *forced perspective*—the exaggeration of *linear perspective,* the apparent converging of parallel lines toward the horizon. Not only are the I-beams in the set placed at an exaggerated angle toward the rear of the stage; they are also specially constructed to be larger at the end facing the audience. The scale of rooms within this cross-sectioned house also varies considerably, with rooms designed to look farther away being actually smaller. This illusionary device cannot be carried too far within the area the actors must use, however, for the false scale would be immediately apparent to the audience if a 6-foot (1.83 m) actor stepped into an area with a 6-foot-high (1.83 m) ceiling and miniature chairs. Another illusionary device involves *aerial perspective*—the use of sharper details, value contrasts, and color intensity in areas represented as being closer to the viewers, with lighting and colors quickly fading toward the rear, as if being affected by the atmospheric haze of great distance.

Space is not just a matter of visual tricks in set design; it can be used to present a metaphor of the play itself. *Going Away* takes place in a steel mill town and concerns the struggles within a family who relate to each other as combatants. Jerry Rojo used space to project his understanding of the underlying meaning of the play:

> I used the image of a factory and the furnaces of a steel town so that everything is an explosion out of these furnaces—a metaphor for the exploding family. The house is broken up—the father is always watching television up in his room, the mother is always in the kitchen, the brothers are making out with girls in their bedroom. Each member of the family has their own kind of room, like a factory. The set is also suspended in space, physically hung, so that when you look at it you see the edges of the set and the world around it. Like the family, it's not stable and grounded; it's exploding out into the world.

In many works, the artist's use of space is thus a subtle vehicle for the content of the piece. Ideas or emotions may be expressed not only by creating metaphorical spatial illusions but also by developing delineated shapes in space, drawing attention to the interaction between forms and the surrounding area or to spatial relationships among forms, confining a form—or the viewer—within a defined space, or altering the scale of the familiar.

5.1 Shapes in Space

Assemble six to eight blocks of soft wood in such a way that they delineate and draw attention to one or more shapes in unfilled space. The pieces of wood should be similar but need not be identical; you can paint them if you choose.

5.2 Activated Surrounding Space

Using materials of your own choosing, create a piece that seems to extend beyond its own physical limits, activating a larger area of the space around it. Refer to the text for ideas about how this subtle effect might be achieved.

144 Confined Space. Found wood, stones. Student work.

Elements of Three-Dimensional Design

5.3 Confined Space

Using any materials including found objects, create a confined space and then develop forms within it. By thus isolating these forms, you will draw special attention to them. In Figure 144, pieces of scrap wood are barely confined within an open-ended box, as if about to burst out of bondage. The box itself can also be perceived as spatially confined by the stones around its base. The predominant feeling is one of inhibited outward expansion: Confinement is actually the emphasis of the piece.

5.4 Scale Change

Using any materials, create a situation in which the viewer is very aware that something has been presented in an unaccustomed scale, much larger or smaller than its usual reality. In the student example shown in Figure 145, a miniature apartment has been constructed within the seat of a chair, some-

145 Scale Change. Stuffed armchair, cardboard, paper. Student work.

thing normally seen within a room. The normal scale of the chair reminds us that everything in the scene that sits within it has been greatly reduced in scale.

5.5 Illusionary Space

Using any materials, create a piece that gives the illusion of behaving differently in space than it actually does. For example, by the way you cut or paint a form, you could make a shallow piece appear to occupy very deep space or could make square contours appear rounded. The piece shown in Figure 146 is actually an absolutely flat piece of cardboard, airbrushed to look like a three-dimensional cube with a gash in it.

146 Illusionary Space. Painted cardboard. Student work.

Elements of Three-Dimensional Design

Line

We tend to identify line as a stroke on a two-dimensional page, yet line also exists in our three-dimensional world. Branches, grasses, late afternoon shadows, icicles, telephone poles, cables, fences, and jet trails all appear as lines. In general, a *line* is an area whose length is considerably greater than its width.

In three-dimensional art, whole works may consist of lines. Lines may also appear within forms or even implied in space. Depending on their character, lines can steer our attention in a particular direction or perhaps help to convey the emotional effect the artist intended. To a certain extent, these experiences are subjective. The degree to which an area is seen as a line depends on the viewer's distance and awareness, and the emotional qualities ascribed to different kinds of line may not affect everybody in exactly the same way. Nevertheless, line can be a powerful and direct tool in the hands of the artist.

Linear Works

Many everyday objects have a strong linear quality. In the Japanese gardener's scissors shown in Figure 147, the gracefully symmetric shear handles appear to be a single line turning back into itself, carrying the eye through its flowing curves. The design is actually quite functional, for it can be used equally well by right- or left-handed people and concentrates the force of the hand-squeeze right where it is needed for nipping off tough plant stems.

Bare trees appear as series of lines in a landscape. Isolated, wooden boards or branches often have a linear effect, as do many things made from lumber and branches. In the *Thonet Rocker* (Fig. 148), wood has been bent into the vinelike curves of Art Nouveau lines. Arms, legs, and frame grow outward together like wild plants continually looking for something to cling to. The lines even terminate in vinelike tendrils curling back on themselves.

Sculptures made from linear materials such as wire often retain a strongly linear quality. Alexander Calder's *The Brass Family* (Fig. 149) uses line almost as a two-dimensional drawing does—as outlines within which we obligingly fill in full-bodied three-dimensional figures with our imagination.

The linear nature of the human figure seen from a distance is often called into play by choreographers, who turn dancers into moving linear sculptures. In *Ciona* by Philobolus (Fig. 150), the organic lines suggested by the dancers' variously joined bodies are accentuated by high-contrast lighting that makes the figures thinner and less recognizable as individual human forms. The difference the high-

147 (top) Gardener's secateurs. Japan.
148 (bottom left) GEBRÜDER THONET. *Rocking Chair*. 1960. Bent beechwood, cane. Height 37½″ (95 cm). Collection Museum of Modern Art, New York (Gift of Café Nicholson).
149 (bottom right) ALEXANDER Calder. *The Brass Family*. 1929. Brass wire, height 64″ (163 cm), width 41″ (104 cm), depth 8½″ (22 cm). Collection Whitney Museum of American Art, New York (Gift of the artist).

Elements of Three-Dimensional Design

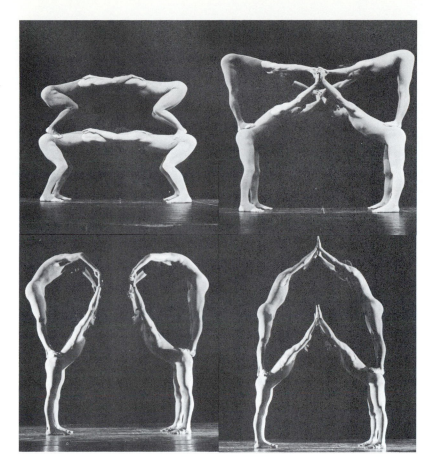

150 (left) Pilobolus Dance Theater. *Ciona*.
151 (below) Alberto Giacometti. *Tall Figure*. 1947. Bronze, 80 × 6 × 5″ (203 × 15 × 13 cm). Hirshhorn Museum and Sculpture Garden, Smithsonian Institution.

contrast lighting makes can be appreciated by its absence in the group shot at upper left; here the bodies look more like muscular human forms and less like linear constructions.

Sculptor Alberto Giacometti elongates the human body into a single thin line in his *Tall Figure* (Fig. 151). From any distance and in any light, this figure's proportions—80 inches (20.32 cm) in height in contrast to only 5 inches (12.7 cm) at its greatest width—will look like a line isolated in space. Indeed, it affects us with a poignant sense of loneliness—of unhappy withdrawal from the other denizens of this planet; the lonely figure even seems to be drawing away vertically from the horizontal surface of the planet itself.

Our distance from certain works plays a big part in whether we perceive them as linear. Seen from the ground, a street looks like a wide slab; from the air, we can see its length in relationship to its width and thus recognize its linear quality. From a distance, Eero Saarinen's *Jefferson Westward Expansion Memorial* (Fig. 152) in St. Louis thrusts a line high into the sky. But seen from its base, it is a massive form, an

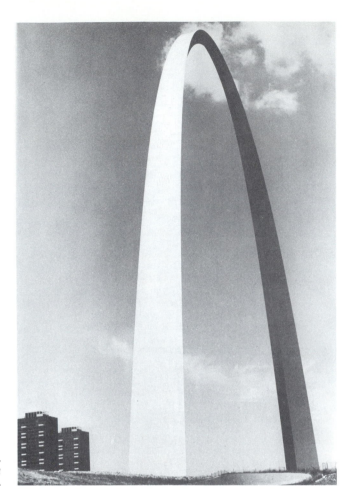

152 Eero Saarinen. *Jefferson Westward Expansion Memorial*, St. Louis. 1966.

arch 630 feet (192.15 m) high with legs broad enough to carry forty people at a time in a lift up to the observation room at the top. Robert Smithson's *Spiral Jetty* (Fig. 153) does not reveal its spiraling line until one is far enough away to get the sort of perspective shown in the photograph. Many such *earthworks*—large-scale, three-dimensional projects involving physical alterations of the earth's surface for aesthetic purposes—are designed to create a monumental line across the landscape.

Lines within Forms

In addition to being used in primarily linear works, lines also commonly appear within forms. Sometimes lines are simply applied to the surface, as in Picasso's *Owl* (Fig. 154). These descriptive lines cannot

Elements of Three-Dimensional Design

153 (top) ROBERT SMITHSON. *Spiral Jetty*. 1970. Black rock, salt crystals, earth, red water (algae), coil 1500′ (477 m) long, approx. 15′ (4.6 m) wide. Great Salt Lake, Utah.

154 (bottom) PABLO PICASSO. *Owl*. 1961. Metal cutout, folded and painted. Height 9⅞″ (25 cm).

Line   123

be considered secondary to the form, for imagine how much of the owl-ness of the piece would be lost if the lines indicating the scraggly feathers had not been added.

In some cases, the lines naturally appearing in the material are revealed and used aesthetically. The grain of wood often adds linear patterns to a work. In sculpting *Adolescence* (Fig. 155), Etienne Hajdu used the fissures within the marble to suggest growth and change. The dark lines are almost like an X-ray view of the circulatory system carrying the hormones that activate the changes of puberty. The organic quality of these lines presents a lively contrast to the more formally controlled outer contours of the figure.

Lines are often created by *edges*—by the lines along which two planes or pieces of material meet—as well as by the distinction between the outer contours or *outlines* of a piece and its surroundings. When people say that a piece has "nice lines," they are usually talking about its edges. What allows us to see edges as lines is differences in *value*—in relative lightness and darkness. Masayuki Nagare's *Wind Form* (Fig. 156) is a form whose edges define a series of lines as the surfaces turn toward or away from a light source. The value differences

155 (left) ETIENNE HAJDU. *Adolescence*. 1957. Marble, 35½ × 11⅞ × 2¼″ (90 × 30 × 6 cm). Hirshhorn Museum and Sculpture Garden, Smithsonian Institution.
156 (right) MASAYUKI NAGARE. *Wind Form*. 1965. Polished Italian travertine marble, 31⅜ × 10¼ × 9″ (80 × 26 × 23 cm). Hirshhorn Museum and Sculpture Garden, Smithsonian Institution.

Elements of Three-Dimensional Design

where two planes meet are accentuated by deep undercutting in the area curving down from the upper left to the center. This entire undercut area becomes a dark line in itself, a visual accent to the broader, lighter plane surfaces.

Implied and Directional Lines

Certain lines are not physically present in a work but can nevertheless be subtly perceived. These *implied lines* may appear as *eye lines* between figures or between a figure and something at which it is gazing. In the ancient bronze *Thorn Puller* (Fig. 157) we can perceive a strong eye line between the boy's eyes and the bottom of his foot where the offending thorn must be.

We may also perceive implied lines as continuations or completions of lines given in a work. The sculptural group *Ugolino and His Sons* (Fig. 158) contains a very dramatic eye line from the largest son to his father. But it also is composed of a series of lines formed by arms and legs that tend to flow together into larger implied lines. For

157 *Thorn Puller (Spinario).*
Bronze, height 28¾" (73 cm). Capitoline Museums, Rome.

125

158 JEAN-BAPTISTE CARPEAUX. *Ugolino and his Sons*. Executed 1865–67 after a model completed 1860–61. Marble, 6'5" (1.95 m) high. Metropolitan Musem of Art (Funds given by the Josephine Bay Paul and C. Michael Paul Foundations, Inc., the Charles Ulrick and Josephine Bay Foundation, Inc., and the Fletcher Fund, 1967).

159 JOAN MICHAELS PAQUE. *Moebius Extension*. 1977. Knotted and woven synthetic fiber, about 8' (2.44 m) long. Collection of Dr. and Mrs. Robert Monk, Waukesha, Wisconsin.

instance, the forward arm of the largest son leads the viewer's eye up to the father's knee and then back across the father's other thigh and down through the son's neck. Alternate visual paths might be traced from the largest son's arm up through the father's knee to the elbow resting on it, up the forearm to the head, or up the upper arm, around the shoulders, and down the opposite arm to the outer leg of the son on the right and thence down into the arm of the smallest child at the bottom, which leads the eye back up into the center. Seen this way, the group becomes a swirl of implied lines leading from one anguished figure to another and tying them all together visually.

Lines may have a strong *directional* quality—the characteristic of pointing the viewer's eye in a certain direction, sometimes creating implied lines thereby. Joan Michaels Paque's *Moebius Extension* (Fig.

Elements of Three-Dimensional Design

159) draws together the edges of the woven forms as pointers, each leading the eye to the next point above. If you follow these directions from bottom to top, a perceptual line is being created up the center of the piece that strengthens and completes the faint line that repeatedly appears where the weaving patterns join along the midline and then disappears into the shadows.

In Chapter 5, we noted that space may be activated by implied lines that direct the eye into unfilled space surrounding a three-dimensional piece. In *N Lines Vertical* (Fig. 128), for instance, the lines given point the eye into the distance beyond. It is inappropriate to be dogmatic in making statements about precisely how people will respond to directional lines, however. Does Paul von Ringelheim's *Endless Force* (Fig. 160) direct the eye up or down along its strong diagonal? Is the "force" rising from or descending to the earth? Perhaps both, for it is actually constructed of two opposing directional lines. Attention is drawn beyond both the upper and lower ends, as indicated by the different directions in which the people in the photograph are looking.

Awareness of directional and implied lines makes it possible to see Nancy Holt's *Sun Tunnels* (Fig. 161) as being "about" lines. For one thing, the sun's rays pierce the holes in the concrete pipes, forming lines of sunlight into the pipes themselves. If a person looks through one of the pipes, what he or she will see will be a defined line into the surrounding landscape, directed "tunnel vision." Furthermore, the pipes are placed to honor the sunrises and sunsets during the solstices in this Lincoln, Utah, setting. At dawn and dusk on the days

160 PAUL VON RINGELHEIM. *Endless Force*. 1978. Stainless steel, 12′ × 2′2″ × 2″ × 14′ (3.66 × 0.66 × 4.27 m). Collection Gerald R. Ford, Palm Springs, California. Conceived within the architectural plan of Welton Becket and Associates.

161 (top) Nancy Holt. *Sun Tunnels*. 1973–76. The Great Basin Desert, Utah. Concrete pipes, 22 tons each; tunnel lengths 18' (5.49 m), height 9'4" (2.8 m), total length 86' (26.23 m). The tunnels are aligned with the sun on the horizon (sunrises and sunsets) on the solstices.

162 (bottom) Michael Heizer. *Circumflex*. 1968. Massacre Dry Creek Lake, Nevada. Earthwork, 120' (36.6 m) long.

marking the height of winter and summer, the sun itself beams directly into one of the tunnels, creating a line of pure light.

Qualities of Lines

Individual artists' use of line is highly varied, as is the background each viewer brings to perception of a work of art. Nevertheless, art does touch us emotionally in ways that are somewhat predictable. Linear elements in works tend to evoke certain responses, depending on the characteristics of the lines.

Our eye tends to move very quickly over simple, smooth lines like those of *Endless Force* (Fig. 160); we scan or *read* complex lines like those of *Ugolino and His Sons* (Fig. 158) or rough edges like those of Giacometti's *Tall Figure* (Fig. 151) more slowly. These natural tendencies lead us to think of lines themselves as being "quick" or "slow," no matter how quickly they were actually made. Michael Heizer's earthwork *Circumflex* (Fig. 162) appears from a distance to be such a smooth and simple line that it seems a quick gesture. This impression belies the work involved in its creation, for it is actually a trench dug across 120 feet (36.6 m) of Nevada desert.

Rough or jagged lines or lines that go in many different directions convey a feeling of emotional upheaval. The ragged lines of the marble fissures and head areas in Hajdu's *Adolescence* (Fig. 155) suggest an emotional turbulence that contrasts with the smooth outlines of the torso.

Curving lines remind us of flowing motion. Single lines that curve, perhaps flaring and thinning as they round corners, may evoke a poignant sense of beauty, even in so mundane an object as the Japanese gardener's shears (Fig. 147), for they tend to mold our awareness itself into a flowing line. No matter how brief the experience, it may be a welcome change from the scattered, frenetic pace of modern life.

The use of many curving lines, as in Antoni Gaudí's *Casa Milá Apartment House* (Fig. 163), may evoke a sense of romance or playfulness. We usually associate living quarters with straight horizontal and vertical lines, so the many ways this building curves in and out, up and down, are a whimsical surprise to the imagination.

Horizontal lines often carry a restful, secure feeling, perhaps through association with the earth's horizon line and our horizontal position when sleeping. The straight horizontal lines that predominate in David Rockefeller's office in the Chase Manhattan Bank (Fig. 164) convey an elegant sense of calmness. Even the chairs are squared off

163 Antoni Gaudi. *Casa Milá Apartment House*, Barcelona, Spain. 1905–07.

164 CMP Interiors. *David Rockefeller's Office*. 17th floor, Chase Manhattan Bank, New York. 1961.

165 Lu Duble. *Cain*. 1953. Hydrocal, height 38″ (97 cm), width 28″ (71 cm), depth 18″ (46 cm). Collection Whitney Museum of American Art, New York.

and low to the ground, adding to the feeling of stability. The message is that one can rest assured that this bank is solid, trustworthy, and comfortable with wealth.

Lines that are predominantly vertical do not convey this feeling of stability unless they are anchored in strong horizontal lines. Rather, they suggest defiance of or escape from the earth's gravitational pull. Strong verticals such as the supporting pillars inside a high-ceilinged cathedral or the exterior lines of Gaudí's Church of the Sagrada Familia (Fig. 92) are designed to give worshipers a sense of being spiritually uplifted above the denseness of worldly concerns.

Diagonal lines introduce a feeling of drama or energy. Lu Duble's *Cain* (Fig. 165) dramatizes Cain's sense of anguish and guilt at having killed his brother by the extreme diagonal thrust of his body. Even his throat is elongated into the thrown back head to emphasize the diagonal line that begins at the foot below his open hands.

Combining different kinds of lines is like composing music for a whole orchestra. If the sounds of different instruments are not blended harmoniously, the result is cacophony. This visual chaos may be intended by the artist. But in Toshio Odate's *Pride of New England* (Fig. 166) differing line qualities are blended into a unified whole that both draws the viewer's attention and issues an invitation to quiet contemplation. Trained as a Japanese *shoji* screen maker, Odate uses line to create three kinds of space-defining screens in this piece: the long section featuring a handsome 18-foot (5.49 m) slab of red oak, a section of vertical slats that can barely be seen beyond and to the left in this photograph, and an opaque panel featuring a translucent rice

Elements of Three-Dimensional Design

166 TOSHIO ODATE. *Pride of New England*. 1982. Red oak plank 18' (5.49 m) long, 3½' (1.07 m) wide.

paper circle with wooden lattice. The slab of oak becomes a directional line leading to the circle panel and the low box set among rounded stones before it that suggests a place for seated meditation. Along the oak slab, the vertical dowels and the negative lines formed by the spaces between them are small enough that they emphasize the horizontal by contrast, rather than fighting with it for dominance. The horizontals and verticals are repeated in the panels and framework at the far end. And the subtle curve of the oak slab is repeated in the circular line around the rice paper, the roundness of the stones, and again in the curve of the natural tree trunk. Lines in nature are rarely perfectly straight, but through balanced use of repetition and contrast, Odate unifies the straight lines of manufactured lumber with the curving lines of organic forms.

STUDIO PROBLEMS

6.1 Wire Sculpture

Use wire to create a line or lines in space that describe a human or animal form. The wire can vary in size and can be painted black so that it can be seen more readily. Bend the wire into curves that encompass fully three-dimensional forms in unfilled space, rather than creating a flat frontal piece that looks like a two-dimensional line drawing.

167 (left)   Directional Line. Wood, steel braces, bolts. Student work.
168 (right)   Line and Form. Wire, U-nails, wood. Student work.

6.2   Directional Line

Using any material, create a work that uses line to lead the eye in a specific direction. The possibilities for solutions are limited only by your own imagination. The larger the piece, the more the eye will follow it. The left-to-right directional thrust of the piece in Figure 167 is accentuated by the large scale of the work and by the effect of bridging a wide gap between the two bases. The pieces of wood used for the bases are movable—when drawn farther apart, expanding the bases visually, the directional line above seems to shrink in length.

6.3   Line and Form

Use wire to create a linear three-dimensional sculpture, fully rounded in space rather than frontal; present it in relationship to a wooden base, perhaps with U-nails used unobtrusively to join the two. The mass of the base should work with the airy linear structure to create a unified, well-balanced whole. Using standard bases available in most art departments, experiment with various sizes and shapes of bases to determine what works best. Would the lines in Figure 168 work better against a larger base, or does the balance between the two seem appropriate? If the linear sculpture extends horizontally beyond the edges of the base, how well do they relate to each other?

7

Texture

The *texture* of a work is the surface characteristics we could feel if we touched it—its hardness, softness, bumpiness, smoothness, sharpness, furriness, or whatever. Our interest in these tactile qualities is part of what draws us into exploring a piece. When we cannot or do not touch an object, impressions of what it would feel like if we touched it are conveyed to us visually. As we will see, our eye can be fooled about texture. Artists may therefore work with *visual texture*—the apparent, rather than actual texture of a surface.

The textural characteristics of a work may not be the first thing we notice. We tend to scan a three-dimensional object quickly with our eyes, streamlining its contours, and then perhaps come in closer to see what it is made of and how. We see distant hills as having smoothly rolling outlines; we do not notice the differences in height and form of individual trees that reveal a jagged textural effect when examined more closely. In certain works of art, however, we are not given a chance to ignore the texture. Louise Nevelson's *First Personage* (Fig. 169) immediately draws our attention to the contrasting surfaces of the two pieces of wood. Our eye registers at once what the surfaces would feel like if we touched them—the torsolike right side would be relatively soft to the touch, while the "back" side warns us not to put a hand near its sharp points. This strong contrast between the invitation of the soft contours and the KEEP AWAY signals of the back points seems to be the subject of the piece, a visual puzzle for us to explore and ponder.

Almost all works of three-dimensional art have an actual surface texture that can be felt. Those we will examine in this chapter tend to make the viewer extremely aware of their textural effects. Although texture cannot be isolated from other elements of design, such as color, form, or line, much attention may be drawn to the natural texture of materials, worked textures, or visual textures that differ from the actual textures of the piece.

Elements of Three-Dimensional Design

Natural Texture

Often artists find that it suits their purposes to use materials exactly as they come from nature. An extreme example of this approach is Walter De Maria's *New York Earth Room* (Fig. 170), which is just what is says: a room filled with dirt. The artist has placed a glass partition in the doorway of the museum to hold the dirt in and allow people to see the depth of the dirt layer. The interest of this conceptual piece lies in seeing so much of a decidedly organic material in an urban setting (how did he cart it all into this museum?), and in contrasting the soft, granular texture of the dirt with the hard, smooth texture of the walls. In addition to textural contrasts, the room and the dirt within it also differ considerably in color and also in smell, an element of design which usually receives relatively little attention. The piece offers no judgments about which texture, smell, and color is "better"—it just presents the contrasts to the viewer's awareness, using such large amounts of dirt and wall that they cannot escape notice.

170 Walter De Maria. *New York Earth Room.* 1977. New York. 250 cubic yards (191 cubic meters) of earth and earth mix (peat and bark) weighing 280,000 pounds (127,000 kg), covering an area of 3,600 square feet (335 square meters) of floor space to a depth of 22 inches (56 cm). Installation commissioned and maintained by Dia Art Foundation.

Sometimes natural textures are used not to call attention to their own identity but rather to refer to other similar textures. The Hawaiian artisan who created the ritual figure shown in Figure 171 conveyed the texture and color of human skin by using feathers and of human teeth by using dogs' teeth. The wet, shimmering surface of the human eye is captured with pearl shells. Usually we must be familiar with the texture of both the natural material being used and the texture it is representing to fully appreciate such pieces. But how familiar are we with what the surface of the eye feels like? We dare not touch this sensitive surface; we know its texture more by what it looks like that by how it is perceived through the touch sensors in the fingers.

Many textures that we consider natural have already been worked to a certain extent. We think of rough-sawn wood as a natural surface, but it is already a step removed from the initial bark surface of its origin: the tree. In her site-specific piece *Split Tongue Pier* (Fig. 172), Jody Pinto draws our attention to both the flat machine-cut surface of the rough spruce and pine used in the pier jutting out over a gorge and the natural textures of the trees in the environment. Both register in our mind as WOOD. Their textures are so closely related that the pier seems at one with the trees, rocks, bushes, grasses, and dirt of the natural environment. And yet their textures are different enough that the contrast is of aesthetic interest. If the pier had been made with whole tree trunks, the effect would have been quite different.

171 Image. Feathers, wicker, dog teeth, pearl shell, wood, height 24½″ (62 cm). Museum für Völkerkünde, Vienna. Collected on Captain Cook's third Hawaiian voyage, 1778–79.

172 JODY PINTO. *Split Tongue Pier.* 1980. Swarthmore College, Pennsylvania. Temporary sculpture project for Swarthmore College Campus, rough spruce and pine, 48′ (14.64 m) long × 2′ (0.61 m) wide.

173 Sheila Hicks. *Ephemera Bundle.* 1975. Silk, 8 × 8 × 3″ (20 × 20 × 8 cm). Collection Mr. and Mrs. Ralph W. Bettelheim, New York.

Certain pieces seem to offer a single natural texture for our exploration, yet a subtle form of contrast or variation is often present to engage our awareness. Sheila Hicks' *Ephemera Bundle* (Fig. 173) appears at first glance to be a tangle of soft, curly silk yarns. Yet closer inspection reveals continual variations among tautly spun linear strands, loosely spun curly strands, thinly straying single fibers, and even bits of coarsely woven cloth. We even have the impression of interior texture here—the suggestion that there are layers upon hidden layers of these textures wrapped around each other from the core outward.

Worked Texture

The surface of a material may be manipulated, or worked, by the artist to create a great variety of textural effects. Materials may be carved, blasted, polished, ground, hammered, built up, or woven together for a number of different reasons. Perhaps the most obvious of these are to shape the material to the desired form and to simulate the texture of an actual three-dimensional object. To create a portrait of *Georgia*

174 Marisol (Escobar). *Portrait of Georgia O'Keeffe with Antelope.* 1980. Charcoal on wood, stone, plaster, and antelope, 4'7 × 4'7 × 3'6½" (1.4 × 1.4 × 1.08 m). Collection Martin Margulies.

O'Keeffe (Fig. 174), Marisol uses the natural texture of weathered wood and rock to convey the qualities of solidity and strength that we associate with these materials; the actual head of a stuffed antelope emphasizes the message that this grande dame of American painting was very much at home among the creatures and landscape of the Southwestern desert. Yet to make the portrait more recognizable as Georgia O'Keeffe, Marisol has carved a likeness of her wise, discerning face into the wood. The textural lines created by the chipping away of the wood become character lines that further describe her venerable subject.

Even in nonobjective works, textural manipulation may be used not only to shape form but also to emphasize it. In *Helixikos #1* (Fig. 175), Hans Hokanson makes us very aware of the chiseled grooves seemingly used to carve the spiraling open form out of a more solid block of wood. We would like to trace these grooves with our fingers; as our eye follows this intention by moving forward across the figure, the chisel lines lead us in the direction the double spiral seems to be moving, thus enhancing the sensation of movement.

Textures may also be manipulated to provide contrasts, either within a work or between the work and its surroundings. Isamu Noguchi's *Stone of Spiritual Understanding* (Fig. 176) presents a beautiful contrast between the raw mineral mass of bronze uncharacteristi-

175 Hans Hokanson. *Helixikos #1.* 1968. Natural wood, elm, wax, length 23″ (58 cm), width 40″ (102 cm), depth 24″ (61 cm) (collection of the artist).

176 (top) Isamu Noguchi. *Stone of Spiritual Understanding.* 1962. Aluminum and bronze. The Isamu Noguchi Garden Museum, Long Island City, New York.
177 (bottom) Sheila Hicks. Wall rugs from the *Sejjada* series, shown at Galerie Bob Rouah, Rabat, Morocco. 1971. Each rug 7′7″ (2.3 m) high.

cally cast into a stonelike lump and the extremely smooth reflective surface of highly polished aluminum. The aesthetic balance between the two is like a spiritual marriage of apparent opposites—lightness and darkness, warmth and coldness, roughness and smoothness, earth and sky. The seeming polarities are so inextricably linked that the polished metal appears to physically pierce the bronze stone, which in turn is mirrored perpetually in the surface of the polished aluminum, where it appears to float.

Some works invite us to compare the textures of a work and its setting. In her *Sejjada* wall rugs (Fig. 177), Sheila Hicks combines the contrasting textural effects of flat-woven areas and deep shaggy areas, unified by the horizontal lines that run across both. What is even more compelling, however, is the repetition of textural contrasts throughout the exhibit: The play of close-woven areas against shaggy areas, and softly woven fiber arts against hard walls echoes the play of the relatively smooth walls against the roughness of the brick arches. In this photograph taken by the artist, even the hoods and robes of the two women repeat the forms and textures seen in the architecture and in the rugs.

Surfaces may be worked to create a surface that is aesthetically pleasing. Marble and wood sculptures that are extremely smooth invite us to caress them with hand and eye, enjoying the sensual flow of the contours. When metal is smooth and highly polished, this manipulation of the material also gives it an extremely reflective quality. The highly polished silicone bronze surface of Ernest Trova's *Study: Falling*

Texture

178 ERNEST TROVA. *Study: Falling Man (Carman)*. 1965. Polished silicone bronze and enamel, 4'8¼ × 6'6 × 2'8¾" (0.53 × 1.98 × 0.78 m). Hirshhorn Museum and Sculpture Garden, Smithsonian Institution.

Man (Carman) (Fig. 178) offers a gleaming accent to the contours of the human form and picks up reflections of whatever is near the piece, adding to its visual interest. The shiny, slick surface also adds to the illusion of speed—a visual image of man as not only a car, but a very fast car. Our eye would move more slowly across a rough surface and we would tend to ascribe this slowness to the object itself: We would not expect a rusty car to move very fast.

The manipulation of the surface of an object to enhance its beauty is intimately bound to cultural and historical definitions of beauty. In body ornamentation, our culture tends to value soft but smooth skin, with surface ornamentation confined to clothes, jewelry, cosmetics, and textural manipulation of the hair. But some peoples have preferred raised textural effects in the skin itself, as in the body scarification shown in Figure 179. The complex details of such body

179 Unmarried girls with filed teeth and scarification. Pende, Zaire. National Museum of African Art, Eliot Elisofon Archives, Smithsonian Institution.

Elements of Three-Dimensional Design

sculpture may be emphasized by the use of oils and cosmetics. Those who have learned to cherish the smooth skin of youth may have a negative reaction to this form of body art. We can easily imagine what it would feel like to run a hand across these raised textures—or to endure the initial pain of the scarification process—and our immediate reaction may not be a pleasant one. It may be very difficult for us to appreciate the point of view of those who consider this worked texture beautiful on a human body or who take pride in being thus adorned. In addition to the fact that beauty is in the eye of the beholder, not all art intends to be beautiful. Though the love of beauty is often a motivating factor, many artists are motivated by the quest for a public or a private truth.

Finally, textures may be worked to create a paradoxically natural effect. The many intricate textures of Norma Minkowitz's *Inner Rhythms* (Fig. 180) flow across the cape like organic forms. But yet they are the result of extremely detailed crochet work that totally alters the straight nature of the single fibers used. Minkowitz explains that in her wearable art she works with fiber to create lines reminiscent of fine pen and ink drawings: "I like to work with fiber as if I were sketching in pen and ink. The pieces become like imaginary landscapes."

180 NORMA MINKOWITZ. *Inner Rhythms.* 1980. Fiber (cotton), 32″ × 29″ (81 × 74 cm). Collection Christine Carter.

Visual Texture

As we noted earlier, many works present an optically perceived *visual texture* that does not correspond with the actual texture of the material. A familiar example is the carving of marble to look like softer textures. Gianlorenzo Bernini's *Louis XIV* (Fig. 181) has been carefully sculpted to give the visual impressions of curling hair, swirling cape, and smooth skin. But if you were to touch the bust, your hand would

181 GIANLORENZO BERNINI. *Louis XIV.* 1665. Marble, height 31¼″ (79 cm). Palace of Versailles.

141

register a different tactile sensation than what your eyes perceived: the cold hardness of marble. The perceptual effect depends not only on the sculptor's skill but also on an historical tradition of portraying transient moments and materials in the more nearly eternal medium of marble. Because we have learned to associate marble with soft visual textures, we willingly ignore our knowledge of its actual hardness to appreciate the softness portrayed.

Visual textures may be used not only to capture the likeness of soft objects in more permanent form but also for other reasons. Sometimes the optical illusions are designed to amaze the viewer with their clever simulation of actual textures. The success of Marilyn Levine's *Two-Toned Golf Bag* (Fig. 182) depends on its perfect replication in stoneware of the textures of worn leather and metal fittings. At this extreme, visual textures become *trompe l'oeil*, or "fool the eye" imagery.

Another way in which visual textures have been used is to make objects more visually pleasing or acceptable. Early in the Industrial Revolution, many people preferred the ornate hand-wrought styles with which they were familiar to the simpler lines more natural to

182 (top) MARILYN LEVINE. *Two-Toned Golf Bag.* 1980. Stoneware with nylon reinforcement, 35 × 10½ × 7″ (89 × 27 × 18 cm)
183 (right) Rose Engine Lathe, c. 1750. German. Science Museum, London (British Crown Copyright).

142

machine-made products. Attempts to satisfy the older aesthetic led to creations such as the German *Rose Engine Lathe* shown in Figure 183. Its elaborate, vinelike visual texture is designed to camouflage the presumed ugliness of its function as a machine. Indeed, it appears almost too fragile to stand up under the stress of continual motion.

Visual textures are not necessarily an attempt to fool the eye, however. In some cases, they grow out of the complexities of reality. David Smith scoured the steel surfaces of *XI Books III Apples* (Fig. 184) to create interesting light-reflecting patterns which happen to have the optical softness of velvet, a nice contrast to the hardness and the hard edges of the steel forms. It is interesting that Smith himself used textural metaphors to describe the creative impetus of the artist. He wrote, "I know now that sculpture is made from rough externals by rough characters or men who have passed through all polish and are back to the rough again." In a sense, art grows out of the textural qualities of the artist's life—the polishing and grinding and reworking, the soft places and the hard, the affinity for nature or for the accretions of civilization, the love of the beautiful surface and the scratching beneath the surface to reveal what lies within.

184 DAVID SMITH. *XI Books III Apples.* 1959. Stainless steel, height (2.39 m), width 31¼″ (0.79 cm), depth 13¼″ (0.34 m). Collection Storm King Art Center, Mountainville, New York (gift of the Ralph E. Ogden Foundation).

7.1 Texture Switch

Taking two already existing objects, create a new surface texture on each that will contradict the previous sense of pleasantness or unpleasantness. For example, the smoothness of a bar of soap might be covered with crushed glass, and the roughness of a cinder block might be covered with terrycloth.

7.2 Three Textures Together

Using worked and/or found textures, create a piece using three different textures that work well together. They may be unified by contrast as well as by similarity. In Figure 185 twine has been wrapped around hay to create a single ropelike texture whose shagginess and limpness is contrasted with the relatively flat surfaces of lumber. The seeming heaviness of the "rope" is a visual texture, for the hay is actually quite light in weight.

185 Three Textures Together. Hay, twine, wood. Student work.

Elements of Three-Dimensional Design

7.3 Visual Textures

Using an existing object or a solution to a previous problem, manipulate its surface to alter its visual texture and affect the way viewers would respond to it. The new optical effects could be created by painting or drawing on the surface, or you could devise some other way of optically changing the visual texture of the piece. In Figure 186, the welcoming texture of the soft chair, accentuated by the homey rug and lamp, is totally contradicted by the sticky fly-paper, complete with flies, draped all over it.

7.4 Soft Sculpture

Manipulate soft material(s) by processes such as sewing, wrapping, stuffing, and tying to create a soft sculpture large enough to work well by itself as a floor piece. What are the possibilities and limitations of each process?

7.5 Contradicting a Form

Using applied or real texture, try to contradict an existing form. The original angular form in Figure 187 is almost obliterated by the visual texture created by spattering of paint. We tend to notice the visual texture first; the underlying form is discovered secondarily.

186 (top) Visual Textures. Stuffed armchair, fly strips, rug, lamp. Student work.
187 (bottom) Contradicting a Form. Styrofoam, paint. Student work.

Texture

8

Light

Light is a rather subtle element of design but nonetheless a very dramatic tool when used consciously. In three-dimensional design, light develops a range of values as it falls across a piece, creating highlights, shaded areas, and shadows stretching beyond the work. These effects will vary considerably depending on the angle and intensity of the light source and whether the lighting is natural or artificial. The effects of light on a piece will also depend on the degree to which its surfaces curve away from the light.

In addition to using the light cast upon a piece as a design element, artists may incorporate reflections into their work. Light itself may even be the medium with which the artist is working.

Value

The light reflected from a surface determines its color. Color is such a rich element of design that we will devote the entire next chapter to it. *Value*, or degrees of lightness and darkness, is a characteristic of color. If you look around you, you can see that surfaces seem to change in color as they curve away from a light source. A wood desk might appear yellow on top where it catches the light and browner on sides away from the light. These differences are actually changes in value: Brown is a dark value of the hue we call yellow. It is useful to separate value from the other characteristics of color we will be studying in the next chapter, for value has a number of specific functions in three-dimensional art.

To study values, we observe the darkness or lightness of areas in relation to each other. Seeing value differences is easiest in black-and-white photographs, for they reduce color differences to a range of values from black through grays to white. In real life, we tend to assign objects a global color label, thus ignoring the actual differences that can be perceived in various areas of their surfaces. If you saw Gaston Lachaise's *Standing Woman* (Fig. 188) in the Museum of Modern Art,

188 Gaston Lachaise. *Standing Woman.* 1932. Bronze, height 7'4" (2.24 m); at base 3'5⅛" × 1'7⅛" (1.04 × 0.48 m). Museum of Modern Art, New York (Mrs. Simon Guggenheim Fund).

147

you might mentally label its color as bronze and thereby overlook the fact that its polished surface reflects light as near-white highlights and then develops darker values ranging to near-black in areas where light is blocked by parts of the figure. The underside of her chin, for instance, is in deep shadow because the protrusion of the face prevents the overhead lighting from reaching this area. The *highlights*—brilliantly lit areas that appear as luminous spots—occur in areas that receive the most direct illumination.

Gradations in value from black to white can be talked about in terms of a *gray scale,* such as the one shown in Figure 189. Here, the range from black to white is represented as ten equal steps. In reality, the range of values is almost infinite; many slight changes in value could occur between each of the ten steps shown. Values nearer the white end of the gray scale are assigned higher numbers. On a ten-step gray scale, white is 10 and black is 1. Since we perceive values in relationship to what lies around them, the gray scale is often shown with middle gray circles to illustrate how our perception of this mid-gray changes depending on its surroundings. It appears far darker on the high end of the scale in juxtaposition to white, and far lighter in juxtaposition to black, but it is in reality the same value throughout.

Although we may be only subconsciously aware of values, artists use them consciously for a variety of purposes. One function of value is to provide clues to three-dimensional form. From our experiences in the three-dimensional world, we have learned to associate gradual value shifts with rounded surfaces. Value changes are far more abrupt across sharply angled surfaces, for they juxtapose areas that catch the light and areas in which illumination is blocked. In the *Standing Woman*, the slowly changing range of gray values across the thighs helps us to perceive their full roundness; the sharper curve of the breasts away from the overhead light is indicated by the much more rapid transition from high values to low values. These areas of high value contrast created by exaggerating the curves of a muscular female figure add dramatic emphasis to the contours of the piece.

In addition to emphasizing forms, value contrasts may be used to create patterns of light and shadow that are interesting in themselves. The visual appeal of Barbara Hepworth's *Two Segments and Sphere* (Fig. 190) is enhanced by the series of semicircular shadows its forms cast. These shadows subtly repeat and vary the theme of sphere and slices of a sphere introduced by the three forms themselves.

Patterns of value contrasts may not only tie a work together but also unite it visually with its surroundings. In Frank Lloyd Wright's *Falling Water* (Fig. 191), the extremely cantilevered forms of the house create dramatic contrasts between brightly lit surfaces and areas of dark shadows that echo the value patterns and forms of the deeply undercut natural rock shelves below. Such devices helped Wright to

190 (top) BARBARA HEPWORTH. *Two Segments and Sphere.* 1935–36. White marble, height 12″ (30 cm). Collection Mrs. L. Florsheim, Chicago.

191 (bottom) FRANK LLOYD WRIGHT. *Kaufman House ("Falling Water").* Bear Run, Pennsylvania. 1936–39.

192 Larry Bell. *The Iceberg and Its Shadow.* 1974. ⅜″ (0.95 cm) clear and gray glass coated with Iconel and quartz. 56 panels 5′ (1.52 m) width, height varying from 5′7″–8′4″ (1.44–2.54 m). Collection Albert and Vera List family (on loan to M.I.T.).

create houses that seemed intimately related to their natural environment.

Values may be used to help us make spatial sense of a piece or to heighten its spatial effects. In Larry Bell's *The Iceberg and Its Shadow* (Fig. 192), the slight optical darkening that occurs when the tinted but transparent Plexiglas panels overlap each other allows us to judge how the panels relate to each other in space. Barbara Hepworth relates this function of value to "stereognosis": the ability to perceive three-dimensional form through the sense of touch. In a sense, values allow us to grasp the three-dimensionality of a form with our eyes rather than our hands. Hepworth writes,

> The importance of light in relation to form will always interest me. In sculpture it seems to be an extension of the stereognostic sensibility, and through it I feel it ought to be possible to induce those evocative responses that seem to be part of primeval life, and which are a vital necessity to a full apprehension of space and volume. There is an inside and an outside to every form. When they are in special accord, as for instance a nut in its shell or a child in the womb, or in the structure of shells or crystals, or when one senses the architecture of bones in the human figure, then I am most drawn to the effect of light. Every shadow cast by the sun from an ever-varying angle reveals the harmony of the inside and outside. Light gives full play to our tactile perceptions through the experience of our eyes, and the vitality of forms is revealed by the interplay between space and volume.

Elements of Three-Dimensional Design

In addition to describing forms, value contrasts allow us to see surface textures. Consider the difference in apparent texture of a surface under dim and bright lighting. On an overcast day, Alberto Giacometti's *Monumental Head* (Fig. 193) would appear to have a much smoother surface than the extremely rough texture revealed by the patterns of light and shadow on a bright day.

Natural Lighting

Any piece that is placed outside will be subject to the vagaries of changing light conditions. Although these are not under the control of the artist, in some cases they can be planned for. And in any case, changes in angle and intensity of natural lighting may enhance the liveliness of the aesthetic experience, for the changes in lighting make the pieces themselves ever-changing in mood and visual impact. To appreciate an outdoor work fully, one should come back again and again to see it under many different lighting conditions. In bright overhead sunlight in the Museum of Modern Art Sculpture Garden, Lachaise's *Standing Woman* (Fig. 188) glistens as though the figure had just emerged from the water. On a gray day she appears far softer, with her muscle structure less prominent. To appreciate her more fully, one should also see her in the warm sidelighting of dawn or dusk, in a dense mist, or bearing new-fallen snow.

The greater the intensity of natural lighting, the stronger the value contrasts created. Under very bright sunlight, the 52-ton granite boulder in Michael Heizer's *Displaced/Replaced Mass* (Fig. 194) is dramati-

193 (top) ALBERTO GIACOMETTI. *Monumental Head.* 1960. Bronze, 37½ × 12 × 15″ (95 × 30 × 38 cm). Hirshhorn Museum and Sculpture Garden, Smithsonian Institution.
194 (bottom) MICHAEL HEIZER. *Displaced/Replaced Mass.* 1969. Granite, 52 tons. Silver Springs, Nevada (dismantled). Collection Robert C. Scull.

151

195 KYU SUNG WOO AND JOHN G. WILLIAMS, with the assistance of Prof. Michael Kim of the Harvard Graduate School of Design. *Shadow study of Jordan Pond Valley,* Acadia National Park, Mount Desert Island, Maine.

cally set off by a well of darkness. Under overcast lighting conditions, both the boulder and the excavation in which it rests would be a less dramatic range of gray tones. Perhaps the siting of the work in desert country was dictated partly by the likelihood of sunny days.

Not only the intensity but also the angle of natural lighting changes. The sun moves from east to west each day, at an angle that is most directly overhead in the summer and closest to the horizon in winter. The shift from morning to afternoon sunlighting means that shadows will shift from one side of a piece to the other. When the position of shadows is of aesthetic importance, the artist must observe where they will fall during the day to determine the most desirable placement of the piece.

Shadows cast by objects other than the work of art may also influence its placement. Buildings themselves may cast shade on a sculpture. Often artists try to avoid the uniform values created by total shade. On the other hand, shadows created by the surroundings may in some cases enhance the work. For example, the architectural firm of Woo and Williams was commissioned to design a new Jordan Pond House to replace the old one which burned down in Acadia National Park on Mount Desert Island in Maine. A much-loved tradition was to be preserved: afternoon tea on the lawn. In siting the new structure, the architects wanted to take advantage of the view up the pond and through the valley to the mountains beyond. They found that the shadow cast by the cliffs west of the pond created a dramatic dark line that spread across the valleys as a mobile aspect of the landscape. Using a contour model of the area and special lighting to approximate the path of the sun, they were able to construct a "shadowstudy" (Fig. 195) that showed where the shadow shape would fall in the valley and

Elements of Three-Dimensional Design

196 *Lincoln Center for the Performing Arts,* New York. 1962–69. Left to right: New York State Theater, Metropolitan Opera House, Vivian Beaumont Theater and Library and Museum of the Performing Arts, Philharmonic Hall (now Avery Fisher Hall), arranged around three interconnecting plazas, seen by daylight. Buildings and the Guggenheim Bandshell in Damrosch Park arranged around three interconnecting plazas.

across the Tea Lawn south of the pond during the afternoon tea. Using the shadowstudy, they oriented the new building not toward the most obvious view but rather toward the changing drama of cliff and shadow, and were able to keep the Tea Lawn itself beyond the reach of the shadow.

Artificial Lighting

The controlled use of artificial lighting is not subject to the daily changes in natural lighting. Used well, it can considerably improve the aesthetic success of a work of art. In Chapter 2 we saw how the mood of Daniel French's *Abraham Lincoln* (Figs. 48 and 49) was dramatically changed by the addition of artificial lighting. In the natural light coming from below, the face appeared soft and perhaps a bit haggard, with light inappropriately concentrated around the chin. When illuminated by artificial spotlights from above, the head developed dramatic shadows beneath the eyebrows and mouth, considerably altering the appearance of the statue.

Whereas daylight tends to flood an object with light from a particular direction—the sun's position—artificial lighting can range from a small, intense spotlight to banks of floodlights, arranged wherever the artist feels they are most effective. Illuminated by overhead sunlight at midday, the *Lincoln Center for the Performing Arts* (Fig. 196) features dark, cavernous arches between brightly lit columns. Attention is also drawn to the lines leading to the fountain in the central plaza. The darkness of the arches almost holds the viewer away, as though the fronts of the buildings were solid. By contrast, artificial floodlighting of

Light   153

the interiors of the buildings by night (Fig. 197) turns them into warmly beckoning pools of light, drawing the viewer's attention inward to the delicate intricacies of the interiors. The effect is so changed that the second picture appears to be almost a photo negative of the first, with black areas transformed into light areas and vice versa.

The use of artificial light to create value contrasts can emphasize spatial and textural qualities of a piece. Leonard Baskin's *Oppressed Man* (Fig. 198) would appear far flatter under uniform lighting conditions than it does in the carefully arranged artificial lighting used in the photograph shown. The sense of the weightiness of knowledge—represented by the owl, which also is known as a symbol of death in some cultures—is dramatized by lighting from above that makes the bottom part of the owl seem particularly strong, pressing downward.

Elements of Three-Dimensional Design

This is not a man whose thoughts are rising. Rather, his thoughts are sitting on him, heavily. Note that the darkness of the background is used to accent the whole piece by contrast with the highlights on the contours. Often museum photographs are trimmed or taken against a white wall so that there is nothing to be seen but the figure itself. But inclusion of background and careful manipulation of lighting can enhance the photographic impact of a piece.

A truly great work of art cannot be killed by any kind of lighting. But even a great work can be enhanced by skillful artificial lighting. Millions have been touched by the beauty and pathos of Michelanelo's *Pietà* (Fig. 199). Yet photographer Robert Hupka manipulated artificial lighting as well as camera angle to take a series of photographs of the work such as the one shown in Figure 200 that make its emotional statement even more compelling. The high value contrast in areas such as the folds of Mary's robe heightens the drama of the sculpture. And to lose Mary's face in the shadows draws attention away from the surface characteristics of her figure and allows us to focus more on the quality of her presence—the tremendous love and sense of loss but yet an eternal serenity that transcends the pathos of suffering.

198 (top) Leonard Baskin. *Oppressed Man.* 1960. Pine painted white, 31 × 13 × 11½″ (79 × 33 × 29 cm). Whitney Museum of American Art, New York.
199 (bottom left) Michelangelo. *Pietà.* 1498–99. St. Peter's Rome.
200 (bottom right) Michelangelo. *Pietà.* 1498–99. St. Peter's, Rome.

Reflected Light

Another way in which artists may use light consciously is to create areas in which reflections may occur. Dull or rough surfaces absorb all light striking them, but shiny, smooth surfaces may reflect light back to the viewer, making the objects seem to glow with inner life. Highly polished flat surfaces will also mirror their surroundings; curving polished surfaces will present a distorted reflection of whatever passes before them. The smooth curves of Lino Sabattini's silver-plated flower vases (Fig. 201) are enlivened by an ever-changing play of abstracted images as life moves around them. Many objects in our three-dimensional world have this reflective quality, yet we rarely stop to enjoy the patterns that develop on their surfaces.

Mirrors, polished glass, or water may also be used by artists as reflective surfaces. Henry Moore's *Lincoln Center Reclining Figure* (Fig. 202) has been placed over a reflecting pool with obvious awareness that when the water is calm, it will provide a mirror for the piece. The reflections in the water below become an active part of the sculpture.

201 (top) Lino Sabattini, designed for Argenteria Sabattini, Italy. *Houn Ohara.* 1974. Silver-plated flower vases, height 14″ and 10½″ (36 cm and 27 cm).
202 (bottom) Henry Moore. *Lincoln Center Reclining Figure* in reflecting pool. Lincoln Center Plaza North, New York. 1965. Bronze.

Reflections of the sky in the water give the sculpture and its reflections the appearance of floating in a displaced sky.

Light glancing off the surface of a highly polished work may dazzle the eye of the beholder. In Brancusi's *Bird in Space* (Fig. 7), this dazzling light helps to create an ephemeral sense of the quick flash of a bird through the sky. Linda Howard in *Round About* (Fig. 203) ground wavy lines to a high sheen along the aluminum surfaces for a slightly different purpose. It is her intent to use light to visually dematerialize matter into a semblance of the energy patterns that actually underlie the apparent solidity of things. The shimmering surfaces almost disappear from view in bright sunlight, as in the upper left corner of the work. At the same time, the shadows cast by the strips balance the disappearing tendency by reinforcing the physicality of the structure. While the sculptural form is created by elements rotating through space, even more compelling than the form is the illusion of energy patterns. These are created by the wavelike *moiré* patterns of the interweaving of brightly lit elements, shaded segments, and unfilled spaces, repeated with ever-changing variations throughout the

203 LINDA HOWARD. *Round About.* 1976. Aluminum, 8 × 8 × 8′ (2.44 × 2.44 × 2.44 m). Photographed at Artpark, Lewiston, New York. Bradley Collection, Milwaukee, Wisconsin.

157

work and even beyond the sculpture to the shadow patterns cast on the ground.

Howard explains that she is using light in an attempt to give visual form to the ideas of contemporary physics and Eastern philosophies:

> I am deeply concerned with the paradox that exists between our experience of physical reality and our scientific knowledge of conceptual reality, with finding connections between these apparent opposites. Light is an important element in my work, for it brings out both sides of the paradox. Ambient light functions may either dematerialize structure into an almost totally ethereal experience of light and energy, reinforce structure, or sometimes even add illusionary structural elements. I want to dematerialize structure because I have always been struck by the ambiguity of matter. It seems physically hard but contemporary physics says that all matter is composed of energy, which simultaneously manifests itself as discrete particles and as waves. I'm working with that balance between our knowledge of matter as anything but solid and our actual experiences with its seeming solidity.

Light as a Medium

In addition to its many ways of dramatizing works of art, light itself may be the medium with which the artist works. In a sense, natural light is being harnessed as a medium in Le Corbusier's Notre Dame du Haut (Fig. 111), for as it pours through the windows it creates highly active forms.

Contemporary technologies have made it possible to build sculptural forms and lines using nothing but directed light. Lasers, for instance, create thin beams of colored light that can be thrown against the sky. The laser beams of Rockne Krebs' *Green Air* (Fig. 204) have no physical substance, but carve quite visible paths through the night sky above the Fort Worth Art Museum. Holography (see Chap. 1) can be used to create insubstantial forms that co-exist with the viewer in three-dimensional space.

In other light sculptures, light is shaped by some outer shell. Normally light travels in a straight line, but neon tubing and fiber optic strands can conduct light in curving paths. Dan Flavin's *Untitled (To My Dear Bitch, Airily)* (Fig. 205) uses straight but offset blue and green fluorescent tubes of light to create an installation piece in which light is the medium. We see three kinds of light: the gaseous light contained within the tubes, the aura that surrounds them, and their reflections on the polished floor of the gallery. The increasingly distorted and ephemeral quality of the reflections seems to extend the work into a strangely unfamiliar reality in which light floats, quite insubstantially.

Elements of Three-Dimensional Design

204 (top)   ROCKNE KREBS. *Green Air.* 1978. Laser installation at Fort Worth
Art Museum, Texas. Sponsored by the Fort Worth Art Museum and the Elmwood
Foundation for the Arts and Humanities.
205 (bottom)   DAN FLAVIN. *Untitled (To My Dear Bitch, Airily).* 1984. Blue and
green fluorescent light (as installed at 142 Greene St.), 4 × 44″ × 86′8″ (0.10 × 1.12 × 26.42 m).

Light is also used as a medium in theater, where stage lighting is as important as set design, costuming, makeup, sound, and acting in creating the desired effects. As stage lighting designer Don Murray notes,

> Most good lighting is so integrated with the wholeness of the theatrical event that it doesn't stand out as a thing in itself. But lighting can expand or contract the illusionary space of the stage, drawing it down to a pinpoint so that everything else fades into oblivion or creating on a 25-foot-deep stage the sense of vista of the great plains of Nebraska. It can be used to dramatize emotional effects or to subdue them. It can also make colors seem to advance or recede. Lighting's ability to be so flexible is one of its great contributions to theater. Whereas the sets are fixed, lighting is an active, hands-on activity that, like the actors, can respond to the moment.

Elements of Three-Dimensional Design

The impact of lighting on theatrical illusion is quite apparent in Franz Merz' lighting design for Sophocles' *Oedipus Rex* (Fig. 206). Here the space of the stage has been divided by lighting into one area of highly concentrated light, beyond which the boundaries of the stage are lost in total darkness. The makeup, costuming, and masks all repeat the high-contrast values, emphasizing the stark black-and-white tragedy of the play. Although all elements work together harmoniously, imagine what a difference it would make if the dramatic lighting were replaced by normal institutional lighting, like that of a supermarket or a classroom. Instead of seeing masklike human faces, masks, and a pool of light against a vast darkness, the audience could be looking at the curtains, the wings, the underpinnings of the sets, and perhaps even at each other. Light, used consciously, is thus a very powerful tool in the artist's control of the aesthetic experience.

STUDIO PROBLEMS

8.1 Natural vs. Artificial Lighting

Use your solution to any previous problem and show how it could be affected differently by artificial lighting and natural lighting. Note the changes that occur as the placement of the light source changes, as in the movement of the sun through the day or intentional shifts in studio lighting to heighten the impact of the piece. Figure 207 is the same work as shown in Figure 40, but with high-contrast lighting rather than the diffuse lighting used in the first photograph. Under the high-contrast lighting coming from the upper left, the thin shadow line in the center is no longer a visual emphasis; instead, emphasis falls on the variations among the angular shadows thrown by the slightly differing fins jutting forward. If your piece has both straight edges and curved contours, note the different ways that they are affected by light.

207 Natural versus Artificial Lighting. Foamcore. Student work.

208 Shadows. Oak, glued and bolted. Student work.

8.2 Shadows

Create an outdoor sculpture in which shadows on and thrown by the form are part of the excitement of the piece. The shadows on the form in Figure 208 create visual variations that make it hard to recognize that the piece is actually made of repetitions of the same shape. The shadows thrown on the ground are so strong that it is also hard to distinguish the solid structure from the shadows it casts.

8.3 Light as a Medium

Using materials of your own choosing, create a piece in which light is used as a "three-dimensional" medium. Some examples might be a series of mirrors reflecting a flashlight beam, a fishtank full of smoke with a light shining in one end, or a light shone through colored water.

9

Color

Color is such a compelling element of design that we have purposely omitted it thus far by using only black-and-white photographs to avoid distracting attention from the other elements. To get an immediate sense of what color adds to three-dimensional design, compare Figure 209 and Plate 1 (p. 179). In black and white, Charles Eames' *Solar Toy (Do Nothing Machine)* is obviously a playful combination of shapes that spin about like a mock space-age machine when the solar collector is activated. Yet how much more humorous and playful the toy appears when we can see the delightful carnival-like atmosphere created through the use of a great many different colors.

Color is an extremely rich tool the artist can use in many ways, whether working with the natural colors of materials or adding color to them. Before we can talk about colors, however, we must introduce the basics of color theory so that we will have a vocabulary to draw on.

CHARLES EAMES. *Solar Toy (Do Nothing Machine).* 1957. Aluminum and silicon disks, solar cells. Base approx. 3 × 4′ (0.92 × 1.22 m), height approx. 2½′ (0.71 m). For Alcoa.

A Vocabulary of Color

Despite the impression that objects "are" certain colors, colors exist not on the surfaces we see but in our brain. Colors exist as invisible energy waves in white light. We pick up these waves of electromagnetic radiation when they are either refracted or reflected. When passed through a prism, light is broken down or *refracted* into the rainbow of the *visible spectrum* (Fig. 210). *Reflection* occurs when light strikes an opaque surface. Waves of certain lengths are absorbed; others are reflected. When these reflected waves are conveyed to the rods and cones in the retinas of our eyes, the sensation is translated as a particular color.

To change the color of a material, artists use *pigments* that reflect the wavelengths associated with the desired color. Mixing pigments together produces a slightly darker color, for each subtracts its energy from the light reflected. Pigment mixing is therefore called a *subtractive* method of mixing colors. The exception is mixing white pigment

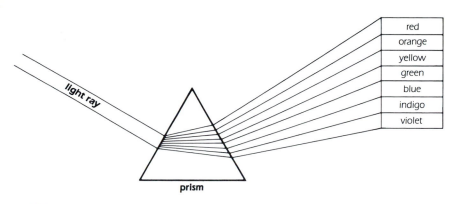

| red |
| orange |
| yellow |
| green |
| blue |
| indigo |
| violet |

light ray

prism

210 The visible spectrum.

to another pigment to create a lighter value, or *tint,* of that color, Adding black produces a *shade,* or darker value of a color.

Although most color mixing is done by the subtractive method, artists who work directly with light—as in photography, television, computer graphics, and laser art—are using an *additive* method of color mixing. That is, each color adds its energy to that of the others used, raising the value of the mixture slightly. *Optical color mixtures* occur when colors are mixed in the viewer's perception rather than on the surface of an object. Optical mixtures may occur when colors lie so close to each other that their energies interact or when colored forms are transparent, allowing one color to be seen through another and thereby mixing with it visually.

Colors can be classified by three main characteristics: hue, saturation, and value. *Hue* is the characteristic we identify by color names: red, blue, green, yellow, yellow-green, etc. Variations between hues are almost infinite, but a simple model of their interrelationships can be expressed by a *color wheel,* such as the one shown in Plate 2 (p. 180). In pigment mixing, all hues can be obtained by mixtures of just three hues. In traditional color theory, these basic hues from which all others can be mixed are red, blue, and yellow, and are called *primary colors.* Mixing two primaries together produces *secondary colors*—green (blue plus yellow), orange (red plus yellow), and purple (red plus blue). Mixtures of a primary and a secondary produced from it create a third set of colors: the *tertiaries* red-purple, red-orange, orange-yellow, yellow-green, blue-green, and purple-blue. Many more hues are created by mixtures falling between these named positions on the color wheel. In light mixtures, the primaries from which all other hues can be mixed are red, green, and blue-violet. Other color theories posit slightly different basic hues, but these will do as an initial vocabulary for our discussion of color.

The third characteristic of the colors we perceive is *saturation* (also called "chroma" or "intensity"). This term is a measure of the relative purity or brightness of a color. When colors lying opposite each other on the color wheel—known as *complementary colors* (such as red and green)—are mixed together, they tend to neutralize each other, producing a grayer version of one hue or the other. Mixed in the correct proportions, they will produce a gray that resembles neither. Gray is shown in the center of the color wheel (Pl. 2), for this position places it between each set of complementaries. Another way to gray a color is simply to add gray or black to it.

Colors are said to be highly saturated when they are very bright. Colors of very low saturation—those that are closer to gray than to the named hues of the outer ring of the color wheel—are sometimes called *neutrals.* They are of interest to decorators and clothing designers, for since they are almost lacking in hue, they can be used next to a variety of more saturated colors without undesired hue contrasts.

Value we discussed in the last chapter: It is the relative lightness or darkness of a color. To represent color relationships in these three dimensions—hue, saturation, and value—colorist Albert Munsell patented a three-dimensional model in which steps of value change along the vertical axis, saturation changes are shown through the horizontal axis, and hue differences are shown around the periphery, as diagrammed in Figure 211. Munsell's system has been adopted as an instrument for measuring and naming colors by many official institutions, including the National Bureau of Standards in the United States. Note that Munsell's classification is based on five primary hues (which he terms *principal hues*), rather than the traditional three. Each pri-

211 Diagram of relationships in hue, saturation, and value.

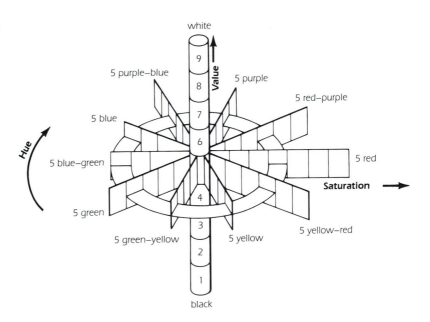

Elements of Three-Dimensional Design

mary and *intermediate* (secondary) hue is designated by its initials. Colors are then given numbers in which the first refers to the step of value and the second refers to the degree of saturation, with higher numbers indicating a higher degree of saturation.

Hues differ in the number of equal steps required to reach maximum saturation. As shown in Figure 211, at value 5, red can take fourteen steps before it is as highly saturated as it can be, whereas blue-green reaches maximum saturation at step 8. Hues also differ in the step of value at which they reach their greatest saturation: Yellow (which is relatively light in its purest form) reaches maximum saturation at step 8 of value, while purple-blue (which is dark in its purest form) reaches maximum saturation at step 3 of value.

The colors we perceive, besides being affected by the pigmentation of a surface, are also a function of the glossiness of the surface, the surrounding colors, and the ambient lighting. A highly polished surface will pick up highlights, which will make colors appear lighter. In a principle known as *simultaneous contrast*, juxtaposition of two colors exaggerates their differences and reduces their similarities. Complementaries intensify each other's saturation if used together— red appears redder next to a green, and vice versa. Butchers often put fake green parsley next to meat to make it appear redder and therefore fresher. Hues optically "subtract" their own wavelengths from hues to which they are juxtaposed, so meat would look a sickly gray on a bright red plate. As for lighting, bright light creates strong value contrasts; an overcast day or dim indoor lighting shifts color perceptions to the middle range of values. The redness of late afternoon sunlight, the yellowness of incandescent lighting, and the blueness of fluorescent lighting produce such different color sensations that colors should always be examined under the lighting in which they will be used.

Natural Color

Although pigments can be carefully mixed to approximate the subtle colors of nature—or natural plant dyes used to the same end—artists often work instead with the natural color characteristics of their chosen medium. It is this use of the *local color* of the material that we are calling *natural color.*

Craftspeople often search for materials that are naturally beautiful and then present them in such a way that this beauty is enhanced. Peter Michael Adams' *Dotoh* (Pl. 3, p. 180) features not only elegant, flowing form but also the sensual visual appeal of laminated walnut. By smoothly sanding and oiling the surface of the wood, Adams has brought out its warm colors and its close-grained striations. The rich colors and smoothness of the surface are like beacons drawing us in to caress and enjoy this coffee table. The beauty of the colors cannot be separated from the other aesthetic and functional aspects of the piece, however. Adams explains the integration of his work: "A successful piece will not only mirror my sensitivity to sight and touch, but give credence to my conviction that functional forms can speak eloquently of sculpture, movement, and sensuousness, and still maintain their practicality."

While the striations of Adams' walnut slabs occur randomly, in Charles Henry Joseph Cordier's *Negro in Algerian Costume* (Pl. 4, p. 181) the creamy body and darker gold bands of color in a block of jasper are used quite consciously to provide decorative detail. The natural lines in the stone become bands of extraordinary richness used to represent woven patterns in some sumptuous material. In places, such as the sleeve to the left in the photograph, the sculptor has even altered the carving to make the occasional deviations of the bands in the stone from the horizontal appear to be plausible curves of the fabric. Selection of just the right piece of stone was obviously very important to this artist. The natural colors of the porphyry used for the base add to the impression of opulence. And silvered bronze provided precisely the skin color the artist was trying to capture, enriched by a range of lighter values as the polished facial features curve to reflect the light.

In contrast to the richly decorative use of natural color in Cordier's statue, natural color may sometimes be chosen for its simplicity. Aesthetically, this simplicity of color may allow attention to be drawn to other elements of design, such as form. During China's Ming Dynasty, porcelain pots and figures were often high-fired to the subtle white of the clay body itself. With no other colors added to distract the eye, one could fully appreciate the forms of the pieces. At the same time, isolating nature's warm eggshell white brought attention to this white itself as a color.

Natural color may also be used conceptually. In George Segal's *The Parking Garage* (Pl. 5, p. 181), the stark natural white of the plaster is used to make a conceptual statement: The attendant appears to lead a bleached-out existence amid the garish colors of contemporary urban life. Here, the material world becomes the vibrant reality; by contrast, the white plaster human figure is the one element in the scene that appears lifeless.

In other works, use of natural color may have the opposite effect—that of linking the work to its natural surroundings. Architect Frank Lloyd Wright's Wisconsin house, *Taliesin North* (Pl. 6, p. 182), expresses his philosophy of the "natural house"—one that appears to be at one with its environment. To tie it in with its site, he has made extensive use of local stone that echoes the pale earth tones of the hill in the background. The wood shingles weather naturally to the dark gray-brown of the shadows across the stone; the wood framing is treated with a preservative that allows it to weather to a pale warm gray. Sand from the river has been mixed with the plaster of the walls to tie in their color and texture with the earth tones. Even the red-brown accents in the window framing fall within the palette of hues reminiscent of the earth, while the green shrubbery on the patio further blurs the boundary between the house and its surroundings. Both seem to flow together as an organic whole.

In landscape design, the natural colors of plants are used because they are what is available to the designer. Planning a garden is actually a manipulation of colors as well as forms and textures in three-dimensional space. When used consciously, the natural colors of plantings can be extremely effective. The designer of the topiary (sculpted shrubbery) garden at Levens Hall in England (Pl. 7, p. 183) used a very limited palette to bring out the richness of variations among a few hues. In summer, the subtly varying greens of the sculpted evergreen shrubs, grass, plants, and surrounding deciduous trees are enriched by contrast with the colors of the flowers. The flower beds have been thoughtfully arranged as bands of single-hued accents. Both flower hues and shrubbery greens are also set off by the warm beige of the stone wall in the background. The colors of gardens change dramatically with daily changes in the weather and seasonal changes in foilage. In winter, only the evergreens and the stone wall would remain of the summer color scheme, but imagine their appearance against the ever-changing color of the sky.

Applied Color

Despite the wide range of effects possible through use of natural colors, artists have often chosen to apply pigments to the surface of their materials or otherwise change the natural color characteristics of the media. Historically, works were colored to bring them closer to physical or mystical perceptions of reality. More recently, artists have chosen colors on other bases to enhance the impact of their pieces and sometimes even to display colors as ends unto themselves.

Although we tend to think of classical marble statues as unpainted, revealing the elegant simplicity of the natural marble, the marble sculptures of ancient Greece and Rome were in fact originally painted. Researchers have determined that they were not painted on all surfaces, however. As suggested by the photograph of *Peplos Kore* (Pl. 8, p. 184), only certain areas were painted with pigments in hot wax (the long-lasting *encaustic* method). These pigmented areas served partly as decorative, eye-catching accents to the white of the marble, which was itself accentuated by waxing and polishing. Slight traces of paint remain on the meandering patterns of the tunic, as well as the startling red of the hair, eyes, and lips. Was this figure really painted with these reds or was this an undercoating for another color that has since worn away? We cannot be sure, but the addition of color does seem to bring the statue to vibrant life. Particularly the painting of the eyes: Instead of being blank, they make direct eye contact with us.

For an example of a fully painted statue in which most of the detail remains, the 16th-century *Virgin and Child* shown in Plate 9 (p. 185) is fairly well preserved. In this *polychromed* (multicolored) wooden piece, the applied colors enhance the realism of the stylized carving, help us to distinguish skin from fabric, and create details such as the border of the robe that are not distinguished at all in the carved form. The bright red applied to Mary's cheeks seems intended not so much to help viewers grasp the spatial modeling of her face as to develop the semblance of full-blooded life. Note that unlike a two-dimensional painting, in which values must be painted explicitly to create modeling effects, classical polychromed sculptures were typically painted in solid colors, with the contours of the form itself creating a range of values as surfaces catch or are hidden from the light. The varying hues seen in the draped fabric across Mary's legs can be attributed to the aging of this 16th-century piece, as the upper layer of paint flakes away to reveal undercoats and the raw wood itself.

Another motivation for adding color to a work is to attract attention. Color is the hook that draws the viewer's eye to the fence running through Alan Wood's 320-acre work called *Ranch* (Pl. 10, p. 185). Without the strong colors used, the fence would tend to blend in with its surroundings. With color added, the fence becomes noticeable as an art form: a procession of vivid lines across the rolling terrain, leading to the spectrum of the "Rainbow Fence," which playfully brings the sky down to earth. The colors we can see from this perspective make us want to become actively involved with the work by walking along the fence to see what other colors it has been painted. Other aspects of the installation, such as stylized haystacks, birds, a bridge, and barns, are painted in similarly bright hues to help bring to viewers' awareness objects that might otherwise be ignored because of their familiarity.

Color may also be added for its decorative appeal to the senses. Lush or pleasing colors may be food for the eyes and perhaps the spirit. Consider the veritable symphony of colors used in the Baroque interior of the Benedictine abbey church in Ottobeuren, Germany (Pl. 11, p. 186). The effect of the golden ceiling areas and pastel marble columns, set off by the pure white of the woodwork, quite overwhelms the worshiper with the splendor of the heavens. Behind the altar, the deeper tones enhance the sense of shrouded mysteries. The viewer's consciousness is drawn both upward by the golds and inward by the muted tones of the altarpiece, creating an architectural environment that encourages exploration of these two dimensions of the human search for the divine.

Sometimes color is used to give visual strength to a form. Linda

Howard chose to paint the steel pieces of her *Cathedral Series VIII—Gothic* (Pl. 12, p. 187) white for this reason. She explains that compared with her earlier scoured aluminum works, such as *Round About,* shown in Figure 202, the multiunit pieces require a more positive surface for aesthetic balance:

> The elements have become thinner, more delicate in proportion to the structure, and more complicated, creating a whole architectural environment. So I had to switch to white to strengthen these elements visually. I was already making a kind of filagree, and the play of reflected light through the pieces would be too great if they were ground aluminum. The structure would be too weak, visually, and too busy. To hold the balance between airiness and solidity I had to go back to white and simplify the individual elements. It's very important to me to hold the balance—to maintain that line, whatever it is, between illusionary and real.

At the same time that painting the steel strengthens the visual impact of the structure, the use of white is sufficiently neutral to allow full appreciation of the complex interplay of lines—constructed lines, shadow patterns, and the lines created by negative areas filled by the sky. And white is often associated with purity, a quality that seems appropriate for leading the eye toward the sky.

In the works we have examined thus far in this section, applied color is secondary to the forms, enhancing them in some way. But in some cases, color itself is the primary consideration; the forms involved are only secondary. In Robert Walker's *Vertical Wedge Form* (Pl. 13, p. 188), for instance, abstract bands of color flow within a simple geometric form. It is the varying optical mixtures of the inner planes of dyed acrylic polymers that are the focus of the work. As an indication of how these translucent color mixtures can change as one moves around the work or the light is shifted, consider Plate 14 (p. 188), which is exactly the same piece, but illuminated from the right rather than the left. Walker explains his choice of simple forms to contain these fascinating, ephemeral colors:

> For one thing, I like the contradiction of forms visually—the hard edge of the sculpture compared to the flowingness of the interior color forms. And that's also a necessity of the optical quality of the material. I'm dealing with a transparent material and creating a plane that you have to see through. If the form of that plane is abstract or distorted, it would distort the internal image. My focus is the internal color image, and I'm trying to provide a relatively simple external form through which to view the internal form. In other words, I've tried to provide a simple geometric shape that your eyes can perceive easily. Since it's simple to comprehend, it allows your eyes to focus on the interior forms.

Within the nearly rectangular outer form, Walker uses optical combinations of three "virtually pure" transparent color dyes to capture the ephemeral beauty of the fleeting patterns that nature so often presents but that we so seldom really see.

Computer graphics take the presentation of color one step further. James Hoffman's *Translucent Surface Colored by a Generalized Lighting Model* (Pl. 15, p. 189) is a lovely study in color variations that have the purity and transparency of light and the *iridescence* of a bubble, the lustrous display of all the colors of the spectrum. These subtleties are particularly surprising since they come from a computer. Until recently computer art was associated with straight edges and solid blocks of color, but high-resolution graphics and expanded color palettes now allow a highly sophisticated range of effects based on varied mixtures of the light primaries red, green, and blue. In addition to the beauty of the colors, the form is quite lyrical, yet it has no physical existence as an actual three-dimensional object. Colors are the only reality here, creating on a flat screen the illusion of a transparent three-dimensional form almost too ethereal to be manifested as a tangible object.

Psychological Effects of Colors

To varying degrees, artists also use colors to control the emotional responses of viewers—to express a certain emotion rather than a literal depiction of the *local color* of an object. In our culture, colors have certain common emotional connotations: Yellow is linked with cheerfulness (though also with cowardice), red with passion (including aggressiveness), blue and green with peaceful meditative states (but also with depression), purple with mysticism, black with death, and white with purity. To a certain extent, these associations are culturally learned—in China, white is the color associated with death. But considerable research has been done on the actual effects of colors on our physiological processes, and thus our emotional state. In general, hues in the red range do tend to be stimulating, whereas blues and greens tend to have a calming effect, though these effects may be reversed over time. Violent prisoners are initially calmed by being placed in pink rooms, but after about fifteen minutes, their fury returns. Blue initially lowers blood pressure and pulse rate, but the opposite effect may later replace this initial one.

In traditional usage, reds, oranges, and yellows are referred to as *warm* colors, while blues and greens are called *cool* colors. These temperature associations are probably based partly on learned visual association of reds with fire and blues and greens with the coolness of water and shade trees, and partly on innate physiological responses to differences between colors. Experiments show that red seems to accelerate tissue healing, whereas blue decreases hormonal activity and retards wound healing. This stepping up and slowing down of metabolism may slightly raise or lower the body temperature, thus validating the "warm" and "cool" labels. People actually feel colder in a room painted in cool colors than in one painted in a warm color.

Spatially, the warm colors seem to advance, giving the impression of reducing the apparent size and weight of objects. When walls are painted in cool colors, they expand the apparent size of a room since they seem to recede. High-visibility orange helps hunters to distinguish one another from the deer not only because this orange is a highly saturated color but also because this hue can be sharply focused by the eye; blue is far more difficult to bring into focus.

While the wealth of research on such effects of color is valuable and fascinating, it is not yet sufficiently refined to account for the great range of colors within each named hue. And factors other than hue may offset the already subtle effects of the colors themselves. In art, they include the size of the colored area, the value and saturation of the hue, its "contamination" by other hues, the forms on which it is presented, manipulation by the artist of other elements of design, and the viewer's current emotional state and learned associations with color.

Consider blue. In George Segal's *Blue Girl on Park Bench* (Pl. 16, p. 189), the blue girl seems suspended in time, quietly waiting, focusing inward rather than outward. Is she depressed? Lonely? Bored? Trying to control her anguish? Meditating? Why is she sitting on the very end of the park bench? What do you feel in looking at her? If you feel a sense of isolation and sadness, or conversely, a sense of peace, how can you determine whether that response is your existing emotional state or what the artist intended? We see our inner state reflected in the outer world, so our judgments of how things "are" are highly subjective.

Now consider the emotional effects evoked by the use of blue in Marjorie Strider's *Blue Sky* (Pl. 17, p. 190). Here we see blue sky oozing playfully down a spiral staircase, in gay disregard for its proper place high over our heads. As it winds upward, the blue becomes paler, emphasizing the distance by the principle of *aerial perspective* (things seen at a distance have less value contrast and less distinct edges than things seen nearby). At its deepest value, the blue is that of children's clay or fingerpaints, a plastic, not-quite-real, just-for-fun quality. Or is this just one person's interpretation? Art critic Donald Kuspit describes a different range of emotional responses to the work:

> Irrepressible, irresistible, this flow seems a comic hallucination, but it also evokes primordial terrors. It is at once a science-fiction fantasy of doom and our own consciousness as it swarms over and swamps things. Strider's ooze is at once the reflex response of mind to a reality gotten out of hand—gone beserk—and a monstrous suppuration from an invisible wound. If Strider's ooze is seen as

static "form," it is a dumb heap; if it is seen as a flow, it acquires powerful being, an insidious ability to insinuate itself everywhere.

Is life so simple that we can identify only one gross reaction in ourselves to each of its events? Are we either happy or sad? Or do many emotional states flow through our awareness as a complex and ever-changing mirror of inner and outer patterns? Can blue be said to inevitably represent any one of these states?

Consider one more blue—that of Noguchi's *Sky Mirror* (Pl. 18, p. 190). Here blue seems to evoke a great serenity, a highly spiritual sensation. Yet how much of this effect can be attributed to the color itself and how much to the ethereal nature of its creation? This extraordinary blue-green does not actually exist on the surface of the piece. Rather, the slanted top of this otherwise rough and earthy stone is so highly polished that if oriented to the sky, it reflects the color mood of the sky. The effect is so delicate and ephemeral that we cease our own noisy mind-games lest we jostle the image. The atmosphere created may be one of hushed sacredness—but only if we are sensitive enough to respond this way.

Color Combinations

Not only do single colors vary in their emotional effects; colors are also varied by their juxtaposition to other colors. In general, color combinations have been traditionally classified according to whether the colors are closely related or contrasting. When hues are closely related, visual interest is usually created by adding certain slightly contrasting notes to the existing harmony. In a contrasting color scheme, contrast is the rule rather than the exception.

These relationships are judged according to the relative position of hues on the two-dimensional color wheel. But as we have seen, a more sophisticated model of the actual complexities of color variations is three-dimensional. Since there are no easy ways to account for relationships among colors that differ in value and saturation as well as hue, artists often combine colors more intuitively than intellectually until they achieve the effect they desire. Public tastes in color combinations change over time. At the turn of the century, the combination of blue with green was considered awful, whereas today color tastes show great diversity. Nevertheless, we will briefly review the standard models of color combinations to explore their characteristics.

The most closely related colors are those that all stem from a single hue but vary in value and/or saturation. This combination is called a *monochromatic* color scheme (Fig. 212). As an example, the room shown in Plate 19 (p. 191) is a series of yellow-greens that are almost identical in hue. In this example of a monochromatic color

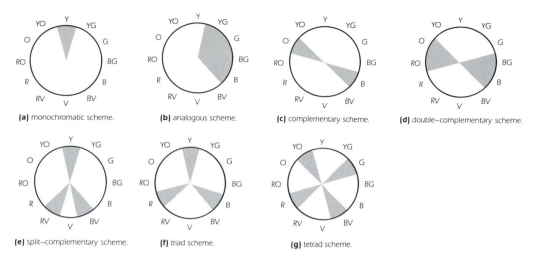

(a) monochromatic scheme.

(b) analogous scheme.

(c) complementary scheme.

(d) double–complementary scheme.

(e) split–complementary scheme.

(f) triad scheme.

(g) tetrad scheme.

212 Color schemes.

scheme, even the values of the rug, built-in furniture, walls, and ceiling are quite similar. The effect is one of quiet coolness, allowing the subtle hues of the window panels by William Gray Purcell and George Elmslie to be appreciated. Monochromatic color schemes often include small areas of other colors as accents, such as the stained glass in the windows and the black of the lamp in this room.

Although it is fairly safe to assume that monochromatic colors will not clash with each other, we cannot assume that the effect will necessarily be restful or pleasing. Imagine this room in values of red, with an abundance of highly saturated reds and pinks. But what would be difficult to live with as a home environment might make a very exciting color scheme for a single piece of three-dimensional art.

Analogous color schemes combine colors that lie next to each other on the color wheel. John Lewis' *Urn* (Pl. 20, p. 192) uses blues, blue-greens, greens, and a small amount of yellow-green. As Figure 210 illustrates, this is a progression of adjacent hues. The effect of the combination is a pleasing, quiet harmony.

Analogous color schemes do not inevitably have quietly harmonious effects, however. The yellow-orange and orange-pink used together on Lawrence Ajanaku's Nigerian Okakagbe costume *Ancient Mother* (Pl. 21, p. 192) are so highly saturated that they almost seem to vibrate. The black-and-white bands allow a bit of space between them, like taking a sip of water between tastes to clear your palate, but they also keep the orange and pink as bright as possible by not allowing them to affect each other. Placed side by side, each would seem to fade somewhat by simultaneous contrast as they optically subtracted their own wavelengths from each other. Emphasizing the brightness of the colors heightens the sense of pageantry. And imagine the added effect of movement as the wearer of the costume dances down the street in the masquerade procession.

Color

Hues that are at farther intervals on the color wheel are in general somewhat more contrasting than closely analogous hues. However, we tend to perceive less contrast between hues when their value is high or their saturation is low. The orange, yellow, and green of John Ferren's *Construction in Wood: Daylight Experiment* (Pl. 22, p. 192) blend quite harmoniously. Although the colors are quite clear (highly saturated), they are all relatively high in value. What we are seeing in juxtaposition are pale color shadows reflected off the painted backs of the wood columns, rather than pigmented surfaces. All the surfaces we can see from the front are actually painted white to act as pure reflectors for the sunlight that comes from behind and then is bounced off the orange, green, or yellow backs of the columns. If we were to look at the piece in reverse, seeing the darker values of the painted backs of the columns rather than their paler shadows, we might see greater contrast between the colors.

Hues are said to show the greatest degree of contrast when they lie opposite each other on the color wheel, as *complementary colors* (Fig. 212). Closely juxtaposed, complementaries intensify each other's brightness. The intensity of the contrast may create a feeling of excitement. The Spanish interior shown in Plate 23 (p. 193) conveys a feeling of exuberance by juxtaposing the complementaries blue-green and orange, both in the fabric used and in the painting of walls and door frames. Another series of contrasts occurs between very dark values, such as the deep brown of the window and chair legs and the black of the planter, and lighter values, such as the lampshade and the walls of the closer room. In not being afraid to combine colors normally considered clashing, the designer has created an atmosphere that surrounds people with a sense of vigorous health.

Some other contrasting color schemes can be identified as *double-complementary* (two adjacent hues and their complements), *split-complementary* (one hue plus the hues on either side of its complement), *triad* (three hues equidistant from each other on the color wheel), and *tetrad* (any four hues that are equidistant on the color wheel), as shown in Figure 212. Such combinations are said to be both stimulating and balanced, since they include both cool and warm hues.

When colors far distant from each other on the color wheel are used together, their physical distance within a piece and their relative amounts will affect their degree of harmony or contrast. In Charles Eames' *Solar Toy* (Pl. 1, p. 179) the spaces between circles of different hues allow us to see each one separately to a certain extent. Furthermore, even though all parts of the spectrum are used, blues, purples, and reds tend to predominate, giving the color scheme a distantly analogous flavor. Yellow and green appear only as brief accents that help to give the whole piece an upbeat carnival atmosphere without destroying its lively harmony.

Elements of Three-Dimensional Design

How can we explain the way Betsy Utting has used many normally contrasting colors together harmoniously in her *Checkerboard Jacket* (Pl. 24, p. 194)? The checkerboard pattern assigns equal amounts to each color, so the quantity factor is not an explanation. To a certain extent, the paler values help modulate the progression from one hue to another, lessening the contrasts between hues. The darker values at the center and outer borders of the design on the front of the jacket seem like peaks toward which the changes in value and hue are progressing, giving the flow of colors a certain logic. But beyond these intellectual attempts to analyze why something works, after the fact, we cannot ignore the power of the artist's instinctive sense of color combining. In today's wide-open world of art, artists are free to use the rich tool of color any way they want, so long as they can make it do what they intend. The "rules" of color combining are useful as general guides to the understanding of color, but the subtleties of the possible spread far beyond.

STUDIO PROBLEMS

9.1 Natural Colors

Find three to five objects with different local colors, such as wood, stone, brick, or fabric. Put them together in such a way that they are harmonious not only in form but also in color.

9.2 Applied Color

Create or find three identical simple geometric forms or use solutions to previous problems. Apply color to each piece in a different way, comparing the effects: (1) Paint the piece in a solid color; (2) Paint each surface a different color; (3) Break up the surfaces by painting them in geometric patterns or splattering paint on them.

9.3 Psychological Effects of Color

Find an everyday object and paint it in such a way that viewers will respond to it in a different way. You could simply change its solid color to another solid color, as in painting a yellow banana purple. Or you could paint its

213 Removal of Color. Mixed media, gray paints. Student work.

surface with nonobjective designs such as stripes or representational images. How can you use color to alter the phychological effect of the object?

9.4 Removal of Color

Increase sensitivity to the effects of color by removing color from a familiar environment. Use objects from our everyday world to create an installation piece in which local colors have been replaced with grays by painting them in values of gray. The values need not be the same as the original color values. Everything in Figure 213 has been painted in grays and presented against a gray wall; even the static on the imageless television screen is gray. In our environment, color adds a certain liveliness; in this scene without color, one gets a depressing sense of the drabness of everyday existence.

Elements of Three-Dimensional Design

Plate 1 CHARLES EAMES. *"Do Nothing Machine"* (*Solar Toy*). 1957. Aluminum and silicon disks, solar cells. Base approx. 3–4′ (0.92–1.22 m), height approx. 2½′ (0.76 m). For Alcoa.

Plate 2 (top)   Color wheel of pigment mixtures.
Plate 3 (bottom)   Peter Michael Adams. *Dotoh.* Coffee table, 1983. Laminated and carved walnut, oil finish, 1′6″ × 4′2″ × 2′4″ (0.46 × 1.27 × 0.71 m).

180

Plate 4 (top) CHARLES HENRY JOSEPH CORDIER. *Bust of a Nubian.* 19th-century France. Silvered bronze and jasper on porphyry, height 38¼" (97 cm). Minneapolis Institute of Arts.

Plate 5 (bottom) GEORGE SEGAL. *The Parking Garage.* 1968. Plaster, wood, metal, electrical parts, and light-bulbs. 10′ × 12′8″ × 4′ (3.05 × 3.84 × 1.22 m) The Newark Museum, Newark, New Jersey.

Plate 6 FRANK LLOYD WRIGHT. *Taliesin North.* 1925. Spring Green, Wisconsin.

Plate 7 Topiary garden, Levens Hall, England. 1680.

Plate 8 *Peplos Kore,* Acropolis, Athens, c. 530 B.C. Acropolis Museum, Athens.

Plate 9 (top) *Virgin and Child,*
c. 1500. Polychromed wood, height
10¼″ (26 cm). Metropolitan Museum
of Art, New York (bequest of George
Blumenthal, 1941).

Plate 10 (bottom) Alan Wood.
"Rainbow Fence," portion of *Ranch.*
320-acre installation outside Calgary,
Alberta, Canada. Total work used 60,000
yards of canvas, 150,000′ (45,750 m) of
wood, 1,200 gallons of paint.

185

Plate 11 Johann Michael Fischer. Interior, Abbey Church, Ottobeuren, Germany. 1736–66.

Plate 12 Linda Howard. *Cathedral Series VIII, Gothic.* 1984. Proposed for steel painted white, scale 24 × 30 × 40′ (7.32 × 9.15 × 12.2 m).

Plate 13 (left) 14 (right)   ROBERT WALKER, *Vertical Wedge Form.* 1977. Cast acrylic, 16 × 16 × 2″ (41 × 41 × 5 cm). Private collection.

Plate 15 (top) JAMES T. HOFFMAN.
*Translucent Surface Colored by a
Generalized Lighting Model.* 1983.
VAX–11/780 using attached Grinnell
Display System (frame, buffer, and
monitor), display resolution 512 × 512
pixels, 4 bits of red, green blue.
35 mm film.

Plate 16 (bottom) GEORGE SEGAL.
Blue Girl on Park Bench. 1980.
Painted plaster and aluminum.
51 × 78 × 44″ (129.5 × 198 ×
111.7 cm). Collection Melvin Golder,
Melrose Park, Pennsylvania.

Plate 17 (left) MARJORIE STRIDER. *Blue Sky.* 1976. Urethane foam and pigment, height 20' (6.1 m), width 8' (2.44 m), depth 5' (1.53 m). Temporary installation at the Clocktower (work destroyed).
Plate 18 (bottom) ISAMU NOGUCHI. *Sky Mirror.* 1967. Basalt.
Plate 19 (opposite) Interior, with rug and built-in furniture by Saskia Weinstein, window panels by William Gray Purcell and George Elmslie. Courtesy *House and Garden.* Copyright © 1985 by The Condé Nast Publications Inc.

190

Plate 20 (top) JOHN LEWIS. *Urn.* 1979. Blown glass, 7 × 7 × 7″ (18 × 18 × 18 cm).

Plate 21 (bottom left) LAWRENCE AJANAKU. *Odogu* (*Ancient Mother*) headpiece and costume. Headpiece: wood frame, applique, and yarn, 19½ × 20″ (49.5 × 51 cm). Costume 41½″ (105.5 cm). Nigeria: Ogiriga village, Okpella people. Collection UCLA Museum of Cultural History.

Plate 22 (bottom right) JOHN FERREN. *Construction in Wood: Daylight Experiment* (*Façade*). 1968. Painted wood, 6′½″ × 4′ × 1′2″ (1.84 × 1.21 × 0.35 m). Hirshhorn Museum and Sculpture Garden, Smithsonian Institution, Gift of the Artist through the Joseph H. Hirshhorn Foundation.

Plate 23 (opposite page) Interior in southern Spain.

Plate 24 (bottom) BETSY UTTING.
Checkerboard Jacket. 1982. Hand-quilted
cotton fabric.

9.5 Color Combinations

Using nine simple wooden forms, create three three-piece sculptures that are identical except for color. Paint each sculpture in a different kind of color combination, choosing from monochromatic, analogous, complementary, split-complementary, triad, or tetrad color schemes. What effects does each create? Which seems to work best for the piece? For comparative purposes, it is helpful to paint each three-piece sculpture identically, except for the colors chosen. If you further limit the variables to combinations that involve one particular hue, you will be better able to judge the effects of different combinations.

10

Time

Thus far we have only talked about elements of design as occupying space. But there is another dimension to experience, and that is time. Aesthetic experiences occupy time as well as space, from subtle or uncontrolled or even illusionary movement through time on the part of the viewer or the work of art, to clearly defined sequences of change through time. Accustomed as we are to being entertained—or bored— by temporal arts such as television and movies, we nonetheless maintain a childlike fascination with things that move and change as we watch. The time element is therefore a dynamic tool at the artist's disposal for involving people with a work of art.

214 AUGUSTE RODIN. *St. John the Baptist Preaching.* 1878. Bronze, 6'6¾" (2 m) high. Collection Museum of Modern Art, New York (Mrs. Simon Guggenheim Fund).

Illusion of Movement

Before we examine actual movement through time on the part of the viewer or the work, we should note that certain works, though stationary, are designed to appear to move and change through time. Rather than appearing to be a single moment frozen in time, works such as Rodin's *Saint John the Baptist Preaching* (Fig. 214) draw us to read successive stages of motion as a time sequence. Rodin created this effect quite consciously, explaining that "movement is the transition from one attitude to another." In a sense, we "see" Saint John walking, for Rodin shows us one movement flowing logically into another. Our eyes are drawn by the saint's pointing left hand down to his left foot, where his weight seems momentarily planted. Reading upward toward his upward-pointing right hand, we see a gradual shift in weight toward his right foot, with his left shoulder raised to unweight the left foot so that it can be swung forward again. This is not a single frame from a motion picture; it is more like a composite of several frames, each represented by a certain part of the body and read in sequence. Rodin contrasts the effect with that of a stop-action photograph:

> While my Saint John is represented with both feet on the ground, it is probable that an instantaneous photograph from a model making the same movement would show the back foot already raised and carried toward the other. Or else, on the contrary, the front foot would not yet be on the ground if the back leg occupied in the photograph the same position as in my statue. . . . It is the artist who is truthful and it is photography which lies, for in reality time does not stop. . . .

Another way of representing the illusion of time-spanning motion in a single stationary work was explored by the Futurist painter and sculptor Umberto Boccioni. As a Futurist, he was interested in representing the fast pace of life in a modern industrial society. In painting, a succession of similar images overlapping was often used to give this impression. But few artists tried to translate the Futurist manifesto into sculpture. Boccioni's *Unique Forms of Continuity in Space* (Fig. 215)

215 UMBERTO BOCCIONI. *Unique Forms of Continuity in Space.* 1913. Bronze, approx. 43½″ (110 cm) high. Museum of Modern Art, New York (bequest of Lillie P. Bliss).

does, however, manage to convey the impression that we are seeing a person striding rapidly through space and time. We see a forward-pressing leading edge to the left, but also slightly separate forms suggesting blurred after-images of previous movement. The forms streaming backward are not literal descriptions of motion, as in *Saint John*. Rather, they are visual metaphors for speed and for describing the optical continuity of perceiving several quickly successive images at once, like the extra legs seen on a galloping horse.

Viewing Time

A more common way that the time dimension enters a work of three-dimensional art is the time it takes to explore the piece. This aspect of time is highly variable, of course. Some people will walk right by a work without paying much attention to it. But to fully appreciate a piece of three-dimensional art, we must take the time to view it from a distance, come in close, and move all around it.

Mark di Suvero's *Gorky's Pillow* (Fig. 216) is over 23 feet (7.01 m)

216 MARK DI SUVERO. *Gorky's Pillow.* 1969–1980. Steel (painted), height 15′6″ (4.72 m), width 9′6″ (2.9 m), length 23′4″ (7.11 m).

217 HARVEY FITE. Portion of *Opus 40.* 1939–1976. Environmental sculpture, bluestone rubble. Covers 6.5 acres on the site of an abandoned bluestone quarry, 7480 Fite Road, Saugerties, New York.

long and 9 feet (2.74 m) wide. To see it from all angles, we must walk over 64 feet (19.52 m) around its perimeter. We could also walk beneath it and around the hanging forms to examine them individually. Their playful quality invites lengthier participation—climbing on and seeing what happens, and perhaps even trying out the bell. If the sculpture has drawn the attention of children, we might stay even longer to watch their ways of enjoying it.

To a certain extent, the length of time people will spend in exploring and appreciating a piece is an indication of the artist's success. It is also a function of the physical size of the piece. Harvey Fite's *Opus 40* (Fig. 217) is an environmental sculpture covering 6½ acres. Not only is it large in scale; it also controls the viewer's movements through time and space by stone steps, walls, and terraces. As they disappear intriguingly out of view, they lead the viewer up and down into deep walled enclosures and around and through the structure as if it were a building. The only point of moving through it, however, is to explore it. The experience stretches across a considerable amount of time simply because the work is so large. A piece small enough to be held may also engage our attention for a long time span, for we can turn it over in our hands repeatedly until our curiosity is satisfied and our appreciation of the experience complete.

Even greater control of viewing time is commanded by narrative pieces such as *Trajan's Column* (Fig. 218). It presents the story of the emperor Trajan's adventures in a series of carvings that wind around the immense marble column. To "read" the story, one must keep walking around the column, reading upward from the bottom.

218 *Trajan's Campaign against the Dacians,* detail of *Trajan's Column.* A.D. 106–113. Marble, height of frieze band 4′2″ (127 cm).

Controlled Time

In contrast to pieces in which it is the viewer who moves through time, certain works are themselves designed to move and change through time. They are referred to as *kinetic art.* A now-classic example is Josè de Rivera's *Brussels Construction* (Fig. 219, p. 202). Its single line flows continuously not only through space but also through time, for the plinth on which it sits is motorized to revolve slowly. As viewers watch from a single perspective, the line curves in and out, up and down, gracefully changing its relationships with other parts of the same line.

219 Josè de Rivera. *Brussels Construction.* 1958. Stainless steel. Courtesy Art Institute of Chicago (gift from Mr. and Mrs. R. Howard Goldsmith).

220 Rikuro Okamoto. *Moving Rock #11.* 1979. Plastic resin mixed with sand; aluminum, stainless steel, and motor. 36 × 76 × 40″ (0.91 × 1.93 × 1.01 m).

Elements of Three-Dimensional Design

George Rickey, whose *N Lines Vertical* (Fig. 129) moves with the wind, points out that the three-dimensional world in which we live is often a world of motion rather than of frozen tableaux:

The artist finds waiting for him, as subject, not the landscape, but the *waving* of the branches and the *trembling* of stems, the piling up or scudding of clouds, the rising and setting and waxing and waning of heavenly bodies, the creeping of spilled water on the floor, the repertory of the sea—from ripple and wavelet to tide and torrent.

Those works of art that are designed to move through a pre-determined sequence of events exist in what can be called *controlled time*. An example of a time-controlled piece of kinetic art whose very simplicity is part of its humorous intent is Rikuro Okamoto's *Moving Rock #11* (Fig. 220). This visually realistic replication of a boulder does something we never expect a rock to do: It moves at a snail's pace back and forth across its stainless steel pad, propelled by a small hidden motor. The sudden recognition that this seemingly inert mass is not stationary is the hook that draws people into enjoying the piece.

Works such as *mobiles* (hanging sculptures activated by the wind) and folk art *whirligigs* such as the bicycling man shown in Figure 221 can move only in preestablished directions, though the speed at which they do so will depend on the wind that propels them. In the whirligig, the paddles of the propeller catch the wind and as they rotate activate wires that cause the man's legs to move as though he were pedaling the cycle. The faster the wind blows, the faster he will

221 *Whirligig: Uncle Sam Riding a Bicycle.* 1850–1900. Artist unknown, New England. Carved and polychromed wood, metal. Museum of American Folk Art (promised bequest of Dorothy and Leo Rabkin).

seem to be pedaling. Even at rest, the piece creates the illusion of movement through the rippled carving of the flag and the flaring of Uncle Sam's coattails, as if blown by the wind. Indeed, the top part of the whirligig is movable, and will always head into the wind.

Another form of controlled time exists in works designed to last only a specified amount of time. Like the subtly moving rock, mobiles, and whirligigs, Jean Tinguely's *Homage to New York: A Self-constructing and Self-destroying Work of Art* (a moment from whose life is shown in Fig. 222) is designed to follow a set sequence of events through time. But unlike the other pieces, Tinguely's machine could carry through the routine only once. It existed for only one performance, in which this zany machine created and then destroyed itself. This category of controlled kinetic art is called a *kinetic sculpture performance*. Self-destruction is not mandatory.

A traditional play or dance performance lasts but a few hours. Although the performance may be repeated, the sequence of events is similar each evening. When the series of performances is ended, the sets are struck and the work no longer exists, except in photographic documentation and the possibility of repetition elsewhere. The same is true of performance pieces, such as Laurie Anderson's *United States Part II* (Fig. 35). Some conceptual art pieces operate within a similarly

222 JEAN TINGUELY. *Homage to New York: A Self-constructing and Self-destroying Work of Art.* Self-destroyed March 17, 1960. Assemblage of piano, machine parts, bicycle parts, weather balloon, fireworks, etc. in the garden of the Museum of Modern Art, New York.

limited time framework: a brief static or kinetic display, sometimes observed only by the artist, with nothing saved for posterity except perhaps some photographs of the event. Christo's *Valley Curtain* (Fig. 43) was only supposed to hang for a few weeks and then be dismantled, a process that began somewhat prematurely. It can be argued that such works faithfully imitate life, for our experiences are fleeting rather than carved in eternal stone. We cannot hold on to a single moment; if we do not appreciate it as it flows by, it is gone forever.

Free Time

Whereas controlled-time pieces can only move within a certain pattern preestablished by the artist, works that exist in what we are calling *free time* are shaped partially by factors beyond the artist's control. These pieces will therefore vary somewhat randomly and unpredictably through time. "Free" is a relative label, though, for all art, no matter how minimal, implies a degree of control on the part of the artist in order to bring some object or experience to the attention of the viewer.

Some artists work with natural forces that change unpredictably through time, such as water or wind. All outdoor pieces are subject to their eroding effects, with changes measured in months, years, or centuries, depending on the durability of the material. Many earthworks are relatively short-lived, soon reclaimed by the earth through natural processes of attrition. Some metals used for outdoor pieces rust to a point and then the rust itself forms a sort of protective coat for the material. Some plastics theoretically have a very long lifespan, being highly resistant to corrosion, but could melt in a fire. Marble, used historically for its great durability as well as its beauty, may be eaten into by acid rain resulting from airborne pollutants.

On a more immediately observable time scale, we can see the movement of water as it flows through channels and around obstructions. James Fitzgerald seems to have intentionally limited his control over the movement of water through his waterfall-like *Fountain Sculpture* (Fig. 223, p. 206). To create a natural, free-flowing effect, Fitzgerald crafted a series of metal planes, each so flat that there is no obvious downward channel for the water to follow in its response to the pull of gravity. The water therefore spills off a little here, a little there, in quantities that change randomly through time. The shapes of the edges of the planes consistently determine the forms taken by water as it spills over the edges, but variations in the amounts coming over any one point will alter the pattern of the water curtain at that point.

We are fascinated by the continual movement and evanescent beauty of such a phenomenon. And watching the freely changing pat-

223 JAMES FITZGERALD. *Fountain Sculpture.* 1961. IBM Building, Seattle. 5,000 pounds of black bronze, 24' (7.32 m) high, fountain with 40 tuned nozzles, activated by a 350-gallon pump.

terns of water tends to free our mind to flow in simple appreciation of the moment.

Watching a fire has a similarly spellbinding effect. And like Fitzgerald's fountain, fires are both controlled and free in their changes through time. John Willenbecher's *Burning Tetrahedron* (Fig. 224) was consumed by flames in a performance controlled somewhat by the shape of the 25-foot-square-based structure and the protective trench encircling the piece to keep the fire from spreading. The hollow center and gradually diminishing circumference created a chimney effect, allowing a draft of wind to rush upward and thus intensify the fire. But the actual process and timing by which the sculpture took to flames was not predictable. When the brush at the base was first ignited, nothing much happened. Seeing mostly smoke, the crowd in attendance ventured closer. But then flames suddenly filled the center of the structure, instantly transforming it into a dynamic, crackling, heat-radiating presence. Awed, the crowd quickly retreated to watch the slow progress of the fire, whose dramatic effects throbbed with the mutual rhythms of life and death. The form of the piece kept changing, but never did it seem chaotic, for the framework was consumed from the top down, leaving a coherent structure almost until the end. As witness Kirk Varnedoe reported,

> The structure collapsed in three major steps, from the top downward. . . . Each fall was discrete, and separated by long intervals during which inevitability and unpredictability tugged at each other in the spectator's involvement. The end could not be in doubt, yet each event in the process was a surprise; and the stochastic rhythm of change was, during long periods of apparent changelessness, mesmerizing.

While the previous two pieces invoke free time through the unpredictability of natural forces, some works involve the unpredictability of human behavior. One quality that sometimes effects public art is the potential for destructiveness. The miniature dwellings that Charles Simonds builds on New York's Lower East Side (Figs. 4 and 26) so fascinate the children of these poor neighborhoods that they try to protect them from vandalism. But sooner or later, all are destroyed. The longest-lived lasted five years, in an inaccessible location. Simonds accepts the temporary nature of his works, for he chooses to construct them in such a way that they cannot be moved and then leaves them for the whole community to enjoy. That they are destroyed is part of the saga of the "Little People," the imaginary ones for whom he builds. Despite the violence to which they are subjected, they survive by moving through the city, always rebuilding. Their determination to survive despite the presence of danger becomes a symbol of hope for the people of the ghettoes who follow their trail.

Another aspect of human behavior that may enter into works is willingness or unwillingness to participate. People readily set mobiles into motion or push buttons designed to activate kinetic sculptures to see what they will do. But being asked to become actively involved as part of a work of art may raise some reluctance. Street theater is an example of an art form that depends partly on viewer participation, which can be provoked but never counted upon. When we are faced with a novel situation, who knows how we will act? When invited to participate actively, sometimes we avoid getting personally involved in unusual experiences for fear of appearing foolish to others. We humans tend to have a herd mentality; many of us are reluctant to plunge into novel situations until others do so first. Art that operates in free time in which the unpredictable variable is human behavior therefore depends on free people in order to work.

Timelessness

All art is finite—it exists only a certain amount of time before it decays or otherwise comes to an end. Some works are created in materials designed to withstand the ravages of time, such as marble, but nothing

224 John Willenbecher. *Burning Tetrahedron.* August 20, 1978. Artpark, Lewiston, New York.

225 Mies van der Rohe. *Barcelona Chair.* 1929.

226 James L. Seawright, Jr. *Mirror 1.* 1984. An array of 225 mirror-faced blocks, 6 × 6″ (15 × 15 cm), outer dimensions 7 × 7′ (2.14 × 2.14 m). Mirror faces are inclined at the precise angles necessary to direct all of the faces to the focal point, 12 feet in front of the center of the array. Collection of David Bermant (shown at Wadsworth Atheneum, Hartford, Connecticut).

made by human beings is truly permanent. But there are ways other than the permanence of an individual piece by which art can transcend chronological time.

One of these is classical appeal. Certain designs last through time because they transcend contemporary aesthetic trends to express more universal standards of beauty or truth. Throughout this book, we have shown numerous very old works that still stand up today as examples of good design. In Chapter 5, for instance, we admired not only Michelangelo's *David* (Fig. 118), sculpted back in 1501–04, but also the figure called *Gudea Worshiping* (Fig. 115), which was created in 2100 b.c. We don't think of Michelangelo as a Renaissance artist; we think of him as a consummate artist whose work will probably always be loved. Some more recent works have also outlasted our society's tendency toward short-lived fads. Mies van der Rohe's lounge chair (Fig. 225)—called the *Barcelona Chair* since it was first shown at the Barcelona Fair in 1929—is still being manufactured. It is already referred to as a classic since its beautiful lines, textural contrasts, pleasing proportions, and elegant workmanship have kept it in continuing demand.

In contrast to the long-lived method of transcending time, certain pieces are outside of time in the sense that they can hardly be said to exist until someone becomes involved with them. James Seawright's *Mirror 1* (Fig. 226) is a series of mirrors turned toward the center of the piece. The design does not come to life until there is something—or someone—for the mirrors to reflect. Then what one sees will vary greatly, depending on what is reflected. The man in this photograph could see only images of the photographer in the mirrors; the photographer could see only the man, reflected as an interesting play of shapes and values across modules that are similar but ever-changing. No two contain precisely the same image. The work does not exist in its "completed" form until someone stands before it, and each time a different person is there to complete the work, it is different.

Finally, much art presents us with the opportunity to transcend time by becoming so fully involved with a work that we forget ourselves, lose track of the passage of time, and experience the vastness of the moment, beyond time. This is an inner experience that cannot be represented in a photograph. But to get some idea of what can happen, consider Beth Galston's *Lightwall* (Fig. 227). The installation consists of two panels of mirrored Plexiglas strips, one on the uneven floor and one suspended from above. Four light projectors trained on the strips create reflected linear patterns on the walls that change subtly through time as the lights change under the control of a computerized dissolve unit. When people enter the installation, the reflections play across their bodies. The combined effects have the potential for lifting participants out of their normal consciousness and into a world

227 Beth Galston. *Lightwall.* 1983. Mirrored Plexiglass strips, projectors, computerized dissolve unit. Size of gallery space: 35 × 35 × 12′ (10.68 × 10.68 × 3.66 m). Installation at Kingston Gallery (collection of the artist).

in which space and time take on entirely different dimensions. Lois Tarlow describes some typical responses:

> Visitors entering the dark room invariably uttered sounds generally reserved for fireflies and falling stars. They approached the strips tentatively, uncertain as to whether they were connected by invisible barriers. Finding easy access, the viewers roamed among the free-hanging mirrors, thereby jostling them and causing the streaks on the walls to lurch about wildly. People spoke in hushed tones. One young man said, "I'd like to live here forever."

STUDIO PROBLEMS

10.1 Growth or Decay

Using any media including found objects, create a piece that is not permanent and that draws attention to processes of growth or decay. Influences such as wind, rain, fire, cold, or heat can be used to alter the physical appearance of the piece through time.

10.2 Kinetic Sculpture

228 Kinetic Sculpture. Wood, string, plumb bob. Student work.

Make a three-dimensional object that moves in a controlled space, in controlled time. Solutions could include wind-up toys or fan-moved works. The plumb-bob in the solution shown (Fig. 228) can be pushed, setting it swinging in patterns that gradually diminish with time. Even the rotation of the earth causes it to swing subtly. Adding a bed of sand or salt crystals would provide a visual record of its movement through time.

10.3 Controlling the Viewer's Movements

Using inexpensive materials, create an installation piece or even an earthwork that controls the movements of viewers, forcing them to become participants in the work. What happens psychologically when one is led through physically awkward or "welcoming" spaces?

10.4 Changes by the Viewer

Design a piece that changes with each viewer's participation in it. Some possibilities include games, processes, forms to be manipulated. Consider

Elements of Three-Dimensional Design

229 Changes by the Viewer. Wood. Student work.

the possibility of motion or movable parts as a primary focus of the piece. Figure 229 offers an assortment of pegs, no two of which are alike, that can be placed in any of the holes drilled in the blocks of wood. There are more holes than pegs, and the holes are at varying distances from each other. Each person who plays with rearranging the pegs may thus change the overall effect of the work considerably.

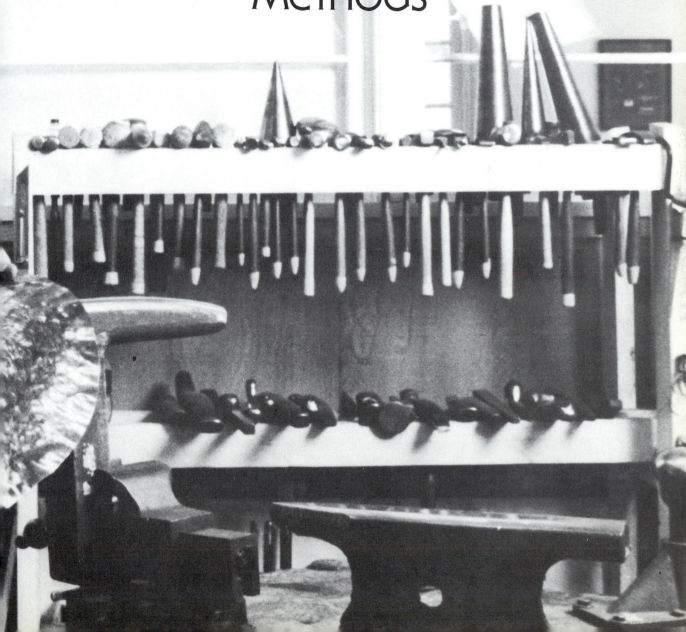

PART 3

Construction
Methods

11

Found Objects

A *found object* is any object not originally created as a work of art but appreciated for its aesthetic qualities or personal meaning. Can there be anyone who has not regarded some kind of found object as a treasure? We pick up rounded stones or shells at the beach, enjoying the way they look and feel, and perhaps keep some for luck or display. A colorful feather found on a path seems worth saving, though we may not know quite what to "do" with it. Some of us dig through old dumps for antique medicine bottles, admiring the aesthetic qualities of the hand-blown glass. Weathered old tools may be appreciated for their interesting forms and textures. And semiprecious stones such as amethysts, rock quartz crystals, and onyx are often displayed in their uncut natural state because of the beauty of their colors or transparent clarity.

The appreciation of found treasures seems universal. Throughout human history, there have been people who have carried this love for the beauty and personal meaning of nonart objects into statements now considered to be art forms. This use of found objects is the first of four major "construction" methods we will be considering.

In some cases, no construction is involved at all; a found object is simply considered worthy of interest in its own right. Sometimes a base is fabricated using art methods and media and then found objects are somehow woven, braided, tied, glued, or otherwise fastened to it. Or found objects themselves may be assembled to create a piece in which the original identity of the objects is a meaningful or humorous counterpart to the overall form. In any case, the main thing the artist brings to these works is an eye for design in unexpected places and imagination in envisioning how found things could be put together.

Individual Found Objects

Nonindustrial societies living close to the earth learn to watch for natural objects that can serve useful functions. Although the objects themselves are found rather than made for the intended purpose, they may be decorated to add an artistic dimension to everyday experiences. The bush people of Southwest Africa find an ostrich eggshell a perfect container for precious drinking water and may carefully engrave and paint ornamental lines on its surface (Fig. 230).

230 (right) Decorated ostrich egg-shell drinking vessel, Luderitz Ray, Nabib Desert, Southwest Africa. Engraved lines filled with red and black pigment, height 5⅞″ (15 cm). University of Zurich.

216   *Construction Methods*

231 (top left) Queen's Head. Yehliu, Taiwan. Naturally eroded rock formation.

Some natural objects are prized simply for their beauty or design interest. When such found objects are not portable, viewers may travel to see them. In the fishing village of Yehliu in Taiwan, erosion of the local sandstone by wind and water has produced fantastic natural sculptures such as the *Queen's Head* shown in Figure 231. The "head" consists of harder rock than the more eroded "neck." The resulting formation bears a great resemblance to the sculptures of Alberto Giacometti (see Figs. 151 and 193). Travelers and scholars who have found these natural sculptures refer to them as "national treasures."

Marcel Duchamp is credited with the discovery that manufactured objects such as industrial bottle racks (Fig. 232) can be displayed as "ready-made" art. Many of us follow his lead by bringing manufactured objects into our homes for uses other than their original

232 (top right) MARCEL DUCHAMP. *Bottle Rack., from a leather case containing reproductions of the artist's* work. Height 16⅛″ (41 cm), width 14¾″ (37 cm), depth 4⅛″ (10 cm). Collection Museum of Modern Art, New York (James Thrall Soby Fund).

Found Objects   217

233 Interior with woodstove and found objects.

functions. In the interior with woodstove (Fig. 233), old fire grates have been mounted on the wall as interesting linear sculptures whose vertical lines repeat the verticals in the wood paneling and woodstove pipe. In addition, age-worn pieces of wood have been used to frame a composition of bare branches whose organic patterns present a pleasing contrast to the straight-edged metal objects. Even the woodstove becomes a found object presented as a work of art in this carefully arranged harmony of woods and wood-burning metal tools.

Assemblages with Spiritual Connotations

When everyday nonart materials are combined to create a work of art, the result is often called an *assemblage.* Some such works are used for special spiritual functions, for the personal or group meaning attached to each thing adds to the spirit of the whole. A handmade quilt may enhance a family's sense of historical kinship, for each bit of fabric may recall incidents in family history: "This one was from the dress Carrie wore the first day of school; this was John's christening dress; here's a scrap of your mother's wedding dress. . . ." Likewise, to put together found objects representing earth, air, water, and fire brings one into symbolic contact with the universe.

In African tribal cultures, assemblages of found materials are amassed for ritual display and power-enhancing purposes. Objects attached to masks, headdresses, or power figures like the piece shown in Figure 234 may carry symbolic social significance—such as indicating wealth and status—as well as invoking the aid of supernatural forces. Cowrie shells connote wealth, for the shells are used as money in many of these groups. Cowrie shells also have intriguing tactile and visual qualities, with a combination of surface smoothness and dark hidden inner recesses that many cultures have linked symbolically with femaleness.

The design of a ritual display or power piece may be informal enough that it can be added to as time goes on and additional materials are found. These range from skulls of small animals, teeth, seed pods, shells, fur, feathers, and claws to mirrors, nails, beads, and shotgun shells, with an emphasis on repetition of many small units. In the accretion of materials, the prevailing feeling seems to be "the more, the better," and many people may bring found things to the piece over time, giving it a variety of textures and forms and a lively organic appearance of growth. Each addition brings a different kind of spiritual power—as well as form and texture—to the piece. The addition of new materials is often accompanied by special chants and spreading of dried blood or the like on the piece to honor and increase the magical powers being drawn into the sculpture. Even if we are not privy to the symbolism involved, we may find such a piece visually and psychologically exciting. It raises questions for which the mind has no answers: Why? How? Where did they get those?

Assemblages may also express devotion. In Naples, devotion to various saints as intermediaries between oneself and heaven is often expressed in homemade roadside shrines. Whatever is available to enhance the love offering is incorporated into the design, from bits of ironwork, plastic, and sculpture, to flowers, candles, and even neon lights. Continual additions to such pieces allow one to maintain a sense of personal contact with the divine. The shrine in Figure 235 includes a skull, perhaps as a reminder that things of the earth are fleeting and that one might better keep one's vision set on the eternal.

The local emotional response to such pieces, be they tribal sculptures or Catholic shrines, stems from a shared spiritual tradition that everyone in the area understands. An outsider untutored in these beliefs may nevertheless experience a certain aura of mystery or sacredness surrounding these assemblages, as though they awaken

234 (top right) Fetish figure. Primitive wood sculpture, African, Zaire, Kongo. Height 11″ (28 cm). Metropolitan Museum of Art (Michael C. Rockefeller Memorial Collection, Bequest of Nelson A. Rockefeller, 1979).
235 (bottom right) Roadside shrine, Naples. 1948. Stucco and marble, height 2½′ (0.76 m). 1978 photograph in Rhode Island School of Design Museum.

Found Objects

236 (top left) Lucas Samaras. *Untitled Box Number 3*. 1963. Pins, rope, stuffed bird and wood. Height 24½″ (62 cm), width 11½″ (29 cm), depth 10¼″ (26 cm). Collection Whitney Museum of American Art, New York (gift of the Howard and Jean Lipman Foundation, Inc).
237 (top right) Pablo Picasso. *Baboon and Young*. 1951. Bronze, height 21″ (53 cm). Museum of Modern Art, New York (Mrs. Simon Guggenheim Fund).

deep-buried memories from what psychologist Carl Jung called the "collective unconscious." Be that as it may, certain artists can evoke the sense of sacrosanct mysteries without referring to any tradition with which we are familiar. Lucas Samaras' *Untitled Box No. 3* (Fig. 236) creates such an effect by suggesting a hidden, secret place. Found materials are used as though collected by a bird to create a nest of sorts, woven of bits of wood and bristling with thousands of pins. The frayed twine hanging below is strangely out of scale for a nest, but its outsized appearance makes it all the more noticeable as something found and brought to this creation. The stuffed bird nestles within, protecting a dark and secret space on which we feel we should not intrude.

Junk Sculpture

Our affluent society's tendency to throw used objects away rather than reusing or recycling things has opened fertile new ground for artists. Sometimes in protest against wastefulness, sometimes in delight at finding creative uses for castoffs, a number of artists turn what is considered junk into assemblages that work as art.

Construction Methods

In some of these assemblages, the discovery that a castoff looks like something entirely different is both the artist's motivation and the viewer's surprise. In Picasso's *Baboon and Young* (Fig. 237), our interest is suddenly captured when we notice that the baboon mother's head is actually a toy car. The relationship between these two forms is totally unexpected, an altogether original perception. That it works so well—with the back tires enlarged as ears—is a tribute to Picasso's imagination, his gift for seeing possibilities in even the most mundane materials.

Sometimes a number of found objects are put together in such a way that the combined image suggests another form. In Richard Stankiewicz's hands, old bedsprings and coiled springs are transformed into grotesque representations of the lacy veil and tender curls of *The Bride* (Fig. 238). Stankiewicz began making junk sculptures when his attempts to turn his yard into a garden unearthed a quantity of old metal things. The artist says he found them so "beautiful" in themselves that he "set them aside as objects to look at . . . , and of course it was only a short step of the imagination to combine various of these things together to make compositions from them." Making abstract peoplelike figures from unwanted machine parts inevitably prompts symbolic associations, as though these grotesqueries are apt metaphors for the human inhabitants of industrial society. As Stankiewicz notes, "visual puns, mechanical analogies and organic resemblances in machinery provide a large and evocative vocabulary for sculpture." It is a vocabulary that may evoke humor or despair, depending on the intention of the artist and the psychology of the viewer.

Although the junk of our civilization often inspires works with a busy variety of lines, forms, colors, and textures, it is possible to create quietly simple art from found objects. An example of this approach is Varujan Boghosian's *Orpheus* (Fig. 239, p. 222). Here a minimum of found objects—an old doll and a vise mounted on a piece of wood— are used to create a wealth of symbolic or psychological associations. With the title as a clue to the content, we can imagine the legendary Orpheus as a figure from the sunlit world traveling into the darkness of Hades to rescue his wife Eurydice. The vise holding the doll in place may suggest Orpheus' attempt to avoid turning back to look at Eurydice until she reaches the sunlight. Those who are unfamiliar with the myth may experience other associations: the dreamlike sense of past remembered; the pathos of a once-loved but discarded child's toy, juxtaposed with and even being held captive by an adult's tool, itself hand-worn. In another sense, the vise becomes more than a vise; it becomes part of the body of the doll, or even a pedestal for the doll. One is also struck by the contrast of the lightness of the doll to the darkness of the wood.

While found objects offer great potential for representational al-

238 RICHARD STANKIEWICZ. *The Bride.* 1955. Steel, 5′9″ × 14″ × 13″ (175.3 × 35.6 × 33 cm). Private collection.

Found Objects   **221**

lusions, certain artists present junk as abstract sculptures to be ap-
praised solely on the basis of their design characteristics. John Chamberlain made a point of using junked automobile exterior parts exactly
as he found them, welding pieces together to create a surprisingly
flowing composition in *Velvet White* (Fig. 240). Such artists do us the
special service of drawing our attention to the beauty of that which
happens by chance in manufactured objects, even when they have
been rejected and deformed, just as other artists draw our awareness
to the beauty of natural objects.

A final motivation for the use of found objects is sheer exuberance for life in all its forms. Simon Rodia's *Watts Towers* (Fig. 241) is
a monumental expression of this all-embracing aesthetic. Trained in
tile setting but unschooled in art, Rodia spent thirty-three years creating his marvelous towers from a framework of concrete and wire mesh,
covered with a rich mosaic of found objects: glass from broken bottles,
shells, mirrors, tiles, shards of dishes. The airy structures rise almost
100 feet into the Los Angeles sky. From close hand, as in the fore-

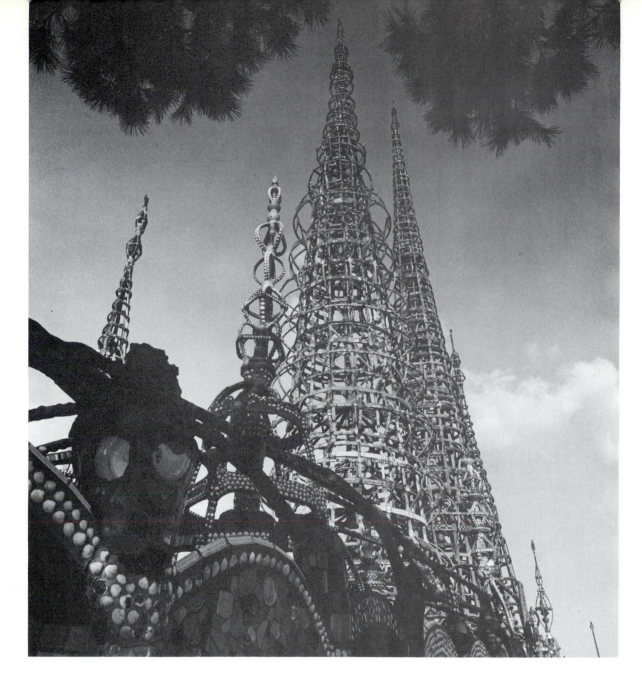

ground of the photograph, the objects' individual identities can be distinguished. But from a distance, they merge into exuberant abstract patterns of color and form. Whether seen as "naive" folk art or the intentional choice of a highly trained artist, the ability to appreciate the design possibilities of whatever is at hand is a compelling motivation for the construction of works from found objects.

241 Simon Rodia. *Watts Towers,* Los Angeles. 1921–1954. Concrete and steel with bits of glass, broken dishes, shells, pieces of mirrors, and other debris from the streets. Height 99′ (30.17 m).

STUDIO PROBLEMS

11.1 Ready-Made

Find an object that suggests a human or animal form, or will if slightly altered. Present it as a sculpture. The student who created Figure 242 found that a head gasket from a car can be bent to look surprisingly like a cow, complete with the appearance of hide and bolt-hole eyes.

242 (top)   Ready-made. Head gasket. Student work.
243 (right)   Assemblage. Snail shell, twigs, safety pin, string, rock, rubber band. Student work.

Construction Methods

11.2 Assemblage

Put together three or more found objects in such a way that they present a coherent whole. The example shown in Figure 243 is an unusually miniature solution whose familiar parts—snail shell, twigs, safety pin, string, rock, and rubber band—are used to suggest something seemingly representational that evokes curiosity, since it cannot quite be identified. In a successful solution, the new whole will be perceived before its components.

Reference Books on Working with Found Objects

Gerald F. Brommer, *Wire Sculpture and Other Three-Dimensional Construction,* Worcester, Massachusetts: Davis Publications, Inc., 1968. Contains a chapter on assemblage with provocative suggestions for projects and some how-to instruction on physical and visual unification of works made from found objects.

Dona Z. Meilach and Don Seiden, *Direct Metal Sculpture: Creative Techniques and Appreciation,* New York: Crown Publishers, 1966. Includes information on soldering, brazing, and welding of metals to each other, combining metal and nonmetal materials, and creating sculptures from found objects.

12

Addition
and
Manipulation

Whereas found objects are often used as is, other techniques for three-dimensional construction involve changing the form of the original material. Those to be explored in this chapter are based on manipulating forms directly without significantly changing their physical volume and/or putting units together to create a larger whole. The two remaining chapters will focus on methods of subtracting excess material to reveal a smaller form or creating desired forms through less direct casting processes. These categories are not mutually exclusive, for many pieces are constructed by a combination of various methods. In addition, the same material may also be handled in a number of different ways. Wood, for instance, may be built up in units for additive sculpture or carved away by subtractive methods.

Manipulating Malleable Materials

One very direct method of working three-dimensionally is shaping *malleable* materials by hand or hand-held tools. These are media that are pliable enough to be stretched, flattened, bent, curved, or twisted without falling apart. Their ability to be worked in these ways is often referred to as their *plasticity*. In the long run, plasticity is not usually considered desirable, so these media are usually worked in a rather soft state and then hardened for durability.

Clay

A highly plastic material that has been used for three-dimensional construction since ancient times is clay. This medium is pliable enough to be shaped between the hands when wet, but is brittle when dry and can be glazed to a variety of finishes. Clays are found as natural deposits resulting from the disintegration of certain kinds of rock, each differing in characteristics such as plasticity, color, texture, and behavior when fired for hardening purposes. Artists who use clays often mix their own *clay bodies* from various types of clay in order to get just the properties they want. Their contact with the clay is quite intimate and direct, for traditional methods of building or throwing a form on a wheel require really getting one's hands into the material. As potter Minnie Negoro (shown at her wheel in Fig. 244) explains,

> You have to like the feel of this very plastic malleable material. It's a sense on your fingertips, moving in and out. When you can control this, when you have the ability to make the clay move just the way you want it to, it's very personal. And since clay is a material that you can compound yourself of different kinds of clays to make the textural feel you want, that becomes very important. Before it's even fired, when it's still in the raw state, you can get that kind of feel that you like to use. You can have it just as smooth and silky or grainy and rough as you want, and then apply force to it to create the form you have in mind.

Although throwing a pot on a wheel is a very direct method of shaping in the sense that the artist's hands guide the growth of the pot from the bottom up, the skills involved are anything but spontaneous. The technology of clay compounding, firing, and glazing is highly technical and subject to endless experimentation. And to create a classical symmetrically rounded form takes great control, developed over years of practice. Clay directly and honestly mirrors the movements of the human hand.

Wheel-thrown forms may be cut, reshaped, or otherwise manipulated into nonsymmetrical forms. There are numerous other means of

244 Minnie Negoro throwing a pot on a wheel.

245 PETER VOULKOS. *Gallas Rock.*
1960. Terra cotta, height 7' (2.13 m).
F. S. Wright Galleries, UCLA (gift of
Julianne Kemper).

working clay other than wheel throwing, such as pinch, coil, slab, and direct modeling techniques. These methods may rely heavily on chance and the inspiration of the moment, or they may involve considerable planning and control, depending on the intent of the artist. Peter Voulkos has used pottery techniques imaginatively to create a huge body of vigorous ceramic sculptures. In his 7-foot-high (2.13 m) *Gallas Rock* (Fig. 245) he pushed clay as far as it can go in height by stacking around a central support about 100 slab-formed and wheel-thrown pieces opened "to let the dark out." Although Voulkos works very quickly and spontaneously, the ability to create such a technical tour de force is based on years of experience and experimentation with clay.

Construction Methods

Whether they emphasize control or happenstance, artists have often chosen to work in clay because of its immediacy. Sometimes clay is used to capture an idea that will later be translated into some more permanent material. If it does not need to be fired for permanency, clay can be built up as a solid mass, with bits added and molded as needed. Models for new cars—both outer bodies and interiors—are typically developed through a series of clay studies, such as the one shown in Figure 246. Rodin did quick clay studies of his models as they moved through his Paris apartment to capture their natural movements, later to be sculpted more permanently in the slow method of carving marble.

Clay is also used as a permanent medium for modeling figures. Andrea del Verrocchio's *Virgin and Child* (Fig. 11) was modeled of terra-cotta back in the 15th century, but it survives in good shape today. This lovely piece is not very thick, because it is a relief. But when clay is used to model thick forms they must be built hollow or hollowed out with an air hole left to the inner cavity before firing, for a thick piece may burst in the kiln when fired. Clay has little strength under tension. And because of its plasticity, clay succumbs rather readily to the tug of gravity. Projecting forms, such as arms held out from the body, are particularly vulnerable. Large works must be carefully supported by an internal armature to avoid unintentional sagging or breaking. The size of works to be fired is also limited by the relatively small size of most kilns. Fairly large works may be created in sections, hollowed, fired, and then reassembled.

Firing (baking to remove moisture and harden the clay) and *glazing* (application of a glasslike liquid that fuses with the clay when fired) require extensive knowledge of complex variables. Most pieces are first fired for several hours at relatively low heat to harden the form but keep the clay porous enough to receive a glaze. This *bisque* ware is then glazed and refired at a higher temperature.

Glazes are used decoratively and also serve the function of making ceramic pieces watertight and nonabsorbent. Glazes also carry

246 Preparing a clay model for a bucket seat for General Motors.

229

pigments to color the surfaces of a piece; they can be brushed, poured, or sprayed on, or the piece can be dipped into a container of glaze. The minerals used to formulate them and their proportions within the formula can be varied for different effects.

In ancient work with clay, pieces were baked directly in the coals of a fire or in covered pits. The contemporary *kiln* is an insulated furnace for firing ceramic pieces which is heated by electricity or by a wood, coal, oil, or gas fire in a separate combustion chamber. Control and even distribution of the heat are critical. *Earthenware,* which uses coarse clays such as terra-cotta to create rough-textured, porous pieces, is fired at a relatively low temperature (about 800° C, or 1470° F). *Stoneware,* made from finer clays, is fired at a higher temperature to form a more glasslike body. *Porcelain,* made from the finest clays, is fired at the highest temperatures (up to 1613.4° C, or 3000° F).

Wax

Another highly plastic medium is wax. Warmed slightly for softening, sometimes just by being rolled in the hands, it can take a great amount of twisting, bending, and reforming without breaking. Additional pieces can easily be attached to a form being built up. The artist simply presses dabs of wax in place or heats both surfaces with a hot tool to allow them to bond without the misshaping of pressing. Like clay, wax can be smooth- or rough-textured in its final form. Edgar Degas did a series of small wax sculptures, like the horse shown in Figure 247, in which the dabs of wax are not fully smoothed into the figure's contours. In addition to creating interesting textures, they increase the

247 EDGAR HILAIRE GERMAIN DEGAS. *Statuette: Horse Galloping on Right Foot.* c. 1881. Bronze cast of wax model, height 11⅞″ (30 cm). Metropolitan Museum of Art (bequest of Mrs. H. O. Havemeyer, 1929. The H. O. Havemeyer Collection).

Construction Methods

liveliness of the figure by conveying a sense of spontaneity, as though the work came so recently from the artist's hands that we can still see his thumbprints. These wax figures were later cast in bronze—for wax melts too easily to hold its shape in warm weather—and the cast retains the fresh quality of the way Degas handled the wax.

Plaster and Cement

Plaster and cement can also be built up directly with the hands and simple hand tools, though they need a supporting understructure to hold projections or curving contours. Some materials commonly used to build up the understructure, or *armature,* include wire, rods, screening, hardware cloth, metal lathe, wood, and foam. Plaster or cement is usually applied to this base in wet layers and finished wet. Rodin's plaster *Young Woman in a Flowered Hat* (Fig. 248) shows obvious signs of having been gouged with pointed tools when the plaster was wet to create textures such as strands of hair and herringbone weaving on the hat. These materials can also be allowed to dry and then chiseled or filed away. Pigments can be added to the mixture for color, and filler materials such as sand, fine gravel, or marble chips may be

248 AUGUSTE RODIN. *Jeune femme au chapeau fleuri* ("Young Woman in a Flowered Hat"). 1865–1870. Plaster. 27 × 13½ × 11.6″ (0.69 × 0.344 × 0.295 m). Musée Rodin, Paris.

231

added to the final layer to produce desired textural effects. Plaster has little tensile strength and may crack when worked dry or chip afterwards. But its low cost and flexibility makes it a common choice for pieces to be used indoors or patterns for projects to be cast or otherwise translated into more durable form. Concrete is somewhat more coarse, but this characteristic is appropriate for certain large, simple outdoor forms.

Malleable Metals

Some metals, while not pliable enough to be totally shaped by the artist's hands, are nonetheless malleable enough to be formed by bending, stretching, twisting, and hammering over a hard flat or shaped surface. As metals are worked, they become harder and therefore less malleable, a condition that can be temporarily reversed by heating, a process called *annealing.* Metals and alloys, or combinations of metals, vary in physical characteristics. In metals, *malleability* is the ability to be readily shaped by hammering; *ductility* is a property permitting the metal to be drawn out into wire or threads. *Hardness* is measured by the depth of a scratch that can be made on a metal by a weighted diamond point. Table 13.1 summarizes variations in these three properties for some common metals.

Metalsmiths and jewelry makers use a variety of tools and techniques to change thin sheets or rods of the relatively soft metals into desired forms and surface textures. Thin wire can be bent into desired shapes; thicker metals may be struck with a variety of tools, each of which leaves its own shape as an impression in the soft metal. In jewelry, *repoussé*—hammering thin sheet metal from the back, using a variety of punches—creates low relief patterns on the front side. These

TABLE 13.1: PHYSICAL PROPERTIES OF METALS

Hardness	Ductility	Malleability
Lead (softest)	Gold (most ductile)	Gold (most malleable)
Pewter	Silver	Silver
Tin	Platinum	Lead
Aluminum	Iron	Copper
Gold	Nickel	Aluminum
Silver	Copper	Tin
Zinc	Aluminum	Platinum
Copper	Zinc	Zinc
Nickel	Tin	Iron
Platinum	Lead (least ductile)	Nickel (least malleable)
Iron		
Steel (hardest)		

(Information based on Jack C. Rich, *The Materials and Methods of Sculpture,* New York: Oxford University Press, 1947, p. 129.)

Construction Methods

249 (top) Douglas Steakley shown raising a piece of holloware.
250 (bottom) Douglas Steakley. *Vase and Bowl.* Vase: silver-plated brass, height
7½″ (19 cm). Bowl: copper, raised with oxide finish, height 4½″ (11 cm).

patterns may be further worked from the front with hammer and punches, a process known as *chasing.* In Figure 249, Douglas Steakley is using the process of *raising*—hammering a flat sheet of metal over a stake, compressing it to create a hollow form. The finished piece can then be left with the texture created by the hammer, as in the vase and bowl shown in Figure 250, or filed and polished to a high finish.

Even iron and steel can be reformed if heated to a relatively malleable state. Long used to create a limited range of functional pieces, blacksmithing is now used as a fine art technique as well. L. Brent Kington's *Rocking Horse* (Fig. 251, p. 234) is not only a delightful child's toy but also a beautiful study in flowing line and positive and negative form. The techniques used to shape the steel are ancient—*forging* (hammering over an anvil or other hard surface), chiseling to define contours, and chasing to provide details on the head. What is new here is the increasing freedom artists and craftspeo-

Addition and Manipulation

251 L. Brent Kington. *Rocking Horse.* 1972. Steel, forged, chiseled, and chased, length 44″ (112 cm). Westwood Art Center, Cincinnati, Ohio.

ple feel to push their media and methods into previously unexplored aesthetic territory.

Fiber Arts

Some of the most exciting redefinitions of the possibilities of specific construction methods are occuring in the *fiber arts.* This label covers all work created by interweaving single fibers of some material to create a larger whole. Conventionally, techniques such as weaving, knitting, and basket making were used solely to create functional objects. In recent years, artists have ranged far beyond the traditional uses and methods of working with fibers. As is true in any area, if creativity is allowed to flow freely, the results will be living, changing, ever-expanding.

Rugs and tapestries were traditionally flat-woven to warm and decorate floors and walls. Some fiber artists are now bringing these techniques off the walls and into three-dimensional space. Woven goods may project outward from the wall or sometimes come off the wall entirely. The richly textured panels in Magdalena Abakanowicz' *Black-Brown Composition in Space* (Fig. 252) hang from rafters, creating an environment of their own through which the viewer may walk, if not totally intimidated by their size. These great woven slabs loom so large and heavy that we feel instinctively wary, knowing that they could crush us if they fell. Imagine the engineering feats involved first in weaving at this scale and then in hanging the pieces. When they choose to work this large, weavers move into nonconventional considerations such as the need for scaffoldings for installation.

Construction Methods

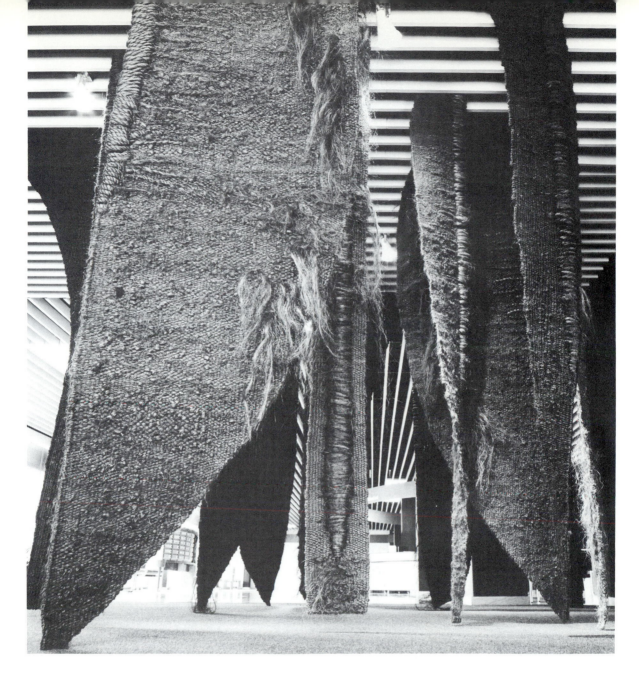

Crocheting, once the province of grandmothers making baby clothes and doilies, offers the inventive artist unbounded opportunities for creating three-dimensional forms. One solution to making a crocheted piece occupy three-dimensional space is to coat it with some stiffening agent such as lacquer; Ewa Pachuka stuffed her crocheted forms to create the extraordinarily lifelike aboriginal scene she calls

252 MAGDALENA ABAKANOWICZ. *Black-Brown Composition in Space.* 1972. Material woven and formed by the artist. 19'8" × 26'2" × 11'4" (6 × 8 × 3.50 m). Permanent installation in entrance space of Huddinge Hospital, Huddinge, Sweden.

Addition and Manipulation

235

253 (top)   Ewa Pachuka. *Arcadia: Landscape and Bodies.* 1977. Woven and crocheted fibre with mixed media, 8′ × 13′ (244 × 396.5 cm). Art Gallery of New South
Wales (gift of Rudy Komon Art Gallery, 1978).
254 (bottom)   Magdalena Abakanowicz. *Self Portrait.* 1976. Mold of linen threads
after a mold in plaster of the artist's face and shoulders, life-size (collection of the
artist).

Arcadia (Fig. 253). Life-size, each of the women and animals is the
result of intricate crocheting of polypropylene yarn. Their surroundings
are made from coir, which is the spun hair of coconut. The resulting
textural effects could not have been created in any other medium.

Some fiber arts even negate the classical traditions by which
fibers are knitted, knotted, crocheted, or woven together. The Polish
fiber artist Magdalena Abakanowicz created her *Self Portrait* (Fig. 254)
of woody plant fibers ("bast"), but rather than interweaving them she
arranged them loosely in a cast of her face and added a hardening
compound. The free-flowing openness of the strands is a fitting metaphor for the freedom with which she and others are exploring the
design possibilities of fibers.

Fabrication with Rigid Materials

Units of more rigid materials such as wood, metals, plastics, and stone
can be assembled into larger wholes. Sometimes these materials are
first reshaped to some extent, though their rigidity limits their malleability.

Construction Methods

255 Edward Livington. *Cradle*. c. 1973. Walnut, width 24″ (61 cm), length 43″ (109 cm), height 36″ (91 cm). Sterling Associates, Palo Alto, California.

Wood Fabrication

In additive sculpture, woods may be used as lumber milled into standard flat shapes, such as sheets of plywood or 2 × 4s. Found woods—such as barnboards or weathered driftwood—may be used as shaped by the elements. Wood can also be steamed to a pliable state and then curved, as in bentwood chairs or the beautifully curving wooden frame of Edward Livingston's *Cradle* (Fig. 255). Curving wooden forms can also be created by *laminating*—gluing thin flat sheets of wood together—and then sanding them in such a way that their outer surfaces form curving contours, as they do in H. C. Westermann's *Nouveau Rat Trap* (Fig. 256, p. 238). In this humorous satire on the curvilinear Art Nouveau approach to functional pieces, woods of varying values have been used. These value striations enhance the interest of the design by accentuating the fact that the form has been built up of many sheets of wood rather than trying to make them blend together into a single tone.

Wood is soft enough to be readily cut with tools such as hand and power saws, lathes, and planes. Pieces of wood can then be attached to each other by nailing, gluing, joinery, or bolting. The strength of the joints is critical. In a piece of furniture, the stress of being sat on and pushed around, added to changes in temperature and

256 H. C. Westermann. *Nouveau Rat Trap.* 1965. Collection Mr. and Mrs. Robert Delford Brown, New York.

257 Gabriel Kohn. *Bird Keys.* 1962. Wood, 39 × 40″ (99 × 102 cm). Courtesy Marlborough Gallery, New York.

humidity, may cause joints to come apart. Outdoor pieces must bear not only their own weight but also stand up to wind, rain, and perhaps snow loads and the weight of climbing human visitors. The larger the piece, the stronger the joints must be.

If bolts, rivets, screws, or other fasteners are needed, how will they affect the aesthetics of the design? Sometimes fasteners are totally hidden; sometimes they are used as subtle counterpoints or accents to the primary form. In Gabriel Kohn's *Bird Keys* (Fig. 257), the ends of the dowels involved in holding the wooden slabs together create subtle implied lines that accentuate the inner curve of the form on the lower right. By contrast, fasteners are sometimes given strong emphasis in themselves. Jackie Winsor chose to accentuate the string she used to bind together her *30 to 1 Bound Trees* (Fig. 258). Each of the scrawny birch trees in the piece is individually bound into a single vertical unit, and then the whole is wound round and round with string to make a single form. It looks mysteriously functional, as though some farmer were storing what little wood was available in this bleak Nova Scotia landscape in the tidiest package possible. Although a single rope wound once around the birches would have served to hold them together, the exaggerated repetition of the string windings creates a strong horizontal that contrasts nicely with the verticality of the piece.

Metal Fabrication

With the growing interest in large-scale outdoor sculpture, many artists have turned to metal fabrication. Many metals have great *tensile strength,* a characteristic that allows thin unsupported pieces to span great distances without sagging or breaking. Metal is also highly durable over time; rustproofing methods can be used for those metals that

238   *Construction Methods*

tend to rust. To sculpt with metals, artists have had to learn industrial techniques not traditionally associated with art. To create his machine-like metal sculptures (see *Wind Chant,* for instance, in Fig. 54), John Matt had to become a highly skilled machinist and equip his studio as a complete machine shop. To fabricate aluminum strips into works such as *Round About* (Fig. 203), Linda Howard had to become a master welder.

Sculptors cut metals using the same techniques as industrial metal fabricators: flame cutting with a torch and mechanical cutting with tools ranging from hacksaws to power bandsaws and shearing machines. The basic techniques for attaching one piece of metal to another are welding, adhesives, and fastening devices such as rivets and bolts. *Soldering* and *brazing* are useful for student projects because they use a minimum of heat from a soldering iron or air-acety-lene torch to melt soft solder or brazing rods to fuse joints between relatively thin pieces of metal.

Plastic Fabrication

Another industrial material whose characteristics are being explored by artists is plastics: synthetic materials that vary considerably in characteristics. The possibilities seem almost limitless, and new plastics are being created continually. Specific plastics may be hard or soft, brittle or flexible, transparent or opaque. Some can be cast in molds since they are capable of being remelted and reformed; others cannot. Plastics tend to expand in hot temperatures and to lack the strength of metals. But reinforcing fibers can greatly increase their tensile and impact strength, and individual plastics offer special characteristics not found in any other usable materials, such as transparency, corrosion resistance, and light conduction. For example, Larry Bell's *The Iceberg and Its Shadow* (Fig. 192) relies on the tintability and optical clarity of clear plastic sheets for its unusual transparency effects.

Modern plastic technologies allow artists to create almost any form they can imagine. Liquid plastics such as epoxies and polyesters can be poured into nearly any configuration or thickness and still be light in weight. Polycarbonates and acrylics can be shaped into large, thick forms with better optical clarity than glass, at a fraction of the weight of glass. Fiberglass-reinforced polyester resin and fiberglass-reinforced epoxies are so flexible that they can take on any shape or curve, as well as being strong enough to be self-supporting and hard enough to take considerable surface abrasion. Foams can span large areas, be formed into huge volumes of any shape, and yet be quite lightweight; some foams are almost indestructible.

Available in many forms such as rods, pastes, tubes, sheets, foams, and films, plastic can be sawed, stamped, sheared, carved, or machine-formed and then assembled by welding, bolting, gluing, rivet-

Addition and Manipulation

258 Jackie Winsor. *30 to 1 Bound Trees.* November 1971. Trees and rope, 5 × 5 × 20′ (1.53 × 1.53 × 6.1 m). Halifax, Nova Scotia. No longer exists.

ing, or other mechanical means. For heat-formed shapes, plastic is heated until it is flexible, bent into the desired shape, and held that way until it is cool. Casting, a common way of shaping plastics, will be described in Chapter 14.

Stonemasonry

While most additive sculpture requires some method of fastening units to each other, artists have in some cases placed units together without bonding them in any way. The hardness and heaviness of stone make it difficult to attach to anything, although stones may be set into mortar to help hold them together. But humans in some stony areas of the world have experimented with additive stone constructions that reach astonishing heights without any bonding agent. Consider the ancient stone construction at Stonehenge (Fig. 130). Massive horizontal stone slabs are set across the tops of enormous rough stone pillars. Nothing but gravity holds them in place, yet the structure has remained nearly intact for centuries. No one knows how the great stones were moved into position, but once placed, they have shifted little through time.

Equally astonishing is the mortarless stonework of the Incas at *Machu Picchu* (Fig. 259). The buildings and terraces they constructed high atop a mountain rising from the Peruvian jungle were built of huge stones that were cut, ground, polished, and fit together like a jigsaw puzzle with such precision that the structures have stood for five centuries, defying earthquakes and jungle overgrowth. So closely are the stones joined that in places a knife cannot even be slipped between them. Perhaps in celebration of their own skill, the Inca stonemasons countersunk their joints so that the faces of the stones bulge outward slightly, accenting by their lightness the darker values of the joints.

Mixed Media

A final category in additive construction is the use of *mixed media—* the assembling of different materials to form a coherent whole. For this approach to work, the varying materials must hold together both physically and visually.

In Carol Hepper's *Lunar Chamber* (Fig. 260), our associations of the materials with those that the Plains Indians once used to build their tipis makes their juxtaposition seem logical. For her structures, Hepper tans hides of deer, cattle, and sometimes rabbit and buffalo and then stretches them across frameworks of willow or chokecherry branches, held together with waxed linen thread or rawhide thongs. All are things of the earth, prized as useful materials for survival on the South Dakota prairies where Hepper's great-grandparents once homesteaded and

259 (top)   Detail of *Machu Picchu* stonework, Machu Picchu, Peru.
260 (bottom)   Carol Hepper. *Lunar Chamber.* 1983. Mixed media, 5′5″ × 6′4″ × 5′ (1.65 × 1.93 × 1.52 m) (collection of the artist).

241

where the artist herself grew up on an Indian reservation. However, her structure transcends its tipilike associations to suggest in its apparent fragility, translucency, and airiness some more delicate reality.

In jewelry, the beauty and magical or wealth-proclaiming properties of certain stones have long been used together with the reflective qualities and formability of precious metals such as gold and silver. The challenge is varied: to fasten stone to metal in a way that is sturdy but does not spoil the design or the beauty of the stone, and to make stone and metal work together visually, complementing rather than competing with each other. Georg Jensen's *Dragonfly Brooch* (Fig. 261) captures semiprecious stones in *bezels* (metal collars) and weaves their oval shapes into the design by creating a continual repetition of oval shapes in space. These shapes are defined by silver lines that move, widen, and narrow continually, with the rhythm of natural forms. Against such a setting, the stones act as rich colored accents, neither overwhelming the design nor being lost in it.

Even the synthetic products of industrialization can be used together so harmoniously that they suggest a single variegated being. Naum Gabo's *Linear Construction* (Fig. 90) marries clear plastic sheeting and nylon thread so perfectly that we have difficulty in perceiving them as two different materials. The thread is added to provide visual textures that allow us to "see" the plastic and to elaborate the forms begun in the plastic. But so subtly are the two joined physically and aesthetically that together they create a single *gestalt,* or whole, that is much greater than the sum of the parts. One of its most beautiful features is the central void defined by the apparent absence of either material.

There is no limit to what materials can be combined with each

261 GEORG JENSEN. *Dragonfly Brooch.* 1904. Silver and semiprecious stones, 3½ × 1.8″ (7.8 × 4.6 cm). Museum of Decorative Art, Copenhagen.

Construction Methods

other. Our everyday lives are full of examples. John Matt, whose *Wind Chant* (Fig. 54) is assembled from metals and woods, discusses the feasibility of additive construction, particularly with mixed media:

It's so obvious it will hit you between the eyes. Your automobile is built in pieces. Jet planes, your house, your watch—everything is assembled. Why can't it be so with sculpture? Why does it have to be one solid form that you subtract from? In the past, I was doing big asymmetrical blocks. I remember sitting in the studio in Rome, looking out a huge window, and all of a sudden I noticed the telephone poles and wires. The telephone poles were wood, the wires were copper, the insulators were glass, there was rubber around certain things. There was aluminum this, galvanized that, Plexiglas. . . . I was looking through a window, which was made of glass and wood, and the walls were concrete and paint, and so it went, all the way down to me! If you think about it, your shoes are glue, leather, cloth, string—all sorts of stuff. Your teeth probably have silver and plastic and maybe gold in them now. It can be the same with art. No holds are barred if you are confident in yourself about visual things. You can use anything in any combination, and if you're convinced you can do it, it's going to work. If your sense of the aesthetics is strong, what's to hold you back except your ignorance of the technical details? Even then, you just find out how to do it, and then you do.

STUDIO PROBLEMS

12.1 Clay or Wax Sculpture

Using clay, plasticene, or wax, model a simple sculptural form whose surface reflects the tools used to shape it.

12.2 Addition with Malleable Materials

Use at least three different malleable materials together—paper, plaster, cement, papier-mâché, fibers, soft metals, clay, wax, or any similarly easily shaped material—to create a three-dimensional piece. How do you use these materials? How can you attach them to each other? What do they do together? In Figure 262, page 244, screening has been laced to itself with twine to create tubelike forms, which were then laced to shaped and cut wire mesh, which in turn is wired to heavy black paper and attached to the wall with double-faced tape. The black offers a strong contrast to the grayness of the screening and wire mesh, whose positive effect against the black is quickly lost in areas where they twist off the black backing and are seen against the wall, reaffirming their light and floating quality.

Addition and Manipulation

262 Addition with Malleable Materials. Wire screen, twine, paper. Student work.

12.3   Fabrication with Rigid Materials

Use three or more materials that are rigid in their final form to create a three-dimensional piece. What effects are typical? Do you choose to contradict these effects? How can you attach the materials to each other? Figure 263 uses welding to hold metal to metal, nails and glues to hold wood to wood in the framework above, and gravity and pressure to hold the large

263   Fabrication with Rigid Materials. Steel, wood, stone. Student work.

Construction Methods

stone in the center of the wood framework and the wood framework within the metal frame. The curiosity-provoking effect is one of some rustic contraption specially created as a carriage for the stone, as if it were a crown jewel.

12.4 Skin and Structure

Use balsa wood and light coverings such as rice paper, sheer fabric, or plastic to create a piece in which the "skin" and the structure that supports it are equally important. References to kites, flight vehicles, or oriental design may develop.

12.5 Wood, Burlap, and Plaster Construction

Build a sculpture using wood, burlap, and plaster of Paris. Using the wood as an armature and then building up plaster forms on it is a common solution. In such a solution, the burlap can be used both to bind the wood joints and as a base for the plaster. Figure 264 shows a unique solution in which the wooden framework is revealed as the emphasis of the piece, with plaster-covered burlap used as struts to hold the wood in dynamic tension.

264 Wood, Burlap, and Plaster Construction. Wood, burlap, plaster. Student work.

Reference Books on Addition and Manipulation

Gerald F. Brommer, *Wire Sculpture and Other Three-Dimensional Construction,* Worcester, Massachusetts: Davis Publications, Inc., 1968. Simply written how-to suggestions for wire sculpture, wood construction, and cardboard and paper construction, illustrated with student works.

Geoffrey Clarke and Stroud Cornock, *A Sculptor's Manual,* New York: Reinhold Book Corporation, 1968. Includes technical descriptions of direct plaster and cement forming, flame and electric welding, plastics, and additive construction methods for plastics, wood, and metal.

Frank Eliscu, *Direct Wax Sculpture,* Philadelphia: Chilton Book Company, 1969. Instructions on where and how to buy wax, wax-working tools, sheet wax techniques, and step-by-step illustrations of specific projects.

Frank Eliscu, *Sculpture: Techniques in Clay, Wax, Slate,* Philadelphia: Chilton Book Company, 1959. Step-by-step illustrations of specific projects, including demonstration of use of armatures as well as self-supporting wet-clay modeling.

Chuck Evans, *Jewelry: Contemporary Design and Technique,* Worcester, Massachusetts: Davis Publications, Inc., 1983. Attractively illustrated, informative guide to jewelry and metalsmithing tools, materials, and techniques, including methods of forming, enriching surface textures, forging, fastening devices, inlays, laminations, and stone settings.

Nathan Cabot Hale, *Welded Sculpture,* New York: Watson-Guptill Publications, 1968. Good discussions of basic tools and techniques of torch and electric arc welding, followed by specific directions for constructing abstract forms, organic forms, and large-scale works, and for modeling solid figures.

R. Bruce Hoadley, *Understanding Wood: A Craftsman's Guide to Wood Technology,* Newtown, Connecticut: The Taunton Press, 1980. Everything you ever wanted to know about wood, from characteristics of different woods such as density and cellular structure, to knots and insect damage, shrinkage and swelling, wood movement, strength properties, types of lumber and plywood, and methods of joining and finishing wood.

Dona Z. Meilach, *Decorative and Sculptural Ironwork: Tools, Techniques, Inspiration,* New York: Crown Publishers, 1977. Illustrated procedures and creative uses of metal forging.

Dona Z. Meilach and Don Seiden, *Direct Metal Sculpture: Creative Techniques and Appreciation,* New York: Crown Publishers, Inc., 1966. How-to instructions and illustrations combined with photographs of masterworks, including discussions of metal-working equipment and metals, soldering and brazing techniques, welded iron and steel sculptures, working with nonferrous metals, combining ferrous and nonferrous metals, and combining metals with nonmetals.

Fred Meyer, *Sculpture in Ceramic,* New York: Watson-Guptill Publications [no date]. Information on kinds of clays, preparing clays, kilns, tools for the ceramic studio from the practical to the whimsical, glazes, considerations of clay's suitability for intended projects, building methods, armatures, firing, and presentation. Includes chapters on specific techniques used by certain artists.

Glenn C. Nelson, *Ceramics: A Potter's Handbook,* New York: Holt, Rinehart and Winston, 5th edition 1984. Excellent, well-illustrated discussions of clay bodies, hand-building techniques, wheel techniques, decorating and glazing, kilns and firing.

Thelma R. Newman, *Plastics as Sculpture,* Radnor, Pennsylvania: Chilton Book Company, 1974. Includes descriptions of various plastics, additive construction processes with sheets, blocks, and rods, manipulation of plastics by foaming, buttering, modeling, and working with fibers, films, and liquid plastics.

Jack C. Rich, *The Materials and Methods of Sculpture,* New York: Oxford University Press, 1947. Technical information on modeling of wax, plaster, papier-mâché, and clays.

John Rood, *Sculpture with a Torch,* Minneapolis: University of Minnesota Press, 1963. Information on oxyacetylene welding, brazing, and arc-welding techniques, illustrated with sculptures by the author.

Sunset Editorial Staff with Robert and Joan Dawson, *Sculpture with Simple Materials,* Menlo Park, California: Lane Books, 1968. Very simple illustrated explanations of wire sculpture, papier-mâché, and clay modeling.

Wilbert Verhelst, *Sculpture: Tools, Materials, and Techniques,* Englewood Cliffs, New Jersey: Prentice-Hall, 1973. Includes chapters on fabrication processes with wood, plastic, and metal, as well as direct modeling of plaster, concrete, plastics, clay, and spray metal.

Arthur Zaidenberg, *Sculpting in Steel and Other Metals,* Radnor, Pennsylvania: Chilton Book Company, 1974. Instructions and safety considerations in welding, soldering, bending rods, creating solid areas, using a cutting torch, forging, and brazing.

William Zorach, *Zorach Explains Sculpture,* New York: American Artists Group, 1947. Includes detailed directions for clay modeling on an armature.

13

Subtraction

The opposite of the additive approach to creating three-dimensional forms is *subtraction.* In this process, the artist begins with a block of material larger than the desired finished piece and then carves away any excess. A very explicit example of this method is Shigeo Fukuda's *Bird Tree* toy (Fig. 265). Areas have been carved out of the upper oval form to give the appearance of open branches. The negative forms thus created accent the rhythm of the piece with an interplay of value contrasts. And because the piece is a standing puzzle, the wooden areas carved away to create the tree are preserved as positive forms: birds that fit precisely into the niches from which each was taken.

We usually think of subtraction in terms of carving away extraneous material from the outside of a form. But subtraction can also refer to the shaping of the interior of a form. A monumental example is the *chaitya,* or Buddhist assembly hall, carved as a cave from the living rock in Karli, India (Fig. 266). Modeled on wood architecture, it is lined

265 (top)   Shigeo Fukuda. *Bird Tree*. Wood, 11″ × 9¼″ × ¾″ without base (27.9 × 23.5 × 1.9 cm). Collection Richard Thornton.
266 (bottom)   Interior of carved chaitya cave, Karli, India. c. A.D. 100.

with huge fluted columns bearing figures riding elephants. Above them a vaulted ceiling soars 45 feet (13.72 m) upward within the hollowed-out cliff.

Qualities of the Materials

Materials most often used for carving are wood and stone. Wood has perennial appeal because of its warm organic feel, texture, and grain patterns. As it ages and is repeatedly handled, it develops a pleasing soft patina. The softest woods include white pine, redwood, spruce, and cedar. Medium-hard woods include birch, butternut, and fruitwoods such as apple, cherry, and pear. The fruitwoods sometimes grow rounded knobs called *burls* with beautiful grain patterns that may be emphasized by the artist. Hardwoods such as maple, walnut, oak, hickory, and teak have attractive fine grain and are very durable. Softness is not directly equated to ease of working, for the soft woods may splinter when chiseled. The artist may have more control when working with harder, more coherent woods.

Like woods, stones used for subtractive sculpture range from relatively soft to extremely hard. At the soft end of the spectrum are rocks such as sandstone, soapstone, and alabaster, which can even be carved with a knife when wet. Marble is harder and more coherent and has long been prized for its beauty. Granite is extremely hard but also extremely durable.

Working these resistant materials is often a slow and painstaking process. Wood may split as it is being carved or check as it dries if it has not been fully dried before being worked; knots and other faults in the wood must be dealt with somehow. Sculptors may encounter unexpected fissures running through the interior of pieces of stone and must either work with or around them or else abandon the work. Some stones are also quite expensive; one doesn't tackle them lightly. In ancient China, an artist might spend his entire life carving a single jade screen such as the one shown in Figure 108.

The initial stages of roughing out a design can in some cases be speeded by power tools, such as chainsaws for wood or electric drills or pneumatic hammers for stone. But for the most part, subtraction is a lengthy process of careful removal of excess material by the use of points, chisels or gouges struck with a mallet or hammer. For a highly polished surface, various abrasives are used for final finishing after the initial roughing-out and intermediate carving.

Although the artist who works subtractively in resistant media is not directly hand-shaping the material, as in modeling clay, the artist's hands are nevertheless closely linked with the material through the tools used. Sculptor Barbara Hepworth notes the very different functions of her two hands, as the right wields the hammer against a point held to the stone by the left hand:

> My left hand is my thinking hand. The right is only a motor hand. This holds the hammer. The left hand, the thinking hand, must be relaxed, sensitive. The rhythms of thought pass through the fingers and grip of this hand into the stone. It is also a listening hand. It listens for basic weaknesses of flaws in the stone; for the possibility or imminence of fractures.

For quicker, less expensive subtractive work, plaster or cement can be cast into blocks and then carved. Even plastic in the form of acrylic, epoxy, or polyester blocks can be carved by sawing, drilling, and filing rather than the chipping and gouging techniques used with wood and stone.

Liberating the Form

It is often said that a sculptor is one who sees a form in a block of material and simply carves away everything that covers the form. In some cases, sculptors do get their ideas from the existing form. But more characteristically, they choose a piece of material that will allow them to develop a form they have imagined. To release the image in the stone or wood then means working the piece to its best advantage.

The before and after photographs of Hans Hokanson's *The Cannon* (Figs. 267 and 268) illustrate a very close relationship between the initial form of the material and the final form of the piece. In Figure

267 (bottom left) HANS HOKANSON, early stage of *The Cannon.*
268 (bottom right) HANS HOKANSON. *The Cannon.* 1965. Wood, height 6′ (1.83 m) (collection of the artist).

267, a large tree trunk has been rough-cut to desired proportions with a chainsaw. In the finished work (Fig. 268), the trunk has been carved into with gouges and chisels to refine the forms and create desired surface textures, and wheels have been attached to the trunk with dowels. Despite these modifications, the divided trunk form is still quite evident in the finished sculpture.

Because the basic form from which the sculptor subtracts is a cylindrical tree trunk, in the case of wood, wood sculptures often retain a strongly vertical linear thrust. In the ancient sculpture of *Sheikh el Beled* (Fig. 269), there is a strong sense of the trunk, which has been carved into only slightly to release the torso, legs, and head. Note that the arms and spear were carved out of separate pieces of wood and then attached at the shoulders. If they, too, had been carved with the rest of the body out of a single piece of wood, it would have had to be very thick, and a great deal of excess wood would have had to be carved away to reveal the form. To carve projecting forms in the full round out of a solid block can be done, but it does take time. Projecting limbs are also highly susceptible to being broken during or after creation of a piece. The great effort and skill needed to release the linear forms of the lyre player (Fig. 270) from a small block of marble also rendered the piece vulnerable to breaking afterward, as evidenced by the many places it has been glued back together or where pieces are missing altogether.

269 (top) *Sheikh el Beled,* from his tomb at Saggara. c. 2400 B.C. Wood, approx. 43″ high (109 cm). Partially restored. Egyptian Museum, Cairo.
270 (right) Classical Cycladic statuette: Seated man with a harp. Marble, height 11½″ (29 cm). Metropolitan Museum of Art (Rogers Fund, 1947).

Construction Methods

Most earlier sculptures from Western civilizations are *monolithic*. That is, they retain the closed form of the original single stone or wood, with arms and legs of figurative works perhaps carved away from the body to a certain extent. In the 20th century, sculptors like Henry Moore introduced *open forms* in which carving into the original material penetrated so deeply as to open voids in its center. In Moore's *Internal and External Forms* (Fig. 271), the center of a trunk has been penetrated only to reveal another trunklike form. In both internal and external forms, the vertical thrust of the original trunk is still apparent, if hollowed out.

Some contemporary sculpture abandons the original form of the material or materials entirely. Fumio Yoshimura's *Bicycle with Parking Meter* (Fig. 272) is carved entirely of wood. This tour de force is so masterfully carved into likenesses of things not made of wood—metal chains, rubber tires, flexible gear cables—that the wood totally loses its identity as tree trunk and instead becomes whatever Yoshimura declares it to be.

When approaching a piece of wood or stone, the artist must have a very clear sense of how the form fits into it. The process of chipping away just enough but not too much to reveal that form has been likened to playing three-dimensional chess: The master plans many moves in advance, even though the form may change as it is developed. Usually a rough guide to where everything will lie is sketched in

271 (top) HENRY MOORE. *Internal and External Forms*. 1953–54. Elm, circumference 9'1" (2.77 m), depth 3' (0.91 m), height 8'7" (2.62 m). Albright-Knox Art Gallery, Buffalo, New York (General Purchase Fund).
272 (left) FUMIO YOSHIMURA. *Bicycle with Parking Meter*. 1978. Linden wood, 5'8" × 4'5½" × 1'4½" (1.72 × 1.36 × 0.42 m). Nancy Hoffman Gallery.

273 MICHELANGELO. *St. Matthew.*
1506. Marble, height 8'11" (2.72 m).
Accademia, Florence.

chalk on the surface of the material. Some artists then work into all
sides of a piece at once, continually shaping areas in relationship to
each other.

An alternative approach is to work one side at a time. This is
more difficult than continually working around the piece. Unless the
form is flexible or one knows precisely where it lies, the sculptor can
carve himself or herself into an impasse for there is not enough mate-

Construction Methods

rial left to develop certain contours. Michelangelo apparently had some such trouble with his *St. Matthew* (Fig. 273), for he abandoned it after carving part way toward the back from the front. The figure appears imprisoned within the marble, unable to open fully. Is there enough marble left to carve the foot on the right side of the photograph, for example? The sculptor can make certain compromises or changes as a piece develops, but beyond a certain point areas simply may not work well in relationship to each other and the piece may seem spatially starved.

A third possibility is for the artist to make a small model of the form in some malleable material such as clay. The model can then be translated into a more permanent material such as stone by master stonecutters taking points from the model to determine how deeply to carve each section.

No matter which approach is used, artists are advised to think of the inside rather than the outside of the form they are modeling. Rodin explains this principle, which he learned from his teacher:

> Never consider a surface except as the extremity of a volume, as the point, more or less large, which it directs toward you. . . . Instead of imagining the different parts of a body as surfaces more or less flat, I represented them as projectures of interior volumes. I forced myself to express in each swelling of the torso or of the limbs the efflorescence of a muscle or of a bone which lay deep beneath the skin. And so the truth of my figures, instead of being merely superficial, seems to blossom from within to the outside, like life itself.

Textures and Values

Although the surface is not the chief consideration in developing the form, its final appearance does affect how a piece works. In Hans Hokanson's *The Cannon* (Fig. 263), the surface is left rough-cut on purpose, for the lines gouged across the grain add rhythmic repetition as well as focusing attention on the crude natural vigor of the wood itself.

In Elbert Weinberg's *Veiled Bride* (Fig. 274), more refined chisel marks are left visible. Our attention is first drawn to the three unusual large shapes, and then to the bare hints of the female figure hidden within them, withdrawn from the world. The rippling, flowing surface texture created by the interplay of chisel marks is a later discovery, tying the coinlike flat shapes to an association with the shimmering surface of hammered metal.

In highly representational works, chisel marks are not designed to be seen as such. Rather, they are blended into the appearance of the visual texture of the object being represented. It is impossible to tell that Fumio Yoshimura's *Bicycle with Parking Meter* (Fig. 272) has been

274 ELBERT WEINBERG. *Veiled Bride.* 1959. Wood, height 5′ (1.52 m). Collection Mr. and Mrs. Albert A. List (courtesy Grace Borgenicht Gallery).

275 (top) *Birdstone.* Hopewell. Slate, length 6½″ (17 cm). Museum of the American Indian (Heye Foundation).
276 (bottom) Machu Picchu, Peru, *Hitching Post of the Sun,* altar for observation and worship of the sun. Carved from the live rock.

created by a carving process, for the artist's tools have left no tracks. Instead, we are presented with many nonwood textures, from the patterns of rubber tires to the slickness of parking meter, each convincingly disguising both the characteristics of wood and the artist's hand at work.

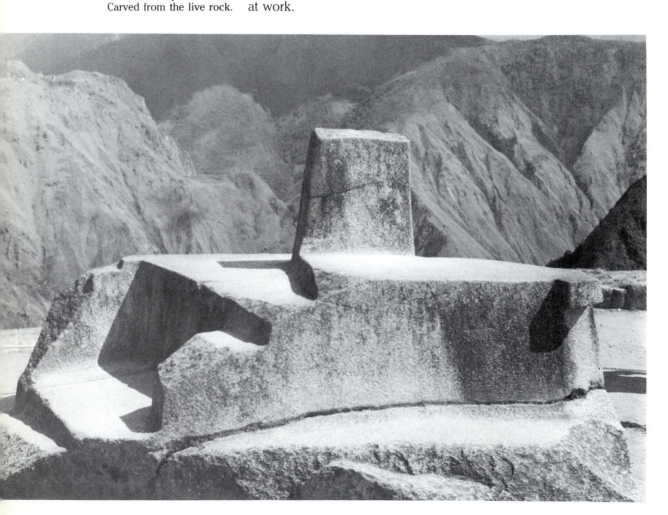

Construction Methods

Sometimes wood or stone is highly polished to bring a pleasing smoothness and glossiness to its surface. In pieces that are handled often over time, such as the slate *Birdstone* in Figure 275, the smooth quality is heightened by the patina of wear. Many touchstones from primitive cultures were clearly designed to be fondled—to be appreciated by hand as well as eye. In our culture, people collect old wooden tools out of appreciation for the hands that used them as well as the hands that carved them.

Surfaces are also used to develop values. Any areas that are deeply undercut will tend to create dark shadows where light cannot penetrate. In the *Veiled Bride* (Fig. 274), the darkness of the deep-cut area in which a bit of the face can be seen heightens the sense of hidden mysteries and contrasts nicely with the shimmering highlights of the finely chiseled surface. At Machu Picchu, the most sacred altar dedicated to worship and observation of the sun (Fig. 276)—the Incas called it *The Hitching Post of the Sun*—is extremely dramatic because of the severe contrasts between light and dark created by the chiseling of sharply angled forms from the living rock of the mountain. Value shifts in the unworked rock below are much more gradual, demonstrating in one picture the artistic potential of the subtractive process in enhancing the impact of one's chosen material.

STUDIO PROBLEMS

13.1 Wood Carving

Carve a simple form in soft wood in such a way that one area flows into another in a continuous series of changes. Concentrate on exploring the subtractive process of creating form by removing excess material. Excess could be carved away with a pocket knife, hammer and wood chisels, file, drill, saw, or sandpaper. Figure 277, page 258, solves the problem with a high relief that demonstrates the process of freeing the form from the material. Deep undercutting almost lifts the form off the remains of the block but retains some of the backing and chisel marks as indications of the process. Depending on the time available, solutions need not be this complex.

13.2 Plaster Carving

Fill a half-gallon milk carton with plaster of Paris mixed according to the directions on the package. After the plaster dries, pull away the carton and carve the mass into a three-dimensional form using tools such as a knife,

277 Wood Carving. Wood. Student work.

file, drill, and/or sandpaper. The piece may be monolithic or open, pierced by a void. Either way, its form must draw the viewer into moving all the way around it to see all sides.

13.3 "Stone" Carving

For an introduction to the experience of stone carving, cast a block of cement or cast stone in a box or carton. Sketch a simple form onto its surface and then work into the material with hammer and stone chisels, always being aware of where the form is within the block.

Reference Books on Subtractive Sculpture

Cecil C. Carstenson, *The Craft and Creation of Wood Sculpture,* New York: Charles Scribner's Sons, 1971. Simple explanations of tools, choice of woods, sculpting and finishing techniques, with helpful observations on subtractive creation of form: avoiding frontality, working all the way around, adding to by taking away, avoiding commitment, working major forms first, and correcting mistakes.

R. Bruce Hoadley, *Understanding Wood: A Craftsman's Guide to Wood Technology,* Newtown, Connecticut: The Taunton Press, 1980. Good discussion of properties of various woods, carving actions, planing, sawing, and finishing.

Malvina Hoffman, *Sculpture Inside and Out*, New York: W. W. Norton and Company, 1939. Old but still valuable discussions of stone and wood carving.

Dona Z. Meilach, *Contemporary Stone Sculpture*, New York: Crown Publishers, 1970. Well-illustrated guide to choosing stones, hand tools, hand carving methods, and power tools and methods.

Jack C. Rich, *The Materials and Methods of Sculpture*, New York: Oxford University Press, 1947. Detailed discussions of carving materials and methods for stone and wood, plus suggestions for subtractive work with inexpensive materials such as brick, concrete, horn and bone, and soap.

John Rood, *Sculpture in Wood*, Minneapolis: The University of Minnesota Press, 1950. Readable accounts of wood-carving tools and techniques, with the step-by-step progress of various works illustrated and discussed.

Wilbert Verhelst, *Sculpture: Tools, Materials, and Techniques*, Englewood Cliffs, New Jersey: Prentice-Hall, 1973. Includes a chapter on carving of wood, stone, plaster, cement, foam, and plastics.

William Zorach, *Zorach Explains Sculpture*, New York: American Artists Group, 1947. Includes several chapters on subtractive sculpture in wood and stone.

14

Casting

The final three-dimensional construction method we will consider is casting. It is an ancient process, sufficiently perfected thousands of years ago to allow production of pieces as aesthetically and technologically advanced as the ceremonial vessel created during the Shang Dynasty in China (Fig. 278). In general, casting involves creation of a *mold*—an outer shell into which another material is poured in a fluid state. When this material hardens, the mold is removed, leaving its imprint in the more permanent material of the inner form—the *cast*.

Casting is an indirect process, with most shaping work done on the mold or the *pattern* from which the mold is made, rather than on the finished piece. It therefore allows artistic use of a number of desirable materials that cannot easily be worked directly into complex forms. The traditional material used for casts is bronze, poured into molds in a hot liquid state. Bronze is prized for its durability and the rich color, seeming translucency and softness of its surface patina, a glow that gets richer with time. Other metals, such as steel, aluminum, and iron, can also be cast, as can wax, clay, and plaster. Many plastics are also readily cast for both artistic and industrial purposes. Even handmade paper, which is a liquid slurry before it dries, can make casts, as in Frank Gallo's *The Faint* (Fig. 279).

278 (top) Ceremonial Vessel, *kuang.* Chinese, Shang Dynasty. Bronze, height 8⅞″ (23 cm), length 13″ (33 cm), width 5″ (13 cm). Metropolitan Museum of Art (Rogers Fund, 1943).

279 (bottom) FRANK GALLO. *The Faint.* Cast in handmade paper, 32″ (81 cm) high × 48″ (122 cm) wide. Edition of 150.

280 ALBERT S. VRANA. Negative mold being prepared from carved sheets of polystyrene foam.

Solid Casts

Casting can be approached in many different ways. Perhaps the simplest is the *direct relief mold* method—preparation of a negative mold into which the desired material is simply poured and then removed when hard. This produces a relief with one finished side. The negative mold can be made of a great variety of materials, including sand, clay, dirt, plaster, wood, cardboard, and styrofoam, with some kind of border added to contain the poured casting material. In Figure 280, a negative mold is being created with sheets of polystyrene foam. The design was then cut into blocks, surrounded with wood sides, and cast stone—a refined concrete—was poured into these shallow molds. In

281 ALBERT S. VRANA, front view of building with sculpture relief. 200 panels pre-cast in carved polystyrene foam for exterior of Professional Arts Building, Miami. 1967. Panels of Chattahoochee stone and sand aggregate in Lehigh Early Strength Cement cover 23,000 square feet. Individual panels are 6″ (15.2 cm) thick and vary from 9 × 12′ (2.7 × 3.6 m) to 17 × 12′ (5.18 × 3.6 m).

the result, used as a facade for a building (Fig. 281), anything that was concave in the mold became convex in the finished cast, and vice versa. The cast picks up the surface qualities of the mold—in this case, a smooth surface—as well as the textures of the materials used in the cast. Cast stone, for instance, can be compounded from cement, sand, and rock aggregates of varying size.

For a form to be cast in the full round, there are several general options. One is to cast the form as a solid, suitable for lightweight, inexpensive materials or small objects. A full-size pattern is first created out of some malleable material. This might be wax or clay; for the sculpture entitled *Mutant,* Elbert Weinberg first created a pattern out of

282 ELBERT WEINBERG. Plaster model for epoxy cast of *Mutant.* 1973. Height 33″ (84 cm), length 31″ (79 cm), width 27″ (69 cm) (collection of the artist).

283 Plaster piece mold.

plaster, shown in Figure 282. Negative molds must then be made from this positive pattern.

For a *rigid plaster piece mold,* the surface of the pattern is divided into separate areas by thin metal *shims* or *fences,* as shown in Figure 283. Each fenced area is coated with plaster to make a partial mold that can be pulled away from that part of the form without breaking. The inner pattern is then removed and the partial molds are reassembled to create a full hollow mold into which the casting material is poured. This process is not suitable for bronze or for casts with intricate details or numerous undercuts.

Plaster piece molds with ball and socket joints for precise assembly are often used for *slipcasting* of ceramic objects or sculptural modules. In this process, clay in liquid suspension *(slip)* is poured into the plaster molds (shown disassembled in Fig. 284). Because the plaster is porous, it absorbs water from the slip, allowing it to harden. Excess slip that does not harden is poured off. When the cast slip is hard as leather, the molds are removed for drying and firing of the piece.

Construction Methods

284 Plaster piece molds for slip-casting, disassembled, with completed cast.

For a *flexible mold,* more suitable for multiple reproductions or more complex forms, the positive pattern is coated with liquid rubber, which picks up all the surface characteristics. A shell of plaster is then applied on top of the rubber for stiffness. The resulting mold (shown diagrammatically in Fig. 285) is then cut in half and removed from the original pattern. The empty halves (plaster outside, rubber inside) may then be reassembled and the material desired for the finished piece poured in to fill the assembled mold. When the molten material hard-

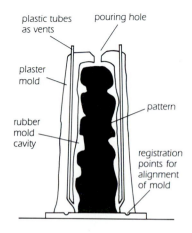

plastic tubes as vents
pouring hole
plaster mold
pattern
rubber mold cavity
registration points for alignment of mold

285 Flexible mold.

Casting

265

286 DUANE HANSON. *Trucker.* 1979. Polyvinyl, polychromed in oil. Life-size. Collection Yellow Freight System.

ens, the two halves of the mold are pulled away, revealing a positive form that exactly duplicates the form of the original pattern. The cast of *Mutant*, which was made of lightweight plastic resin, looks exactly like the pattern in Figure 282, except that the material is different.

Sculptors have sometimes gone directly to the real thing for their patterns. Duane Hanson uses real people as his patterns, coating them with cutaway molds of silicon rubber, and then filling these molds with a melted plastic—polyvinyl acetate. This material, colored with oil paint to match human skin tones, becomes astonishingly lifelike when painted and clothed in human likeness and surrounded by familiar objects such as ashtrays and catsup bottles, as in *Trucker* (Fig. 286).

Construction Methods

Hollow Casts

If a piece is large or the material to be used for the cast is very heavy, as is the case with metals such as bronze, the *lost-wax* process is often used to create a hollow cast. In the *direct lost-wax method,* the original pattern is built of some nonmelting material such as clay or plaster with its final surface modeled in a layer of wax of the same thickness as the ultimate metal cast. A negative mold is constructed over this wax surface, with vents here and there to allow air to escape during the later casting process. Provisions are made for breaking the mold in half and reassembling it after the cast has set. The piece is then heated to the point that the wax melts, leaving a cavity that duplicates the contours of the pattern. The material for the final piece is poured into this cavity and allowed to harden. Once it is hard, the negative molds are pulled away from each side, the hollow walls of the cast are separated, the inner core of the original pattern is removed, and the pieces of the cast are reassembled, leaving a hollow core.

The more complex *indirect lost-wax* procedure, shown in Figure 287, page 268, involves first creating a negative plaster or gelatine mold of the positive pattern. The pattern is then removed and wax is applied to the inner surface of the negative mold. Wax lines to form vents are added and a core of some material such as ground brick and plaster mixed with water is poured or tamped into the wax shell. Metal pins are added to hold the layers together. Layers of fire-resistant material are also built up around the outside of the wax shell. The finished mold is then baked to melt the wax and molten metal is poured into all the cavities once occupied by the wax.

Yet another process uses *sand molds,* frames of sand mixed with a binder to create negative molds. Sand is often porous enough that complex venting is not needed to allow gases to escape when molten material is poured into the mold. The sand mixture is packed in halves or sections around a positive pattern to receive its imprint. The molds are then taken apart, the pattern is removed, a core is added if the piece is to be hollow, the sand molds are reassembled, and the molten casting material is poured in. Like all mold materials, the sand must be sufficiently fine-textured to recreate fine details and strong enough to hold its shape when the heavy metal or other casting material is poured in. Although sand molds can be used to make many duplicates of a piece, they tend to lose fine details; lost-wax processes yield a single cast since the original wax modeling is lost in the process, but they register finer detail than sand molds.

No matter what process is used, large and/or complex pieces must often be cast in sections with ends designed to be rejoined after casting. The *Great Buddha* at Kamakura, Japan (Fig. 288) is 53 feet (16.16 m) tall, so huge that it could only be cast by breaking the form down into pieces. Some of the lines along which they were reassem-

Casting

(a) positive pattern

(b) negative mold

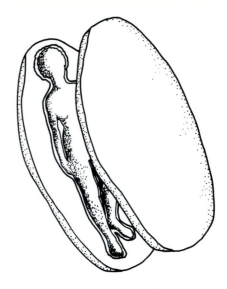

(c) negative molds coated
with wax layer

(d) cross–section of assembled
molds with core tamped
into wax–lined shell

pins

vents

core

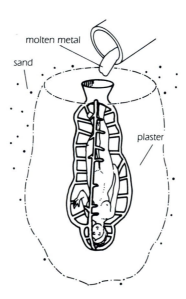

molten metal

sand

plaster

(e) assembled molds encased in
fire-resistant materials and baked
to melt wax, leaving cavity into
which molten metal is poured

rods left
where metal
filled vents

(f) extra metal and core
removed, pieces of metal
cast reassembled into
hollow cast

287 Stages of lost-wax casting.

Construction Methods

288 *Great Buddha,* Kamakura, Japan. 1252. Bronze, height 53′ (16.17 m).

bled can be seen in the photograph as horizontal marks across the chest, arms, and folded legs.

Foundries and Editions

Because of the exacting technology, skill, and time required for casting and the great cost of some casting equipment, many artists now send their work to foundries to be cast. At every stage of the process, certain qualities of the original model may be lost, so provision is often made for retouching molds as well as the finished piece. In Figure 289 (p. 270), workers at the Johnson Atelier are chasing a cast sculpture by Andrea Grassi to bring out the grooves in its surface. Some artists choose to turn over all such details to the foundry; others rework both molds and finished piece.

   With some casting processes, it is possible to create small editions of a piece by saving the molds and repeating the procedures several times to create several more or less identical copies of a work.

Casting   **269**

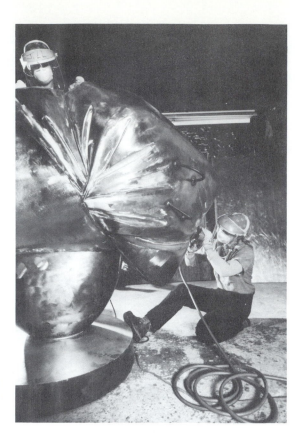

289. Apprentices Betsy Bowen and Jill Rednor chasing piece by Andrea Grassi at the Johnson Atelier, Princeton, New Jersey.

Each is an original work of art, and by casting an edition, the artist is able to lower the per-unit cost of casting by spreading certain fixed costs across many units. Industrial casting processes are designed to allow a great number of copies to be cast from the same mold. The Spode plate shown in Figure 290 is cast of high-grade earthenware from molds that allow quantity production of fine design. Certain casting procedures do not allow deep undercuts, which would prevent detaching the mold from the cast without breaking the mold; industrial designers must sometimes work within the limitations of this consideration, beveling all angles with ease of separation from the mold in mind.

The Outsides and Insides of Casts

Casts can be used to create a great range of surface textures, for they duplicate the surface of whatever is used for the mold or the pattern, depending on the process used. A sand casting will have the granular texture of the sand mold. Pieces cast from a pattern made of a mallea-

290 Spode plate, cast earthenware.

ble material such as wax will retain the freshness and immediacy of the modeling without the impermanence of the original material. Picasso's *Goat* (Fig. 291) is a permanent copy of an assemblage of

291 PABLO PICASSO. *She-Goat.* 1950. Bronze, cast 1952. 3′ 10⅜″ × 4′8⅜″ (1.18 × 1.43 m). Collection Museum of Modern Art, New York (Mrs. Simon Guggenheim Fund).

ceramic flower pots, metal elements, a palm leaf, and a wicker basket, with plaster added to create all the textures of goathood, from the scraggly fur of an ill-kept animal to the coarse undulations of the horns to the smoothness of the udder. The casting process allows considerable surface detail to be elaborated, as in the Shang ceremonial vessel (Fig. 278). Textures can also be developed on the surface after casting, as in Andrea Grassi's piece shown in Figure 289, which is polished to an extremely smooth, reflective sheen.

Traditional hollow bronze casts also reflect the unique quality of hollowness, of being merely the outer covering bulging out around an inner void. As metal is poured, it thrusts outward into every cavity of the mold. This outward thrust may give casts a curiously alive quality, as if instead of being merely empty, they are bursting with inner life.

STUDIO PROBLEMS

14.1 Paper Casting

Manipulate a piece of paper and then use it as a mold into which plaster of Paris is poured. After the plaster has hardened, cut away any undesired edges of the cast with a saw. The result, like the example shown in Figure 292, can be put together with other students' solutions to make a modular wall piece.

292 Paper Casting. Plaster. Student work

Construction Methods

14.2 Plaster Casting in Clay

Build a simple wooden frame with a plywood floor, not too large (anywhere from 12" × 12" [30.48 × 30.48 cm] to 18" × 22" [45.72 × 55.88 cm]), to hold clay and liquid plaster. Place a layer of nonhardening clay or plasticene on the floor of the frame. Shape the clay by pushing, pounding, squeezing and drawing it into a desired "terrain" whose concave areas will be convex in the finished piece, and vice versa. Concentrate on the process of working in reverse. Any tools or materials may be used to create desired textural effects. Then prepare plaster of Paris according to the directions on the package and pour or scoop it quickly into the clay mold, smoothing the upper surface of the plaster, which will become the back of the piece. When the plaster dries, lift the plaster and clay out of the frame and peel away the clay, exposing the surface of the plaster as a low relief that is the reverse of the contours of the clay bed.

An alternative is to use wet sand rather than clay to create the mold. Sand will not hold fine details as well as the clay but is good for rough work.

14.3 Cast Hands

Mix a quantity of plaster of Paris, grease your hands well with Vaseline after removing any jewelry, and then make a cast in your hands by holding the plaster in your cupped and joined palms until the plaster sets. Experiment with different ways of holding your hands to create interesting effects. Once the plaster is dry, cut off the rough edges with a saw. Can the hands of the whole class be combined as an effective modular construction?

Reference Books on Casting

Arnold Auerbach, *Modelled Sculpture and Plaster Casting,* Cranbury, New Jersey: A. S. Barnes and Co., 1977. Directions for clay modeling with and without an armature, plaster casting, and waste molds, for both figures and reliefs.

Geoffrey Clarke and Stroud Cornock, *A Sculptor's Manual,* New York: Reinhold Book Corporation, 1968. Sections on plaster casting, sand casting, lost-wax processes, and techniques for making editions, with some technical drawings,

Chuck Evans, *Jewelry: Contemporary Design and Technique,* Worcester, Massachusetts: Davis Publications, 1983. Detailed, well-illustrated chapter on casting techniques used in jewelry making.

Christian Hauser, *Art Foundry,* Geneva, Switzerland: Les Editions de Bonvent, 1972. Illustrated discussions of metals, foundries, lost-wax processes, and sand casting.

Malvina Hoffman, *Sculpture Inside and Out,* New York: W. W. Norton and Company, 1939. Contains a chapter on plaster and terra-cotta with numerous simple processes suitable for inexpensive student projects in casting.

Dennis Kowal and Dona Z. Meilach, *Sculpture Casting,* New York: Crown Publishers, 1972. Beautifully illustrated explanations of casting techniques, including latex and rubber flexible molds, lost-wax casting, gelatin molds, ceramic shell molds, sand casting, and casting of concrete, plaster, and plastics.

Thelma R. Newman, *Plastics as Sculpture,* Radnor, Pennsylvania: Chilton Book Company, 1974. Descriptions of various plastics and methods of casting them.

Jack C. Rich, *The Materials and Methods of Sculpture,* New York: Oxford University Press, 1947. Includes detailed discussions of numerous casting techniques.

Sunset Editorial Staff with Robert and Joan Dawson, *Sculpture with Simple Materials,* Menlo Park, California: Lane Books, 1968. Includes directions for very simple casting projects: casting from clay with rubber molds, casting papier-mâché from clay, and negative casting.

Wilbert Verhelst, *Sculpture: Tools, Materials, and Techniques,* Englewood Cliffs, New Jersey: Prentice-Hall, 1973. Includes three detailed chapters on the stages of casting: modeling and pattern-making, mold-making techniques, and casting and reproduction.

William Zorach, *Zorach Explains Sculpture,* New York: American Artists Group, 1947. Includes chapters on plaster casting with waste molds, cast stone, lost-wax casting, sand casting, piece molds, and gelatin molds.

Glossary

Words used that are defined elsewhere in this glossary are *italicized*.

abstract   referring to art that simplifies, emphasizes, or distorts qualities of a real-life image rather than trying to represent its surface details accurately. In some cases, the intent is to present the essence of an object rather than its outer form.

activated space   the area controlled by a three-dimensional piece, including not only its form but also perhaps a subtly energized but physically unfilled area in or around the work.

additive color mixing   mixtures of light to create colors, called "additive" since each colored light adds its energy to the mixture, raising its *value* slightly.

additive sculpture   three-dimensional work made by putting pieces of material(s) together to build up a form.

aerial perspective   the optical illusion that areas closer to the viewer are sharper in detail, color *intensity*, and *value contrast* than areas farther away, sometimes used intentionally by artists to create illusions of spatial depth.

analogous colors   *hues* lying next to each other on a *color wheel*, sometimes used together in color schemes.

annealing   heating of metal during the process of shaping it by techniques such as hammering, to return work-hardened metal to a *malleable* state.

applied color   color added to a material, concealing or changing its original color.

applied design   use of the principles and elements of design to create functional pieces.

armature   a simple inner skeleton that provides support for *modeling* with more pliable materials, such as clay or wax.

artificial lighting   use of light from human-made sources such as incandescent or fluorescent bulbs to illuminate an area or a work of art.

assemblage   a work made from objects or pieces of objects originally intended for other purposes.

asymmetrical balance   placement of nonidentical forms to either side of a balancing point in such a way that the two sides seem to be of the same visual weight.

bas-relief   see *low relief*

bezel   a metal collar designed to hold a stone in a piece of jewelry.

box set   in set design, the illusion of a room with one wall cut away so that the audience can see in.

cast   a form made by any of various techniques of creating a mold into which a material is poured in liquid form, allowed to harden, and removed from the mold.

ceramics   decorative or functional pieces made from clay and *fired* for permanence. Also, the art of making ceramic pieces.

chasing   engraving of the surface of a piece, often to help define contours or details.

chroma   see *saturation*

clay body   a mixture of clays compounded for specific characteristics.

closed form   a relatively solid volume with little *negative space*.

color wheel   a two-dimensional circular model of relationships among *hues*.

complementary colors   *hues* that are opposite each other on a *color wheel*. When mixed, they gray or neutralize each other; when juxtaposed, they intensify each other.

conceptual art   works or events in which idea is more important than outer form.

confined space   a spatial field with clearly defined enclosing boundaries.

content   the subject matter of a work of art, plus its emotional, intellectual, symbolic, spiritual, and/or narrative implications, as opposed to its physical form.

controlled time   referring to the movement of works of art through a predetermined sequence of events.

cool colors   *hues* in the green and blue range.

crafts   disciplines in which functional pieces are made by hand or as if by hand, with the individuality associated with handmade objects. In a broader sense, crafts are occupations requiring manual skill and aesthetic sensitivity to create objects that may or may not be functional.

delineated space   an unfilled area described by filled areas of a three-dimensional work.

directional line   a line that seems to guide the viewer's eye along a particular visual path.

dominance   emphasis placed on a particular area or characteristic of a work, with other areas or aspects given subordinate or supporting roles.

ductility   the ability to be stretched or extended without breaking.

dynamic form   a three-dimensional work that conveys an illusion of movement and change.

earthenware   ceramics made from the coarsest clays, usually fired at the lowest temperatures.

economy   deletion of nonessential details to reveal the essence of a form.

elements of design   those qualities of a design that can be seen and worked with independently of its figurative content. They include *line, form, value, space, texture*, color, and time.

emphasis   stress placed on a single area of a work or a unifying visual theme.

encaustic   a method of painting with pigment-bearing hot wax.

ergonomics   the study of how people relate physically to their environment, of particular interest to those seeking to increase job efficiency and decrease workers' fatigue.

exterior form   the surface shape of a work of art.

eye line   the illusionary line between a figure's eyes and something at which it appears to be looking.

fabrication   assembling of rigid materials into units by techniques such as welding, bolting, or *lamination*.

fiber art   work created by manipulation of strands of varying materials by any of a variety of methods.

figurative   representing human or animal forms.

firing   the baking of ceramic pieces to make the clay's form permanent.

focal point   the area in a work to which the eye is most compellingly drawn.

folk art   works that are created by people without aesthetic training but that may be appreciated for their vigor, humor, and highly personal style.

forced perspective exaggeration of the illusionary convergence of parallel lines toward the horizon, used in set design to make a shallow space appear deeper.

forging shaping of metal by hammering it over a hard surface, often after first heating the metal to a *malleable* state.

form the volume and shape of a three-dimensional work, perhaps including unfilled areas that are integral to the work as a whole.

found object an object not originally created as art but used in or appreciated as a work of art.

free time referring to art that moves and changes somewhat unpredictably through time.

frontal seen or made to be seen only from the front, as opposed to pieces that encourage viewing in the *full round*.

full round works designed to be appreciated from all sides, in fully three-dimensional space.

gestalt in a successful work of art, a whole that has properties that transcend the sum of its parts.

glaze in *ceramics*, a colored or transparent liquid applied to pieces made of clay; when *fired*, it bonds to the clay and forms a hard, glassy coating.

gray scale the representation of gradations of *value* as a series of equal steps from black to white.

half-round three-dimensional works in which only 180 degrees of a full circle is presented as being of aesthetic interest.

high contrast in *values*, dramatic juxtaposition of very light and very dark areas.

high relief three-dimensional *form* raised considerably off a flat background.

highlight a brightly lit area that appears as a luminous spot on a work.

hologram a record of laser-light patterns that allows three-dimensional perception of a three-dimensional object on a two-dimensional surface.

hue the characteristic of color identified by color names, such as red and blue. It corresponds to a particular wavelength within the spectrum of visible light.

idealized in representational art, the portrayal of objects as approaching some imagined rather than actual appearance of perfection.

implied form see *negative form*

implied line a line in a work that is subtly perceived by the viewer but that has no physical form; the overall flow of one line into another in a work, with continuation from one to the next suggested by their common direction and/or juxtaposition.

industrial design design of the mass-produced products of our everyday environment, from sinks and furniture to computers.

inner form see *interior form*

installation pieces designed environments installed in museums, sometimes temporarily.

intensity see *saturation*

interior form the shape of the inside of a hollow work of art; an inner form that appears to be emerging from or contained within the outer form.

intermediate hues Albert Munsell's term for *secondary colors*.

junk sculpture three-dimensional works of art created from the castoff products of our society.

kiln an oven, furnace, or other enclosure used for the *firing* of *ceramics*.

kinetic art works designed to move and perhaps change through time.

laminate to create a larger unit by gluing together thin sheets of a material or materials.

line an area whose length is considerably greater than its width.

linear of or relating to a line or lines.

linear perspective the optical illusion that parallel lines converge toward a distant vanishing point.

local color the natural color of an object.

lost-wax any of several *casting* processes by which a layer of wax is melted away from surrounding positive and negative *molds* to create a space into which the material for the cast can be poured.

low relief three-dimensional form that is barely raised from a flat background.

malleable capable of being shaped, pliable.

maquette a small-scale model of a work, usually developed to aid the planning process.

mass see *form*

minimal art *nonrepresentational art* using very few forms and colors.

mixed media combinations of different materials to create a visually and physically coherent whole.

mobiles hanging sculptures that turn when moved by air currents.

modeling shaping pieces from a pliable material such as clay by using the hands and hand tools.

moiré an illusory wavelike pattern.

mold a hollow form created for casting materials that flow into the form when in a liquid state and then duplicate it in reverse when hardened.

monochromatic a color scheme using closely related colors derived from a single *hue* but perhaps varying in *value* and *saturation*.

monolithic having a relatively closed form that reflects the single stone or block of wood from which it was carved.

monumental works very large, imposing works of art that may or may not serve memorial purposes.

narrative art pieces that tell a visual story.

natural lighting the use of existing outdoor lighting rather than artificial lights to illuminate a piece.

negative form a shaped space that has no physical existence but is enclosed or defined by *positive forms*; a void.

negative mold a receptacle for *casting* that is the reverse of the finished form. See *mold*.

negative space a physically unfilled area in a three-dimensional work; in *subtractive sculpture*, a previously filled area that was cut away to reveal the *form*.

neutrals colors of very low *saturation*, approaching grays.

nonobjective art works that have no apparent relationship to objects from our three-dimensional world; nonrepresentational art.

nonrepresentational art see *nonobjective art*

open form a *mass* penetrated by *negative spaces*.

optical color mixture colors mixed visually, as when *hues* are closely juxtaposed in space or when transparent layers of different colors are overlaid.

outline the line described by the outer boundary of a *form*.

participatory sculpture three-dimensional art designed to engage the viewer physically.

patina the sheen produced on a surface by aging or handling; the thin layer of corrosion, usually green or brown, that appears on a bronze surface as it oxidizes.

performance piece a live experience conducted or set up by the artist.

pigment a powder that is the coloring ingredient for paint or other color media.

point of view the distance and angle from which something is seen.

plastic capable of being shaped; polymerized organic compounds that can be shaped in many different ways.

polychromed (polychromatic) multicolored.

porcelain usually white ceramic pieces made of very fine clay and fired at the highest temperatures.

positive form a solid area that physically occupies space in a three-dimensional work of art.

primary colors in color theory, those basic *hues* from which all other hues can be mixed. Different color theories suggest different primaries. In traditional color theory about pigment mixtures, the primary colors are red, yellow, and blue.

primary contour(s) the shape of the outermost extremity of a three-dimensional work.

principal hues Albert Munsell's term for *primary colors*.

principles of design basic aesthetic considerations that guide organization of a work of art.

proportion a sense of appropriateness in the size relationships of different parts of a work.

raising in metalworking, the hammering of a flat sheet of metal over a stake, thus compressing and curving it into a hollow form. In ceramics, one of the stages of the throwing process.

read to scan or perceive a work of art in a particular way or with a particular understanding.

ready-made a functional manufactured object that is displayed as a work of art for its unintentional aesthetic qualities.

realism visual accuracy in artistic representation of known objects.

reflected light the light waves that bounce back to our eye from a surface rather than being absorbed into it. These reflected waves determine what we call the "color" of the object.

refracted light the bands of color seen when white light is passed through a prism.

relief three-dimensional form raised from a flat surface.

rhythm unification of parts of a work through measured repetition of visual accents.

saturation a measure of the relative purity and brightness or grayness of a color, also called "chroma" or "intensity."

scale   the size of an object in relationship to other objects and to its surroundings.

secondary colors   in color theory, the *hues* created by mixing two *primary colors* together.

secondary contours   the forms developed within the outer boundaries of a work.

shadow study   an analysis of where natural lighting will create shadows at different times of day and different seasons at a particular location.

simultaneous contrast   the principle that the juxtaposition of two colors exaggerates their differences and reduces their similarities.

site-specific   referring to works expressly designed for and installed in a particular location.

space   the three-dimensional field with which the artist works, including both filled and unfilled areas.

spatial presence   the size and impact of the field in which a three-dimensional work is experienced. This field may not stop at the physical boundaries of the work.

static form   a three-dimensional work that appears stationary.

stoneware   *ceramic* pieces made of medium-fine clays and fired at medium temperature ranges.

stylized   altering the visual characteristics of an object to fit a desired way of design or cultural aesthetic.

subtraction   creation of a work of art by carving away the excess from a larger piece of material.

subtractive color mixing   mixing of *pigments*, producing a slightly darker *value* since each pigment subtracts its energy from the light reflected by the mixture.

superrealism   extremely accurate representation of actual three-dimensional objects.

symmetrical balance   the placing of identical forms to either side of the central axis of a work to stabilize it visually.

temporal   relating to existence in and perhaps change through time.

tensile strength   the resistance of a material to a force tending to tear it apart.

tertiary colors   in color theory, the *hues* created when a *primary* and a *secondary color* are mixed.

texture   the tactile surface characteristics of a work of art that are either felt or perceived visually.

thermoformed   in plastics, a shape created by bending when hot.

thermoplastic   capable of being remelted and reformed, a characteristic of some resins, metals, and glass.

thermosetting   not capable of being remelted after initial shaping and setting, a characteristic of certain resins and clay.

three-dimensional   having height, width, and depth.

trompe l'oeil   "fool the eye" optical illusion.

two-dimensional   having height and width, but not depth.

undercutting   creation of an overhanging surface by carving material beneath away.

unity   organization of parts so that all contribute to a coherent whole. The term is sometimes listed as one of the organizing principles of design, but in this book it is used to connote the combined result of all principles of design (repetition, variety, rhythm, balance, emphasis, economy, and proportion).

value   degree of lightness or darkness.

value contrast   juxtaposition of light and dark areas.

vertical balance   distribution of *visual weights* in a piece in such a way that top and bottom seem to be in equilibrium.

video art   use of television techniques for purely aesthetic purposes.

visible spectrum   the humanly perceptible bands of colored light created when white light passes through a prism.

visual economy   see *economy*

visual texture   the apparent rather than actual tactile quality of a surface.

visual weight   the apparent lightness or heaviness of a work or a portion of a work.

void   see *negative form*

volume   see *form*

warm colors   red, orange, and yellow *hues*.

Index

References are to page numbers. Bold-face page numbers indicate illustrations. Works of art are listed under the names of their creators. Student works are listed under Studio Problems titles. Many technical terms are included in the Index, with references to their text definitions. Also consult the Glossary for technical terms.

Abakanowicz, Magdalena:
   Black-Brown Composition in Space,
     234, **235**
   Self Portrait, 236, **236**
acrylics, 239
Activated Surrounding Space, 116
Adams, Peter Michael, *Dotoh,* 167–168,
   180
Addition with Malleable Materials, 243;
   student work, **244**
Ajanaku, Lawrence, *Ancient Mother,* 175,
   192
alloys, 232
Anderson, Laurie, *United States,* 27–29,
   28, 204
Andre, Carl, *Way North/South,* 92–93, **92**
applied design, 30
Arp, Jean, *Aquatic,* 41, **42**
art:
   African, 216, 219
   applied or functional, 48
   beauty and, 51, 141
   children's appreciation of, 17, 19, 200
   commissioned, 38–39
   computer, 172
   conceptual, 9–11
   control of, 11
   crafts vs., 44, 48–49, 51, 167, 233–234
   critics of, 30
   fine, 48, 51
   folk, 27, 203–204, 223
   Futurist, 198
   Greek, 74
   illusion and, 85–86
   incongruity in, 30
   intent of, 11–13, 33, 59–60, 65
   kinetic, 201, 204–205, 207

art *(cont.)*
   minimal, 74, 205
   "nonart" activities and, 48–49
   nonobjective, 138
   performance, 27–29
   photographs as, 9–11
   public, 207
   purchase of, 36
   realistic, 22–23, 51, 59, 94–95
   religious, 25–26, 174, 218–220
   stylized, 95
   superrealistic, 94
   video, 29
   wearable, 141
   see also three-dimensional art
Art Nouveau, 93, 120, 237
Asher, Michael, installation at Pomona
   College Art Gallery, 27, **28**
Assemblages, 218–220, 221, 225, 243;
   student work, **224**

balance:
   asymmetrical vs. symmetrical, 68–70
   horizontal vs. vertical, 70–71
Barber, Joseph, Jr., slate gravestone of
   Polly Coombs, 12, **13**
Baskin, Leonard, *Oppressed Man,* 154–
   155, **155**
bas reliefs, 13, 32
"bast," 236
Bauhaus designs, 51
Bell, Larry, *The Iceberg and Its Shadow,*
   150, **150**, 239
Bernini, Gianlorenzo:
   The Ecstasy of St. Theresa, 25, **26**, 41
   Louis XIV, 141–142, **141**
   Triton Fountain, 54, **54**
bezels, 242
Bill, Max, *Monoangulated Surface in
   Space,* 67–68, **67**
birdstone, 256, **257**
bisque ware, 229
blacksmithing, 233
Blenheim Palace, 111, **111**
Boccioni, Umberto, *Unique Forms of
   Continuity in Space,* 198–199, **198**
Boghosian, Varujan, *Orpheus,* 221, **222**

Boyer, Cynthia, *Hand-felted jacket with
   knit sleeves,* 65, **65**
Brancusi, Constantin:
   Bird in Space, 8–9, **9**, 157
   The Miracle (Seal), 95, **95**
brazing, 239
Brodsky, Joyce, 20
burls, 250

Cage, John, 29
Calder, Alexander, *The Grass Family,*
   120, **120**
Carpeaux, Jean-Baptiste, *Ugolino and
   His Sons,* 125–126, **126**, 128
casting, 260–274
   bronze, 260, 264, 267, 272
   of hands, 273
   hollow, 267–269, 272
   industrial, 269–270
   lost-wax, 267, **268**
   paper, 272; student work, **272**
   patterns for, 260, 264
   plastic, 260
   reliefs from, 262
   shims or fences for, 264
   slip-, 264
   solid, 262–266
   studio problems, 272–273
   texture and, 270–272
   venting in, 267
   see also molds
cave sculpture, prehistoric, 13
Cellini, Benvenuto, *Saltcellar of Francis
   I,* 50–51, **50**
cement, 231–232, 251
chaitya cave, 248–250, **249**
Chamberlain, John, *Velvet White,* 222,
   222
Changes by the Viewer, 210–211; student work, **211**
Chartres Cathedral, 24, **24**, 25
chasing, 233
chiseling, 233
choreography, 120
Christo, *Valley Curtain,* 35–36, **35**, 43–
   44, 49, 205
"chroma," 165

Photographic credits The authors and publisher wish to thank the custodians of the works of art for supplying photographs and granting permission to use them. Photographs have been obtained from sources listed in the captions, unless listed below.

A/AR   Alinari/Art Resource, New York   M/AR   Marburg/Art Resource, New York
A/Ma   Alinari, Mansell Collection, London   OKH   O.K. Harris Works of Art, New York, N. Y.
MLF   M. Lee Fatherree, Oakland, CA.   PR   Photo Researchers, New York, N.   Y.
H   Hirmer Fotoarchiv, Munich, Germany   JV   Jeanne Victor, Coventry, Conn.

References are to **boldface** figure numbers

Color   Plate 1: Charles Eames. Plate 3: Dan Bailey, Penland, North Carolina. Plate 6: Pedro Guerrero, New Canaan, Connecticut. Plate 7: British Tourist Authority, London. Plate 8: H. Plate 10: Mark Kauffman, San Francisco, CA. Plate 11: Sandak, Inc., Stanford, Connecticut. Plates 13–14: Robert Walker. Plate 15: James T. Hoffman. Plate 16: Sidney Janis Gallery, N. Y., N. Y. Plate 17: Rob McDougle. Plate 18: Lee Boltin Picture Library, Croton-on-Hudson, N. Y. Plate 19: *House & Garden.* Copyright © 1985 by the Condé Nast Publications Inc., N. Y. N. Y. Plate 20: Kee Fatherree, San Francisco, CA. Plate 23: Michael Dunne/Elizabeth Whiting & Associates, London. Plate 24: © Betsy Utting, Terryville, Connecticut

Chapter 1   **1–2**: Tom Forma, Storrs, Connecticut. **3**: Robert E. Mates, New York, N. Y. **4**: Charles Simonds, New York, N. Y. **8**: John Cliett / © Dia Art Foundation, 1980. **9**: Ralph di Capua, Storrs, Connecticut. **10**: © Ann Parker, 1985. **13**: Al Mozell/Pace Gallery, New York, N. Y. **16**: William Howland. **18**: Will Brown/Philadelphia, PA. **19**: MLF. **20**: Nathan Knobler, Philadelphia, PA. **23**: OKH. **26**: Charles Simonds, New York, N. Y. **27**: Public Information Office/Redevelopment Authority of the City of Philadelphia. **28**: M/AR. **29**: Bates Littlehales © 1964 National Geographic Society, Washington, D. C. **30**: A/Ma. **32**: Hans Namuth, New York, N. Y. **33**: Salk Institute, San Diego, Ca. **34**: Galleries of the Claremont Colleges, Claremont, Ca. **35**: Paula Court. © 1980, New York, N. Y. **36**: Electronic Arts Intermix, New York, N. Y. **37**: Daniel Sinclair, Long Island City, New York. **39–41**: JV.

Chapter 2   **42**: A/Ma. **43**: Harry Shunk © Christo, New York, N. Y. **44**: George Tanier, Inc., New York, N. Y. **47**: Carollee Pelos, from *Spectacular Vernacular: A New Appreciation of Traditional Desert Architecture* by Jean-Louis Bourgeois and Carollee Pelos, Salt Lake City, Utah: Gibbs M. Smith Books, 1983. **48–49**: Chesterwood Archives and Daniel Chester French Papers, National Trust for Historic Preservation, Stockbridge, Mass. **50**: Errol Jackson, London. **51**: Herman Miller, Inc., Zeeland, Michigan. **52**: Elyn Zimmerman, New York, N. Y. **54**: Beverly Dickinson, Storrs, Connecticut. **58**: Skidmore, Owings & Merrill, New York, N. Y. **59**: Darrell Acree, Washington, D. C. **62**: Atelier Teigen, Oslo, Norway. **63**: Diane Sheenan, Madison, Wisconsin. **64**: Louis Mervar/Adams & Flock, Inc., New York, N. Y. **66**: Kurt Naef, Grendelweg, Switzerland. **67**: Reinhart Wolf, Hamburg, West Germany. **69**: Mario Carrieri, Milan, Italy. **70**: Albert Squillace, Bronx, New York. **71**: Andrew Popper, New York, N. Y. **72**: SITE Projects, New York, N. Y. **73–74**: JV. **75**: Robert E. Mates, New York, N. Y. **76**: David Allison, New York, N. Y. **77**: Jerry Spearman, Montreal, Canada. **79**: MLF. **80**: © Mary Noble Ours, Washington, D. C. **81**: Eugene Gordon/PR. **84**: Richard di Liberto, Fresh Meadows, New York. **92**: MAS, Barcelona, Spain. **93**: from *Hans Coper* by Tony Birks, Published by Harper & Row. Photograph by Jane Gate. **95**: Betty Gerich, Enfield, Connecticut. **96**: Consulate General of Japan, New York, N. Y. **97–99**: JV.

Chapter 4   **100**: Paula Cooper Gallery, New York, N. Y. **102**: Burt Sky, Dallas, Texas. **103**: Marlborough Gallery, New York, N. Y. **104**: A/AR. **105**: Hideyuki Oka, Tokyo. Japan. **107**: Reproduced by kind permission of the Board of Trustees of the Royal Armouries, London. **108**: Maurice Max, Inc., New York, N. Y. **111**: from *The New Churches of Europe* by G E Kidder Smith. **113**: H. **114**: Paula Cooper Gallery, New York. **115**: H. **117**: Erven Jourdan, Los Angeles, Ca. **119**: OKH. **122–125**: JV.

Chapter 5   **127**: Terry Dintenfass, Inc., New York, N. Y. **130**: Fritz Henle/PR. **133**: Xavier Fourcade, Inc., New York, N. Y. **134**: P. Goodwin/Records & Archives, City Hall, Toronto, Canada. **135–137**: Ezra Stoller. © ESTO Mamaroneck, New York. **139**: *House & Garden Guide:* © 1968 by the Conde Nast Publications Inc., New York, N. Y. **140**: British Tourist Authority, London. **142**: Elaine Horwitch Galleries, Scottsdale, Arizona. **144–146**: JV.

Chapter 6   **150**: Tim Matson, Thetford Center, Vermont. **152**: Arteaga Photos, St. Louis, MO. **153**: John Weber Gallery, New York, N. Y. **154**: Arts Council of Great Britain, London and John Hedgecoe, Ltd., Burgates, England. **157**: A/AR. **159**: Henry Paque, Shorewood, Wisconsin. **161**: John Weber Gallery, New York, N. Y. **162**: Xavier Fourcade, New York, N. Y. **163**: MAS, Barcelona. **164**: Alexandre Georges/Chase Manhattan Archives, New York, N. Y. **167–168**: JV.

Chapter 7   **170**: John Cliett / © Dia Art Foundation, 1980. **172**: Drew Vaden/Hal Bromm Gallery, New York, N. Y. **173**: Mildred Constantine, New York, N. Y. **174**: Sidney Janis Gallery, New York, N. Y. **175**: Peter Moore/Grace Borgenicht Gallery, New York, N. Y. **177**: Marc Riboud, Paris. **180**: Bob Hanson, New York, N. Y. **181**: A/Ma. **182**: OKH. **184**: Derek St. John, Kingston, New York. **185–187**: JV.

Chapter 8   **190**: Barbara Hepworth Museum (Tate Gallery), London. **191**: Hedrich-Blessing, Chicago, Illinois. **192**: Ben Lux, Taos, New Mexico. **194**: Xavier Fourcade, New York, N. Y. **195**: Woo & Williams, Cambridge, Mass. **196**: Bob Serating/© Lincoln Center for the Performing Arts, New York, N. Y. **197**: Morris Warman/Lincoln Center for the Performing Arts, New York, N. Y. **199–200**: © 1975 by Robert Hupka from *Michelangelo: Pietà,* Crown Publishers, New York, N. Y. **202**: Bob Serating/© Lincoln Center for the Performing Arts, New York, N. Y. **203**: Max Hutchinson Gallery, New York, N. Y. **205**: Leo Castelli Gallery, New York, N. Y. **206**: German Information Center, New York, N. Y. **207–208**: JV.

Chapter 9   **209**: Charles Eames. **213**: JV.

Chapter 10   **217**: Howard F. Dratch, Saugerties, New York. **218**: Fototeca Unione at the American Academy in Rome. **220**: Ruth Bermant, Rye, New York. **221**: Helga Photo Studios, New York, N. Y. **223**: John Schoettler, Seattle, Washington. **224**: Sarah Milstead. **225**: Knoll International, New York, N. Y. **226**: Beverly Dickinson, Storrs, Connecticut. **227**: Beth Galston, Somerville, MA. **228–229**: JV.